A STATISTICS PRIMER FOR MANAGERS

A STATISTICS PRIMER FOR MANAGERS

How to Read a Statistical Report
Or a Computer Printout and Get the Right Answers

John J. Clark
Margaret T. Clark

THE FREE PRESS
A Division of Macmillan Publishing Co., Inc.
NEW YORK

Collier Macmillan Publishers
LONDON

The Free Press
A Division of Macmillan Publishing Co., Inc.
866 Third Avenue, New York, N.Y. 10022

Collier Macmillan Canada, Inc.

Printed in the United States of America

printing number

2 3 4 5 6 7 8 9 10

Library of Congress Cataloging in Publication Data

Clark, John J.
    A statistics primer for managers.

    Bibliography: p.
    Includes index.
    1. Statistical decision.   2. Management—Statistical methods.   I. Clark,
Margaret T.   II. Title.
HD30.23.C575   1982   519.5′024658   82-70999
ISBN 0-02-905800-7   AACR2

Contents

Preface   **vii**

Section I—Managerial Statistics   1

    Chapter 1—What Is Statistics . . . . and Managerial
          Statistics?   3

Section II—The Several Varieties of Averages   7

    Chapter 2—Averages: Ungrouped Data   9
    Chapter 3—Averages: Grouped Data   35

Section III—Is it Probable?   55

    Chapter 4—Probabilities in Business Decisions   57
    Chapter 5—Probability Distributions   79

Section IV—Sampling   111

    Chapter 6—Designing a Sample   113
    Chapter 7—Testing the Evidence   129

Section V—Time and Association   147

    Chapter 8—Time Series Analysis: Dynamic Factors in
          Business Data   149
    Chapter 9—Associations and Correlations   169

Section VI—Classifying Things   191

    Chapter 10—Discriminant Analysis   193

Section VII—Another Approach   203

    Chapter 11—Nonparametric Statistics   205

**Section VIII—The Computer and Quantitative Analysis for
Business Decisions** 221

   Chapter 12—The Computer and Managerial Statistics 223

Appendix A—Bibliography 247

Appendix B—Glossary 251

Index 255

Preface

Managerial statistics treats the contribution of statistics to decision making in typical business situations. Business decisions generate new data and managers in turn rely upon the analysis of data to provide a basis for taking decisions. Yet the analysis of data, however sophisticated, does not ineluctably point to preferred decisions. Decisions ultimately result from the experience and acumen of managers. This book attempts to help in the formation of *informed* management judgments.

The position of managers vis-a-vis statistics is analagous to that of the accounting system. Managers need not be accountants but few managers would realize their potential lacking the ability to interpret intelligently the firm's financial statements or to raise pertinent questions concerning accounting data. Similarly, managers need not be statisticians. Yet the successful manager should possess an understanding of statistical methods sufficient to question the appropriateness of the data presented in support of decisions under consideration. Herein lies the central theme of this volume. Each section and chapter offers an introduction to one of the topics that comprise managerial statistics and concludes with a series of questions that managers can pose when presented with similar data. The resulting dialogue between manager and statistician should foster enhanced appreciation by the executive of the data's strong points and limitations. As a corollary, such give and take helps to define the areas of uncertainty where managerial judgment plays a crucial role.

Statistics can lead or mislead. The latter is generally a result of inaccurate data, erroneous interpretation of valid data, or the application of statistical techniques without regard to underlying assumptions. Statistical methods assume particular characteristics about the data under study. For example, if a firm plans to forecast sales, the input data should exhibit a behavior consistent with the assumptions underlying the statistical method applied or the forecast will fall wide of the mark. Statistical techniques rest upon assumptions that should agree with the reality to be described. To the extent that assumptions

vii

deviate from reality, justifiable suspicion attaches to the conclusions of the investigation. Therefore, in each chapter, we have delineated the underlying assumptions of the method discussed in order to alert the manager of the necessity to examine the assumptions behind the statistical analysis supporting a decision.

To accomplish these purposes, the illustrating problems, or "mini-cases," in each chapter typify business applications of statistical techniques. Thus the assumptions underlying statistical methods are seen in the light of business data and the questions that should be raised by the manager are made concrete in business situations. Hopefully, some situations will be immediately relevant to the reader, while others will only require modification to fulfill present or future needs.

The raw material of statistics is numerical data; this conjures up an image of countless formulae to be mastered by rote without comprehension. We have attempted to minimize the use of formulae. In all instances, whether a formula is stated or not, we have solved the problem in familiar column fashion plus written instructions. The approach rests upon the notion that if the reader can understand what is being done and why—if he can verbalize the method illustrated—then he can construct his own formulae. After all, a formula represents a kind of shorthand comprising a set of instructions to accomplish some end. The end is always: what is to be done; why it is to be done; how it is to be done; and the significance of the results.

The emergence of managerial statistics has coincided with the growing complexity of business operations and the size of the marketplace. The demand for information and the advent of the computer began the "information revolution." Formerly the province of big business, the appearance of microcomputers and time-sharing arrangements have made these capabilities available to all business, large or small, at cost-effective rates. Consequently, it is hardly possible to discuss managerial statistics without reference to the computer. The statistical methods described in our chapters can be solved by computer. Moreover, in business situations, computer capabilities add new dimensions to statistical analysis. It behooves every manager, therefore, to ascertain how the computer might assist him in tackling those decisions that confront him in the performance of his duties. By the same token, the installation of computer facilities imposes on the manager the responsibility to acquire some of the basics about computer performance. Essentially, the manager should be able to interpret computer outputs, intelligently question computer solutions, and comprehend the limitations that attend use of computer data in decision making. The last chapter, dealing with managerial statistics and the computer, has these objectives.

The *Primer* is not a text in the conventional sense. It is plainly an introduction to those topics which are more immediately useful in business situations. Other topics could have been added and the discussion of the topics chosen could also have been expanded. These are matters of selectivity with which some will disagree. However, Appendix A contains a bibliography of academic and business publications. The sources cited introduce other topics in managerial statistics and/or offer advanced treatments of the topics included in the *Primer*.

The *Primer* contains many illustrating problems. To facilitate retention and understanding of the concept illustrated by the problem, the reader will do well to follow the solution using a pocket calculator. Appendix B, containing a glossary of key terms, should also prove useful in the learning process.

A STATISTICS
PRIMER
FOR MANAGERS

SECTION I
Managerial
Statistics

chapter 1

What Is Statistics . . . and Managerial Statistics?

Statistics is essentially concerned with mass phenomena, with aggregates, not with individual observations. The characteristics of some aggregate are sought, such as average family income in the United States, price movements on the New York Stock Exchange, business expenditures on new capital equipment, or changes in the size of the nation's money supply. The investigator looks for a *statistic*—a total, an average, a rank, or a percentage—to typify a mass of data. This perspective also conveys the idea that a statistic is a fact stated numerically.

Statistics focuses on aggregates because the stability of mass data makes it feasible to describe and/or predict. Although chance factors can shape the behavior of individuals, thus eroding the ability to predict, valid statements can still be formulated about aggregate behavior. We may not be able to predict next year's capital expenditures for a given company but we do, with a degree of success, annually forecast capital expenditures for *all* business firms. Statistical theory postulates the *stability of mass data*.

However, although definable, and to some degree predictable, the uniformities appearing from the analysis of mass data are not always perfect. An element of uncertainty is involved in the statistician's assertions about the aggregate under study. Thus statistics can also be viewed as a method of decision making in the face of uncertainty, on the basis of numerical data, and at calculated risks. Now, the statistician couches his generalizations in terms of probabilities and may employ methodologies congenial to managerial situations. When these methodologies are applied in a business context, we have identified the field of managerial statistics.

The uncertainty coloring statistical generalization emanates from the concept of randomness. A random variable is one that assumes different values because of chance. Consequently, random samples taken from the same population (for example, samples on business capital expenditures) may each show different results. Nonetheless, such chance fluctuations in sampling outcomes, while they create uncertainty, do not prevent the possibility of statistical generalization. Probability theory offers a method of dealing with these uncertainties and allows us to make inferences about the population from which the sample was taken.

Another source of uncertainty can arise from a deficiency of knowledge concerning the "state of nature," or how the laws of randomness apply in a given situation. In the case of capital expenditures, there already exists a body of statistical literature on the past behavior of the variable and the interpretation of changes in the numerical data. This provides a frame of reference when judging future sample results. For other variables, there may not exist a similar set of signposts pointing, tentatively at least, to the parameters of the problem. The investigator may have to formulate and test his own hypotheses aided by the sample information to arrive at a statistical generalization.

The difference is this: if you toss a fair coin a given number of times, you know that in the long run the number of heads and tails will *tend* to be equal; any given toss could go either way (hence the presence of risk) but the state of nature is known to be a 50–50 distribution. On the other hand, if the coin is biased, more heads or tails will appear; if you are not sure whether the coin is biased, you can run a sample number of tosses and test the results against the outcome that would have resulted were the coin a fair one. What is the *probability* of a similar result using a fair coin? You now have a basis for stating whether the coin is fair or biased—but you will never be sure. Herein are the elements of managerial statistics: decision making under conditions of uncertainty; use of numerical datas; the presence of risk expressed in probabilities.

It is convenient to define a few key terms used in the preceding paragraphs. *Population* refers to the totality of data that can be collected on the problem being studied, the group or aggregate about which the investigator will state relevant generalizations. For determining average family income in the United States, the population consists of all family units (as defined by the investigator). Thus average family income might be measured simply by looking at the income of each family unit—*a complete enumeration*.

This is likely to involve substantial expense, however. Instead of a complete enumeration of all family units, the investigator might survey only a portion of the population, that is, draw a *sample*. The size of the sample, the type of data collected, and the method of collection are appropriately left for later discussion. For the moment, we shall define a *random sample* as one in which every item in the population (that is, family unit) has an equal chance of being selected for the survey. *Only random samples permit the use of probabilities and create the basis for inferring statistical generalizations about the population surveyed.*

On the other hand, a complete enumeration of the population, where possible, eliminates or vastly reduces the risk of incorrectly describing the characteristics of the population. With a complete enumeration it is no longer necessary to make assumptions concerning the population in order to formulate statistical generalizations based on sample information.

SECTION II
The Several Varieties of Averages

chapter 2

Averages: Ungrouped Data

The world of business is beset by averages of all kinds. The daily prolif-eration of economic, business, and financial data makes it necessary for management to grasp quickly and concisely, the significance of vol-umes of statistical information. As a result there is great reliance by management staffs on the use of averages that summarize and typify large arrays of individualized information. Administrative services may use averages for comparative wage and salary studies; marketing may use averages in divisional sales analysis; in the financial area anal-ysis is replete with averages of earnings, stock prices, income, operating statistics, and so forth. Undoubtedly, averages form the basis for much "communication" between management, staff, and stock-holders concerning the company's profile.

However, although averages are widely used in business and are relatively uncomplicated, it behooves the manager to use caution in in-terpreting an average as typical of a data group. There are many types of averages, each with a distinct meaning and set of limitations.

TYPES OF AVERAGES

A valid average is representative of the individual values from which it is calculated. It aggregates numerical values into a single capsule. Hence, *an average measures the central tendency of the data, the point where the values cluster to typify the series.* But how typical is the average and how much reliance can be placed in this one number? The answer depends upon the type of average and the method of calculation.

Averages can be broadly classified as computational or positional:

1. *Computational averages.* These include the arithmetic mean, the geometric mean, and the harmonic mean. They are determined by computation of all the values in the data series and are subject to further manipulation.

9

2. *Positional averages.* These comprise the median, mode, and quartile averages. They depend upon the location of a single value in the series and hence cannot be further manipulated.

The most familiar and widely used averages are the arithmetic mean, the median, and mode. The geometric and harmonic means are less frequently seen and then primarily to average growth and time rates, respectively. We first consider the meaning and formulations of these averages and then their applications and limitations both for ungrouped data and grouped data.

COMPUTATIONAL AVERAGES FOR UNGROUPED DATA

Arithmetic Mean

The arithmetic mean ($\bar{X}$) is popularly considered synonomous with the term average because of its frequent usage. It is the sum of the inclusive values divided by the number of observations. For example, if management wants to obtain the average yield on high-quality corporate bonds for ten periods to determine the most representative yield per annum, they perform the operations shown in Table 2-1.

Table 2-1   Arithmetic Mean Corporate Bond Yields[a]

1 Year	2 Yield (X)
1961	0.0435
1962	0.0433
1963	0.0426
1964	0.0440
1965	0.0449
1966	0.0513
1967	0.0551
1968	0.0617
1969	0.0703
1970	0.0804
	Total = 0.5371

$$\bar{X} = \frac{0.5371}{10} = 0.05371$$

[a] *Source:* hypothetical data.

Uses and Limitations of the Arithmetic Mean

The arithmetic average has several advantages. These stem from its *algebraic properties*, which follow from its definition. It allows us to perform a number of useful calculations, which are discussed below.

Averaging the Averages. The average annual yield $(\bar{X})$ for the high-quality bonds shown in Table 2-1 is 0.05371, the arithmetic average of individual yields. Now assume individual spot averages of two bond portfolios—one contains ten bonds with an average price of $950, and the second consists of five bonds with an average price of $1,050. These portfolios can be averaged together in this manner—[10($950) + 5(1,050)]/15—to obtain an average price for the fifteen bonds of $983.33.

Determining the Total Value of the Series. The mean $(\bar{X})$ can be multiplied by the number of observations (N). Since the mean is defined as the sum of values divided by the number of observations, the average times the number of observations equals the total value. For example, if the average dollar value of accounts receivable is estimated at $100 and 1,000 accounts exist, the total value is readily calculable at $100,000; or the total of the yields on corporate bonds is the average yield of 0.05371 multiplied by 10, that is, 0.5371. It also follows that the average yield of 0.05371 can be substituted for all the values in the series and summed without changing the totals.

Measuring Dispersion or Variability of the Data in the Series. Since the mean is taken to be typical of the data from which it is computed, the validity of the mean depends upon the tendency of the individual datum to cluster around the mean. To the extent the individual datum disperses away from the mean, confidence in the mean as a representative figure declines. The closeness of the individual datum to the mean is measured by the standard deviation (described below). Suffice to say, the standard deviation is an important measure of risk in modern portfolio management.

Limitations. The limitations of the arithmetic average also stem from its definition. It includes all values in the series. Therefore, extreme values at either end of the distribution influence the average, pulling the mean in the direction of high and low values that may not be typical of the series. For example, if the 1970 bond yield in Table 2-1 is changed to 0.25 instead of 0.0804, it raises the average annual yield to 0.071 and distorts the picture for the ten-year period, since yields for eight periods are below 0.071 percent. Or suppose in the mythical kingdom of Zealot, there were 100,000 automobiles registered to 50,000 families. There are 200,000 families in Zealot Land. Accordingly, one might compute the mean ownership as 0.5 cars per family (100,000/200,000), or one car to every other family! In fact, only 25 percent of the Zealot families own cars. You might bear the lesson in mind when the government releases similar data on home ownership, per capita GNP, and the like. Every average has its uses and limitations, and these must always be kept in mind.

Weighted Arithmetic Average

The arithmetic mean is a weighted average in the sense that each value in the series has an equal weight of one. In the case of corporate bond yields in Table 2-1, each bond yield has a weight of one, since it is included only once in the total. When the arithmetic mean is calculated from a frequency distribution (Chapter 3), the frequencies are considered weights.

In general, when some values have greater influence than others because of their importance or magnitude, they can be weighted (included more than once in the total) to obtain a more accurate estimate of the average.

The weighted average ($\bar{X}_w$) is defined as the sum of the individual items multiplied by their weights and divided by the sum of the weights. For example, since the current yield is the ratio of dollar interest to price, assume a set of corporate bond yields are weighted by prices paid for the bonds. Yields are multiplied by bond prices to determine the dollar yield. The weighted average yield of the portfolio ($\bar{X}_w$) is the sum of these products divided by the total value of the portfolio (see Table 2-2).

Table 2-2   Weighted Average of Corporate Bond Yields[a]

1[b] Year	2 Yield (X)	3 Bond Price (W)	4 (2 × 3) Dollar Yield (WX)
1961	0.0435	$1,150	$50.03
1962	0.0433	$1,155	$50.22
1963	0.0426	$1,100	$46.86
1964	0.0440	$1,100	$48.40
1965	0.0449	$1,115	$49.84
1966	0.0513	$1,000	$51.30
1967	0.0551	$ 950	$52.35
1968	0.0617	$ 930	$57.38
1969	0.0703	$ 800	$56.24
1970	0.0804	$ 700	$56.28
		Total weights = $10,000	Sum of yields times weights } = $518.90

$$\bar{X}_w = \frac{\$518.90}{\$10,000.00} = 0.0519$$

[a] *Source:* hypothetical data.
[b] To facilitate comprehension of this table, and all others in this text, the columns have been numbered.

An alternative method of calculating the weighted average lies in expressing the weights as percentages. Table 2-3 uses dollar averaging—a common technique in portfolio management—to illustrate percentage weights.

If an equal number of shares are purchased at four different price levels in column 2 of Table 2-3, the problem reduces to a weighted average: the average price per share is then $55 ($220/4). However, if the prices per share are weighted by the proportionate representation of each purchase in the total portfolio (for example 40/177 = 0.226), the weighted average price per share falls to $45.22. Dollar averaging permits an investor who commits a constant sum of money to his portfolio in each time interval to take advantage of price variations in the security markets to lower his average cost per share. The commitment of a fixed sum to investment purchases a larger number of shares when prices fall and fewer shares when prices rise. But the weighted average cost is lower.

Geometric Mean

The geometric mean (GM) is defined as the Nth root of the product of N numbers. In statistical shorthand the formulation becomes

$$GM = \sqrt[N]{X_1 \cdot X_2 \cdot X_3 \ldots X_n} \tag{2-1}$$

where: X = value of a single observation or item,
N = number of observations or items,
n = and so on to the last observation or item

The formula tells us simply to multiply all the observations or items in a series by one another and take the Nth root of the product. The calculation can be easily accomplished by any pocket calculator that performs log functions.

Assume observations on bond yields, 0.0845 and 0.20 for the dates 1970 and 1980. *It is further presumed that the rate of change per year grows at an increasing rate.* If an estimate for 1975 is desired, the geometric mean will provide the correct solution:

$$\begin{aligned} GM &= \sqrt[2]{0.0845 \times 0.20} \\ &= \sqrt[2]{0.0169} \\ &= 0.13, \text{ or } 13\% \end{aligned} \tag{2-2}$$

By contrast, the arithmetic mean would yield a rate of 0.14225, or 14.2 percent [(0.0845 + 0.20)/2] for 1975. The difference in results traces back to the assumptions of the problem. The arithmetic mean ($\bar{X}$) assumes that yields are increasing at the same rate each year; the geometric mean (GM) presumed a forecast of increasing annual growth rates.

This basic problem illustrates the essential characteristic of the geometric mean. Although less frequently used than the arithmetic mean,

Table 2-3 Weighted Average Cost of Stock Shares: Percentage Weights[a]

1 Period	2 Price Per Share (X)	3 Number of Shares Purchased (N)	4 (N/ΣN) Percentage Weights (W)	5 (2 × 4) Weighted Average Cost (WX)	6 (2 × 3) Total Cost
January	$50	40	0.226	$11.30	$2,000
February	$100	20	0.113	$11.30	$2,000
March	$40	50	0.282	$11.28	$2,000
April	$30	67	0.378	$11.34	$2,000
		177	Total weights = 1.000	Sum of price times weights } = $45.22	$8,000

Proof:

$$\bar{X}_w = \frac{\$45.22}{1.00} = \$45.22$$

[a] Source: hypothetical data.

the geometric mean provides the only theoretically correct solution for averaging rates of change.

Logarithms

For more complex problems requiring the geometric mean, the use of logarithms can facilitate solution. The system of logarithms is based upon 10, that is, the log of a number is the *power* to which 10 must be raised to obtain that number. Thus the log of 10,000 is 4, since 10^4 (ten to the fourth power, or $10 \times 10 \times 10 \times 10$) = 10,000. Four is also called the exponent, indicating the number of times 10 is repeated as a factor. Likewise:

$$\text{log of } 0.1 = -1, \text{ because } 10^{-1} = 0.1$$
$$\text{log of } 0.01 = -2, \text{ because } 10^{-2} = 0.01$$
$$\text{log of } 0.001 = -3, \text{ because } 10^{-3} = 0.001$$
$$\text{log of } 0.0001 = -4, \text{ because } 10^{-4} = 0.0001$$

Characteristic. The number that refers to the integral power of 10 is the characteristic. To determine the characteristic apply the following rules:

1. If the number is greater than 1, the characteristic of the log is one less than the number of digits to the left of the decimal. For example, the characteristic of all numbers from 1 to 9.9 is 0 (1 − 1 = 0); for 10 to 99.9, the characteristic is 1 (2 − 1); from 100 to 999.9, 2 (3 − 1); and so on for higher numbers.
2. If the number is less than 1, the characteristic (negative) is 1 greater than the number of zeros between the decimal point and the first integer other than zero. For example, 0.677 has a characteristic of − 1; 0.0677 has a characteristic of − 2.

Mantissa. The Mantissa of each of the numbers lying between the integral powers of 10 will be fractional and can be obtained by use of Table 2-4 (alone, or in combination with *interpolation*, discussed below). The logarithm is formed by placing a decimal point before the mantissa and then adding the characteristic, as shown in Table 2-5.

Interpolation. Logs of variables with more than 3 digits require interpolation between two values in the table of common logarithms. What is the log of 1205? It must lie in Table 2-4 between 12 in the 0 column and 12 in column 1. Hence,

$$\text{log of } 1200 = 3.0792$$
$$\text{log of } 1205 = ?$$
$$\text{log of } 1210 = 3.0828$$

First we compute the difference in log values,

$$3.0828 - 3.0792 = 0.0036$$

A STATISTICS PRIMER FOR MANAGERS

**Table 2-4   Common Logarithms
(Selected Numbers)**

N	0	1	2	3	4	5	6	7	8	9
10	0000	0043	0086	0128	0170	0212	0253	0294	0334	0374
11	0414	0453	0492	0531	0569	0607	0645	0682	0719	0755
12	0792	0828	0864	0899	0934	0969	1004	1038	1072	1106
13	1139	1173	1206	1239	1271	1303	1335	1367	1399	1430
14	1461	1492	1523	1553	1584	1614	1644	1673	1703	1732
15	1761	1790	1818	1847	1875	1903	1931	1959	1987	2014
16	2041	2068	2095	2122	2148	2175	2201	2227	2253	2279
17	2304	2330	2355	2380	2405	2430	2455	2480	2504	2529
18	2553	2577	2601	2625	2648	2672	2695	2718	2742	2765
19	2788	2810	2833	2856	2878	2900	2923	2945	2967	2989
25	3979	3997	4014	4031	4048	4065	4082	4099	4116	4133
35	5441	5453	5465	5478	5490	5502	5515	5527	5539	5551
36	5563	5575	5587	5599	5611	5623	5635	5647	5659	5670
45	6532	6542	6551	6561	6571	6580	6590	6599	6609	6618
54	7324	7332	7340	7348	7356	7364	7372	7380	7388	7396
55	7404	7412	7419	7427	7435	7443	7451	7459	7466	7474
56	7482	7490	7497	7505	7513	7520	7528	7536	7543	7551
67	8261	8267	8274	8280	8287	8293	8299	8306	8312	8319
74	8692	8698	8704	8710	8716	8722	8727	8733	8739	8745
75	8751	8756	8762	8768	8774	8779	8785	8791	8797	8802
95	9777	9782	9786	9791	9795	9800	9805	9809	9814	9818
96	9823	9827	9832	9836	9841	9845	9850	9854	9859	9863
97	9868	9872	9877	9881	9886	9890	9894	9899	9903	9908
98	9912	9917	9921	9926	9930	9934	9939	9943	9948	9952
99	9956	9961	9965	9969	9974	9978	9983	9987	9991	9996
N	0	1	2	3	4	5	6	7	8	9

Then we compute the spread between the numbers above and below 1205:

$$1210 - 1200 = 10$$

and the spread between preceding number and 1205:

$$1205 - 1200 = 5$$

Table 2-5   Forming the Logarithm

1 Number	2 Characteristic	3 Mantissa[a]	4 Logarithm
6770	3	8306	3.8306
677	2	8306	2.8306
67.7	1	8306	1.8306
6.77	0	8306	0.8306
0.677	−1	8306	−1 + .8306 = −0.1694
0.0677	−2	8306	−2 + .8306 = −1.1694
75.0000	1	8751	1.8751
999.0000	2	9996	2.9996
10.5	1	0212	1.0212

[a] For each number in column 1 the mantissa is found by taking the first two digits as the row and the following digit as the column and reading across and down in Table 2-4. Since the first digit must be nonzero the first six numbers in column 1 have the same mantissa. The difference in their log will result from their different characteristics (see column 2).

Then we multiply the difference in log values by the ratio of the above spreads:

$$\frac{5}{10} \times 0.0036 = 0.0018$$

and add this number to the log of 1200:

$$3.0792 + 0.0018 = 3.0810, \text{ the log of 1205.}$$

Antilog. Logarithms facilitate the manipulation of original numbers but business usage normally requires reconversion of the log values back to the original data format. What is the antilog of 3.6580? The mantissa 6580 is found in the row 45 under the 5th column. The characteristic of 3 indicates that there are four digits to the left of the decimal point. Hence the original number is 4550. What is the antilog of −0.5918? When finding the antilog of a negative number you must first subtract it from the next integer in order to obtain the mantissa (1 − 0.5918 = 0.4082). The mantissa is found in the row 25 under the 6th column. The characteristic is −1 because the integer from which 0.5918 was subtracted was 1 (had we been seeking the antilog of −1.5918 it would have been necessary to subtract from 2 and the characteristic would have been −2). The characteristic of −1 tells us that there are no (1 − 1) zeroes between the decimal point and the first significant digit, so the original number is 0.2560. Other examples of antilogs appear below:

Log	Antilog (Original Data)
2.4133	259
0.7490	5.61
1.0128	10.3
−1.2644 (= −2 + 0.7356)	0.0544

Use of Logarithms. A little practice with the preceding examples will allow the reader to become quite knowledgeable in the use of logs. They are able to ease the burden of tedious computations.

1. To multiply original numbers, add their logs and obtain the antilog. The addition of logs is the equivalent of the multiplication of original numbers.
2. To divide numbers, subtract their log values and get the antilog. Subtraction becomes the equivalent of division.
3. To raise a number to a certain power, multiply the log of the number by the exponent and obtain the antilog.
4. To extract the root of a number (square root, cube root, fifth root, tenth root, and so on) divide the number by the index of the root (2, 3, 5, 10, and so on) and the quotient is the log of the desired root.

All of this is made easier still by the use of the typical pocket calculator which enables you to obtain the log and antilog of a number without resorting to tables. Nonetheless, you must understand the concept and use of logarithms before you can intelligently employ a calculator.

We are now ready to use logarithms for the computation of the geometric mean (Table 2-6).

The average rate of growth per annum in the Table 2-6 example approximates 11.17 percent. By contrast, the GM of the bond yields (Table 2-6, column 2) is 5.9 percent while the arithmetic mean is 6.1 percent.

Uses and Limitations of the Geometric Mean

The GM treats relative changes for increasing (decreasing) values in a series, whereas the arithmetic mean treats changes as absolutes. For example, the overall percentage change in bond yields from 1965 to 1970 is 0.791 [(0.0804 − 0.0449)/0.0449]. The annualized rate of change, calculated from the arithmetic mean is 0.1582 (0.791/5), a rate that compounds to a value higher than 0.0804 in 1970.

The GM considers all values in a series, like the arithmetic mean but is less affected by large values. It has a lesser upward bias than the arithmetic mean because it considers relative, not absolute, values. Note that the geometric mean of 11.17 percent is lower than the arithmetic mean, which is the usual relationship between the two averages.

Table 2-6 Computation of Geometric Mean by Formula and by Log Values[a]

1	2	3	4
Period	Yield (X)	Growth Factor	Logs of Growth Factor
1965	0.0449		
1966	0.0513	0.0064/0.0449 = 0.1425	−0.8462
1967	0.0551	0.0038/0.0513 = 0.0741	−1.1302
1968	0.0617	0.0066/0.0617 = 0.1070	−0.9706
1969	0.0703	0.0086/0.0703 = 0.1223	−0.9126
1970	0.0804	0.0101/0.0804 = 0.1256	−0.9010
			Total = −4.7606

Geometric Mean of Growth Factor

By formula:

$$GM = \sqrt[5]{(0.1425)(0.0741)(0.1070)(0.1223)(0.1256)}$$

$$= \sqrt[5]{0.00001736}$$

$$= 0.1117, \text{ or } 11.17\%$$

By logarithms:

$$GM = \frac{\Sigma \text{ logs of Growth Factor}}{N}$$

$$= \frac{-4.7606}{5}$$

$$= -0.9521$$

$$\text{Mantissa} = 1 - 0.9521 = 0.0479$$

From Table 2-4, 0479 by interpolation yields 1117, giving an antilog of 0.1117, or 11.17 percent.

[a] *Source:* hypothetical data.

The GM provides the best solution for rates of change, although the arithmetic mean gives the correct solution for *amounts of change.* For example, the total amount of change in bond yields is 0.0355 (0.0804 − 0.0449), or 0.0071 amount of yield change per year (0.0355/5).

The GM can be substituted for each value in the series to obtain the same product. For example, in Table 2-6, substituting 11.17 for each observation (X) gives a product—0.00001736—identical to that obtained in the GM "by formula."

The GM gives logically consistent results when applied to averaging ratios while the arithmetic mean does not. The latter is biased upward, for it is influenced by extreme values and it is the nature of ratios to give preponderance to extreme values. The geometric mean does not suffer the same distortion.

The GM is used when the data is limited in one direction but not in the other. Prices, for example, rarely go below zero but may rise to extreme magnitudes.

An important limitation to the geometric mean is that it cannot be determined if there are zero or negative values in the series. Logically, a number cannot decline by more than 100 percent.

Harmonic Mean

The harmonic mean for a series of numbers is the reciprocal of the arithmetic mean of the reciprocals of the individual values. Since the reciprocal of a number X is equal to $1/X$, the formulation for the harmonic mean is

$$\frac{1}{H} = \frac{1/X_1 + 1/X_2 + 1/X_3 + \ldots + 1/X_n}{N} \div 1 \qquad (2\text{-}3)$$

where:

$$\frac{1}{H} = \text{harmonic mean}$$

N = number of observations or items
X = values of the observations
n = the nth value

Uses and Limitations

The harmonic mean is the statistic to use in averaging time rates and ratios, but the appropriate use of the harmonic mean depends on the conditions set forth in the problem. When time is treated as a variable and other values are constant in relation to time, the harmonic mean should be employed. For instance, assume two departments are charged computer time per printout, and that department A uses 30 seconds per printout and department B 45 seconds per printout. *The average time required per printout should be solved by the harmonic mean, since time is varied,* and weighted with an equal amount of printouts. If the problem is expressed as thirty printouts per second and forty-five printouts per second, *the average number of printout per second is determined by the arithmetic mean.*

The harmonic mean is especially feasible where the data are expressed inversely to what is required in the average, that is, when average cost per unit is desired but the data show the number of outputs per amount of cost. An investor may spend $1,000 for 10 shares of stock at one time, $1,000 for 20 shares at another, and $1,000 for 50 shares at another. The average price per share in the three different periods is $100, $50, and $20. The arithmetic mean is $56.67 per share. A moment's reflection will show that the answer is ludicrous. If the average price per share is $56.67 and the investor has 80 shares, then his total investment must be \$4533.60. Yet we know he invested only \$3,000! The appropriate average results by resorting to the harmonic mean.

$$\frac{1}{H} = \frac{1/\$100 + 1/\$50 + 1/\$20}{3} \div 1$$

$$= \frac{\$0.01 + \$0.02 + \$0.05}{3} \div 1 \qquad (2\text{-}4)$$

$$= \frac{3}{\$0.08}$$

$$= \$37.50$$

Now, multiplying the price per share (\$37.50) by the number of shares (80), we obtain \$3,000, the correct total investment. The reader will properly observe that in this case a weighted arithmetic mean would also produce accurate results.

Also bear in mind that characteristically the value of the harmonic mean is smaller than the geometric and arithmetic means when all are computed from the same basic data.

POSITIONAL AVERAGES OF UNGROUPED DATA

Median (Md)

The median is the "centralmost" item of the series when data are arranged by order of magnitude from the smallest to the largest value. When the "central" or "middle" value is selected, the series is divided so that 50 percent of the values are equal to or lie above the median and 50 percent are equal to or fall below. When the series contains an equal number of observations, the median represents the average of the two central values.

Table 2-7 arranges our corporate bond yields in order of magnitude. Since the median consists of an even number of values (10), the median yield equals the average of the two central values (0.0449 and 0.0513), or 0.0481. If 0.0804 were dropped from the series, an odd number of values would remain and the middle value (0.0449) would denote the median.

Should the same value occur more than once in the middle of the series—that is, 0.0426, 0.0433, 0.0433, 0.0433, 0.0433, 0.0440, and 0.0449—the central yield (0.0433) is still the median. Fifty percent of the values lie above and below 0.0433.

Uses and Limitations

Unlike the arithmetic mean, the median is not affected by extreme values. In Table 2-7, if the 0.0804 yield were instead 0.25, the median would remain unchanged at 0.0481. By contrast, the arithmetic mean would shift from 0.0537 to 0.0707. *The median reflects the location of the*

Table 2-7   Median Average Corporate Bond Yields[a]

Order of Magnitudes	Yield
1	0.0426
2	0.0433
3	0.0435
4	0.0440
5	0.0449
6	0.0513
7	0.0551
8	0.0617
9	0.0703
10	0.0804

$$\text{Med} = \frac{0.0449 + 0.0513}{2} = 0.0481$$

[a] *Source:* hypothetical data.

items in the series rather than the magnitude of the values at the ends of the distribution. Thus, depending on the characteristics of the data, the median may better typify the series than the mean. The advantages of the median are discussed below:

An excellent measure of central tendency, particularly with business data where larger numerical values tend to appear at the ends of the distribution. The number of U.S. corporations listed by asset size will tail off at the upper end of the distribution into a few extremely large corporations.

An average closest to all the values in series. The sum of the absolute deviations (Σd) of the observations (signs ignored) from the median is less than the sum of the absolute deviations from any other point in the distribution (see Table 2-8). The sum of the deviations is less from the median than from any other bond yield in the distribution and less also than the sum of the deviations from the arithmetic mean.

This attribute of median—a minimum total deviation—enhances the business usefulness of the median in certain situations such as setting automobile insurance rates to approximate actual claim costs or in selecting a plant site where the objective is to pick the location closest to other operational facilities of the company.

Apropos of total deviations, the reader should bear in mind that, although the sum of the deviations, *ignoring signs,* is less for the median than the mean, *the algebraic sum* of the deviations around the mean is always zero ($+ 0.05266 - 0.05266 = 0$). The same generalization does not hold for the median.

The disadvantages of the median follow from its definition:

The median lacks mathematical formulation. It is a positional average not subject to further algebraic manipulation. Mathematically speaking,

Table 2-8   Sum of Deviations From the Arithmetic Mean and the Median[a]

1	2	3
	Deviations (d) from the	Deviations (d) from the
Yield (X)	Mean $(X - \bar{X})$	Median $(X - Md)$
0.0426	−0.01111	−0.0055
0.0433	−0.01041	−0.0048
0.0435	−0.01021	−0.0046
0.0440	−0.00971	−0.0041
0.0449	−0.00881	−0.0032
0.0513	−0.00241	+0.0032
0.0551	+0.00139	+0.0070
0.0617	+0.00799	+0.0136
0.0703	+0.01659	+0.0222
0.0804	+0.02669	+0.0323
	Total deviations = 0.10532 (signs ignored)	Total deviations = 0.1005 (signs ignored)
	$\bar{X}$ = 0.05371	Median = 0.0481

[a] *Source:* hypothetical data.

after we have obtained the median, there is not much more we can do with it. The "averaging of averages" does not give meaningful information in the case of positional averages. The medians of two or more series cannot be averaged to secured a single figure which typifies the group. If the purchase costs of two bonds portfolios were expressed in median prices, the two averages could not be combined to secure a pertinent average price.

Use of the median for sample and other incomplete data does not produce a reliable estimate. The data are incomplete per se, and the median does not embody all the values in the sample. The mean would be the preferred average in these situations.

Mode (Mo)

The mode or modal average represents the value that appears most frequently in a set of observations. It identifies the most probable value in the series. The term average is frequently (and wrongly) equated to the mode. Too often, for example, the average wage in the United States is believed to be the wage rate paid to most employees. The association of mode and average arises because the former conveys the impression of what is a common characteristic of the series. For example, in a series of yields—0.0426, 0.0433, 0.0435, 0.0435, 0.0435, 0.0440, 0.0449, and 0.0480—the modal value is 0.0435.

Uses and Limitations

The frequency of the modal value opens the way to many useful business applications. For instance, an engineering firm designing campers for the average family might find the modal average of 3 more helpful in their design plans than the arithmetic average of 3¹/₄ persons per household. Or a company manufacturing paints would prefer the modal average as a guide to the most popular color of house paint—a determination that could not be made from the median or arithmetic average. Other illustrations include the need to know the frequency of certain qualitative variables as style, size, fabric type, color, and so forth.

Extreme values in the distribution do not effect the modal average.

However, the mode has its limitations, too:

It may be difficult to locate the mode if the data are given as a continuous series, such as temperatures, rates of production, product durability, and so on. Variations in the data take place along a continuum and can be measured to some specified degree of accuracy. In these instances, the mode becomes more of an approximation. The problem, however, is mitigated by the use of grouped data.

If the series is bimodal, a conflict of modes can exist. To illustrate, take the following bond yields in a portfolio: 0.0426, 0.0433, 0.0433, 0.0433, 0.0440, 0.0625, 0.0750, 0.0803, 0.0803, 0.0803, and 0.0825. What is the mode? Examination of the data shows two points of concentration, 0.0448 and 0.0803. The condition suggests the data are not homogeneous, that the series mixes noncomparable variables. In the case of the

Table 2-9   Modal Average Corporate Bond Yields[a]

1 Order of Magnitude	2 Average Yield	3 Rounded Yields	4 Second Rounding
1	0.0426	0.043	0.04
2	0.0433	0.043	0.04
3	0.0435	0.044	0.04
4	0.0440	0.044	0.04
5	0.0449	0.045	0.04
6	0.0513	0.051	0.05
7	0.0551	0.055	0.06
8	0.0617	0.062	0.06
9	0.0703	0.070	0.07
10	0.0804	0.080	0.08

Methods of selecting mode:

  A—col. 2 has no mode; all numbers differ.

  B—col. 3, Mo = (0.043 + 0.044)/2 = 0.044

  C—col. 4, Mo = 0.04

[a] *Source:* hypothetical data.

bond yields, the data may be mixing yields on high-quality and low-quality bonds. The investigator should, accordingly, break the series into two groups and determine the mode for each group.

Similar to other positional averages, the mode cannot be subjected to further mathematical manipulation.

These difficulties in the determination of the mode appear in our hypothetical bond yields (Table 2-9).

The erratic behavior exhibited in Table 2-9 raises doubts about the validity of the mode in like situations.

HOW GOOD IS THE AVERAGE?

Although averages summarize aggregate data and facilitate comparisons for business decisions, separate series may exhibit the same average but have the individual observations (X) differently dispersed from the average. Some observations may cluster close to the mean and show little variation therefrom; in other series, observations may disperse widely from the average and show larger variations. In evaluating an average, the manager needs to know something of the variability or dispersion of the individual items around the average.

When dispersion is high, the average is less significant; low dispersion enhances the meaningfulness of the average. For instance, a comparison of earnings per share in two firms may show the same mean and median of $3.00 per share. But quarterly earnings can differ significantly. Firm A's quarterly earnings are $2.95, $3.00, $3.00, and $3.05; firm B's are $1.00, $3.00, $3.00, and $5.00. If the investor strives to minimize risk, the lower variability of A's stock, given the same average earnings, would constitute the preferred selection.

MEASURING VARIABILITY

The dispersion of data from the mean or median can be measured in several ways. Some methods utilize only the extreme values in a series (the range and quartile deviations); others include all values in the data group (mean absolute deviation and standard deviation). Each method has its particular advantages and limitations.

Range

The range is the difference between the lowest and highest values in the series. For example, corporate bond yields in two portfolios have equal means of 0.0537. Table 2-10 computes the range deviation for each portfolio. A comparison uncovers a marked difference in yield spreads. Portfolio B has less risk for the same average yield.

Table 2-10   The Range: Bond Yields of Portfolio A and B[a]

1 Portfolio A Yields	2 Portfolio B Yields
0.0426	0.0487
0.0433	0.0497
0.0435	0.0499
0.0440	0.0525
0.0449	0.0535
0.0513	0.0545
0.0551	0.0550
0.0617	0.0570
0.0703	0.0575
0.0804	0.0588
$\overline{X} = 0.0537$	$\overline{X} = 0.0537$

Range:
   Portfolio A: $0.0804 - 0.0426 = 0.0378$
   Portfolio B: $0.0588 - 0.0487 = 0.0101$

[a] *Source:* hypothetical data.

The range is simple and easy to compute, always an advantage to any statistic. It has business applications in continuous data series, where every value is represented and usually very large or small values that distort the range are absent. An example would be testing product temperatures. Also, in assembly-line quality control, reliable comparisons of samples can be made using the range deviation.

The major drawback to the range involves the influence of extreme values at the ends of the distribution. Moreover, the values between the ends of the distribution have no effect on the range. Thus the range may not truly reflect the dispersion of the series.

Quartile Deviation

The suffix iles designates values that divide the series, such as quartiles, deciles, percentiles. These are all computed in the same manner, the only difference (illustrated in the Chapter 3) involving the denominators: for quartiles, the denominator is 4; deciles, 10; and percentiles, 100.

Calculation of the quartile points for ungrouped data is determined by first arranging the data in an ascending order, and then dividing the total number of observations (N) as follows:

$$\text{Quartile 1 } (Q_1) = \frac{N+1}{4} \quad \text{or} \quad \frac{10+1}{4} = 2.75$$

$$\text{Quartile 2 } (Q_2) = \frac{N+1}{2} \quad \text{or} \quad \frac{10+1}{2} = 5.5 \qquad (2\text{-}5)$$

$$\text{Quartile 3 } (Q_3) = \frac{3N+1}{4} \quad \text{or} \quad \frac{3(10+1)}{4} = 8.25$$

In the case of equation (2-5) and in Table 2-11 below, $N = 10$. Q_1 is the point in the series below which there are 25 percent of the observations. Seventy-five percent of the observations lie above Q_1. The median, represented by Q_2, designates the value above and below which lie 50 percent of the observations; Q_3 is the point below which there are 75 percent of the observations and 25 percent above.

The difference between the third and first quartiles denotes the interquartile range, containing the middle 50 percent of the observations: $Q_3 - Q_1$. The quartile deviation (QD), or the semi-interquartile range, divides the interquartile range by 2; QD is a better measure of disper-

Table 2-11   Quartile Deviations Corporate Bond Yields[a]

Yields

0.0426
0.0433

$\longleftarrow Q_1 = \dfrac{10+1}{4} = 2.75;$ $(0.0435 - 0.0433) \times 0.75 = 0.00015;$
$0.0433 + 0.00015 = 0.04345$

0.0435
0.0440
0.0449

$\longleftarrow Q_2 = \dfrac{10+1}{2} = 5.5;$ $(0.0513 - 0.0449) \times 0.5 = 0.0032;$
$0.0449 + 0.0032 = 0.0481$

0.0513
0.0551
0.0617

$\longleftarrow Q_3 = \dfrac{3(10+1)}{4} = 8.25;$ $(0.0703 - 0.0617) \times 0.25 = 0.00215;$
$0.0617 + 0.00215 = 0.06385$

0.0703
0.0804

$$\text{Interquartile range} = Q_3 - Q_1 = 0.06385 - 0.04345 = 0.0204$$

$$\text{Quartile deviation (QD)} = \frac{Q_3 - Q_1}{2} = \frac{0.06385 - 0.04345}{2} = 0.0102$$

[a] *Source:* hypothetical data.

sion than the range because it encompasses only the middle half of the series. Therefore, unlike the range, QD does not consider the extreme values at both ends of the series. Table 2-11 illustrates the calculation of Q_1, Q_2, and Q_3 using as data the Portfolio A yields of Table 2-10.

The interquartile range is 0.0204 (0.06385 − 0.04345) from Table 2-11. The semi-interquartile range (QD) is 0.0102 (0.0204/2). Accordingly, if K denotes a value halfway between Q_1 and Q_3, then 50 percent of the observations in the distribution fall within the range $K \pm QD$. From Table 2-11, for example, $K = Q_1 + QD$ or 0.05365 (0.04345 + 0.0102). Then 0.05365 ± 0.0102 describes a range containing the middle 50 percent of the observations.

Mean Absolute Deviation (MAD)

MAD represents the arithmetic mean of the deviations of individual values from the average. It captures in one value the deviations of all observations from the average and offers an indicator of typical variation. The calculation is rudimentary:

1. Determine the mean or median of the series.
2. Take the difference between the mean or the median and each observation in the series.
3. Add up the differences (ignoring signs) and divide by the total observations (N).

The mean absolute deviation of our two portfolios is calculated in Table 2-12.

With the same average yield (0.05371), portfolio A has a larger average deviation than portfolio B. As we saw in Table 2-10 (using the range) investing in A is riskier, despite the equality of yield with B. Actually, A should provide a higher yield to compensate for the added risk.

Since its formulation includes all values in the series and does not limit the measurement to certain points, MAD constitutes a more extensive measure of dispersion than the range or quartile deviation. Along with ease of calculation, these attributes make MAD a useful calculation in less complex analysis. However, because MAD measures absolute deviations and ignores plus and minus signs, it is not amenable to further mathematical manipulation.

The most reliable and widely used measure of dispersion is the standard deviation, which overcomes many of the difficulties associated with other measurers.

Table 2-12 Mean Absolute Deviation Corporate Bond Yields[a]

Portfolio A		Portfolio B	
1 Yield (X)	2 Deviation $(X - \bar{X})$	3 Yield (X)	4 Deviation $(X - \bar{X})$
0.0435	−0.01021	0.0487	−0.00501
0.0433	−0.01041	0.0497	−0.00401
0.0426	−0.01111	0.0499	−0.00381
0.0440	−0.00971	0.0525	−0.00121
0.0449	−0.00881	0.0535	−0.00021
0.0513	−0.00241	0.0545	+0.00079
0.0551	+0.00139	0.0550	+0.00129
0.0617	+0.00799	0.0570	+0.00329
0.0703	+0.01659	0.0575	+0.00379
0.0804	+0.02669	0.0588	+0.00509
$\bar{X}$ = 0.05371	Sum of deviations } = 0.10532 (signs ignored)	$\bar{X}$ = 0.05371	Sum of deviations } = 0.0285 (signs ignored)

$$\text{MAD} = \frac{0.10532}{10} = 0.010532$$

$$\text{MAD} = \frac{0.0285}{10} = 0.00285$$

[a] Source: hypothetical data.

29

Standard Deviation [SD or Sigma (σ)]

Sigma is the square root of the mean of the individual deviations squared. The steps to calculate the standard deviation are similar to MAD, except that the deviations are *squared,* summed, divided by N, and the *square root* taken. Thus,

$$\sigma = \sqrt{\frac{\Sigma (X - \bar{X})^2}{N}} \qquad (2\text{-}6)$$

where, Σ is the sum of the observations; in this case, the sum of squared deviations.

Using the data in Table 2-12, we can calculate the standard deviation of portfolios A and B (Table 2-13).

Comparison of the two portfolios again suggests that A bears a heavier burden of risk using the standard deviation as the index of risk. A large standard deviation implies an investor should be less confident of attaining the portfolio's average yield.

The standard deviation shares the advantages of the mean absolute deviation. Both are precise measures of dispersion that take in all the values contributing to the computation of the mean. Nevertheless, the standard deviation is, overall, a superior measure. The negative and positive signs are eliminated by squaring the deviations. In the mean absolute deviation, the plus and minus signs are simply ignored. If they are not ignored, the sum of the deviations (plus and minus) will be zero if the mean is the reference point or nearly zero where the median serves as the reference point. The consequence is an average with no dispersion—an illogical result with business data. Also, where the data are dissimilar, measures of absolute dispersion have no significance for comparison purposes.

Finally, we should take note of the term, *variance,* especially common in business statistics. The term is the square of the standard deviation. (As such, it is merely the next to last step in the calculation of σ—see Table 2-13.) For example, the variance of portfolio A is

$$\sigma_A^2 = (0.0125)^2 = 0.000156 \qquad (2\text{-}7)$$

The analysis of variance is an important topic in our subsequent discussion of correlations (Chapter 9).

RELATIVE DISPERSION

Relative dispersion relates the standard deviation to the mean of the series from which it is computed. If the standard deviations of two proposed capital expenditures, C and D, are $1,000 and $3,000 respectively, and the average cash flows of C equals $10,000 and D, $40,000, one

Table 2-13 Standard Deviation Corporate Bond Yields[a]

	Portfolio A			Portfolio B	
1 Yield (X)	2 $(X - \overline{X})$ Deviation (d)	3 d^2	4 Yield (X)	5 $(X - \overline{X})$ Deviation (d)	6 d^2
0.0435	-0.01021	0.0001042	0.0487	-0.00501	0.0000251
0.0433	-0.01041	0.0001083	0.0497	-0.00401	0.0000160
0.0426	-0.01111	0.0001234	0.0499	-0.00381	0.0000145
0.0440	-0.00971	0.0000942	0.0525	-0.00121	0.0000014
0.0449	-0.00881	0.0000776	0.0535	-0.00021	0.0000441
0.0513	-0.00241	0.0000058	0.0545	+0.00079	0.0000006
0.0551	+0.00139	0.0000019	0.0550	+0.00129	0.0000016
0.0617	+0.00799	0.0000638	0.0570	+0.00329	0.0000108
0.0703	+0.01659	0.0002752	0.0575	+0.00379	0.0000143
0.0804	+0.02669	0.0007123	0.0588	+0.00509	0.0000259
$\overline{X} = 0.05371$		$\Sigma d^2 = 0.0015667$	$\overline{X} = 0.05371$		$\Sigma d^2 = 0.0001157$

$$\sigma = \sqrt{\frac{0.0015667}{10}} = \sqrt{0.0001566} = 0.0125$$

$$\sigma = \sqrt{\frac{0.0001157}{10}} = \sqrt{0.0000115} = 0.0034$$

[a] *Source*: hypothetical data.

might conclude that D bears a heavier burden of risk. The statement is valid in absolute terms ($3,000 > $1,000) but relatively D is the less risky project. The Coefficient of Variation (V) provides a relative measure of dispersion by dividing the average into its standard deviation. Therefore, for projects C and D, the coefficients of variation are:

$$V_{\text{proj. C}} = \frac{\$1,000}{\$10,000} = 0.10, \text{ or } 10\%$$

$$V_{\text{proj. D}} = \frac{\$3,000}{\$40,000} = 0.075, \text{ or } 7.5\%$$

(2-8)

Relatively, D is the less risky project, given the size of the cash flows.

SUMMARY

Chapter 1 emphasized that from one perspective statistics is primarily concerned with masses of data or aggregates and seeks to identify a single figure that will typify the mass. Averages are one aspect of this aggregative function. But the term average covers a variety of measures, each of which has its particular characteristics, uses, and limitations. From the same basic data, the result will differ, depending on the average applied. For our basic bond yield data, the following data were found:

$$\begin{aligned}
\text{Arithmetic mean } (\bar{X}) &= 0.05371, \text{ or } 5.37\% \\
\text{Weighted arithmetic mean } (\bar{X}_w) &= 0.0519, \text{ or } 5.19\% \\
\text{Median average } (Md) &= 0.0481, \text{ or } 4.81\% \\
\text{Modal average } (Mo) &= \text{(A) No mode, or} \\
& \text{(B) } 0.044, \text{ or } 4.4\%, \text{ or} \\
& \text{(C) } 0.04, \text{ or } 4.0\%
\end{aligned}$$

For the measures of dispersion, the following figures were obtained:

$$\begin{aligned}
\text{Range} &= 0.0378, \text{ or } 3.78\% \\
\text{Quartile deviation } (QD) &= 0.0102, \text{ or } 1.02\% \\
\text{Mean absolute deviation } (MAD) &= 0.01053, \text{ or } 1.053\% \\
\text{Standard deviation } (\sigma) &= 0.0125, \text{ or } 1.25\%
\end{aligned}$$

Clearly, the correct average to use depends on the circumstances, the nature of the data, and the objectives of the inquiry. Certainly, management should not accept any average without raising questions relating to the computation of the average:

1. What are the characteristics of the data to be averaged? Do the data contain extreme values? Are the data homogeneous? Do they comprise rates of change or ratios?

2. How is the average to be used by the business? Is the average relevant to the objective of the investigation?
3. Is the average computed from a complete enumeration or a sample?
4. Is the average computational or positional?
5. Is the average weighted? If so, what weights were used?
6. What measure of dispersion was used to validate the average? What was the rationale for selecting a measure of dispersion?
7. What is the Coefficient of Variation?

chapter 3

Averages: Grouped Data

Business firms generate vast amounts of data, comprising a broad spectrum of information on the inputs and outputs of the production process from purchasing to distribution. Decision making requires the data be arranged for analysis and interpretation. Where the volume of data is limited, the methods described in Chapter 2 for ungrouped data suffice. However, if the quantity of data is large, the simple *array* (Table 3-1) does not convey its full significance to the manager. Even if the array were accompanied by an appropriate average and measure of dispersion, the format would not display other pertinent intelligence embodied in the data.

In these cases, the *frequency distribution*, which groups data into classes, constitutes a preferred format. Not only can the usual averages and measures of dispersion be calculated but the distribution of wages by different classes offers additional substantive information to the decision maker. Table 3-1 puts the raw data into *array*, ranging the data from lowest to highest values. Table 3-2 groups the arrayed data into a *frequency distribution*. Note class limits run from $10 to $59.99.

The classes in a frequency distribution can be quantitative or qualitative. As an example of the latter, a personnel department might require a classification of employees by mode of payment—weekly, bimonthly, monthly—with the corresponding number or frequency of employees in each class. When qualitative classes are used, the display is termed a *categorical frequency distribution.*

CONSTRUCTION OF A FREQUENCY DISTRIBUTION

Before attempting to calculate the various types of averages from a frequency distribution, a few basic steps will illustrate the construction of a frequency distribution:

1. *Collection and tallying of raw data.* Assume management wishes to analyze wages of employees in one of its offices. The information on wages or *raw data* is collected from the files and arrayed from the lowest to the highest wage (Table 3-1).
2. *Grouping of data.* Data are condensed into suitable classes or class intervals, in practice usually five to fifteen classes having lower and upper limits. The number of employees falling into each class is then tallied to secure the class frequencies.
3. *Class interval determination.* The appropriate number of classes (or the class intervals) rests to some degree on the exercise of judgment. The frequency distribution condenses large amounts of data to provide an overall view. Therefore, the interval should be small enough that significant trends are not submerged in a few large classes and large enough that generalizations are not rendered difficult by the existence of too many classes. If the interval were too large for the hourly wage rates in our example—say $10 to $29.99 and $30 to $59.99—important characteristics of the data would be lost in the broad groupings. On the other hand, smaller intervals might create too many classes and make interpretation equally difficult.

A common method of determining the *number of classes* involves assuming a class size (for example, $10) and dividing the class size into the difference between the highest and lowest values in the series:

$$i = \frac{H-L}{K} \qquad (3\text{-}1)$$

where: i = number of classes
H = largest value in the series
L = lowest value in the series
K = class interval

Table 3-1   Array of Hourly Wage Rates ($) of Eighty Employees[a]

10.50	22.50	32.00	37.50	39.50	45.00	49.50	54.00
11.00	24.00	32.50	37.50	39.50	45.50	49.50	54.50
12.00	25.50	33.00	38.00	40.00	46.00	50.00	55.00
15.00	26.00	33.50	38.00	41.50	46.50	51.00	55.50
16.50	27.50	34.00	38.00	42.00	47.00	51.50	56.00
18.50	28.00	34.50	38.50	42.50	47.50	52.00	57.00
19.50	29.00	35.00	39.00	43.00	48.00	52.50	58.00
20.50	30.50	35.50	39.00	43.50	48.50	53.00	59.00
21.50	31.00	36.00	39.50	44.00	49.00	53.50	59.50
22.00	31.50	36.50	39.50	44.50	49.50	53.50	59.50

[a] *Source:* hypothetical data.

**Table 3-2   Frequency Distribution
Hourly Wages Rates, Eighty Employees**[a]

1 Wage Rates	2 Number of Employees
$10–$19.99	7
$20–$29.99	10
$30–$39.99	25
$40–$49.99	20
$50–$59.99	18
	Total = 80

[a] *Source:* hypothetical data.

For our hourly wage example

$$i = \frac{\$59.50 - \$10.50}{\$10} \tag{3-2}$$

$$= 4.9, \text{ or } \approx 5 \text{ classes}$$

An alternate method assumes an appropriate number of classes instead of a class interval as follows:

$$K = \frac{H - L}{i}$$

$$= \frac{\$59.50 - \$10.50}{5} \tag{3-3}$$

$$= \$9.8, \text{ or } \approx \$10 \text{ class interval}$$

With five classes in the denominator, the class interval is $10 and the *stated class limits* range from $10 to $19.99, and so forth. To find the class interval, however, subtract the lower class limit of the preceding class from the lower class limit of the next class. With the wage data in Table 3-2, $30 − $20 = $10, the class interval. Therefore, the *midpoint of the second class* M_2 ($20 − $10) becomes:

$$M_2 = \frac{L_2 - L_1}{2} + L_2$$

$$= \frac{\$20 - \$10}{2} + \$20 \tag{3-4}$$

$$= \$25$$

where: M = midpoint of a given class
L_2 = lower limit of next higher class
L_l = lower limit of current class

Grouping data into frequency distributions involves certain inconveniences in the use of statistics for decision making:

1. *Identification of individual values.* The midpoint of each class *de facto* serves as the "original" or exact value for that class, and it is not possible to identify the actual lowest and highest values of the class.
2. *Loss of accuracy.* Averages calculated from a frequency distribution will differ from the true average calculated using the entire series of individual values.

All the same, the minimal loss in precision is more than outweighed by the enhanced informational content and the ease in handling large quantities of data.

COMPUTATIONAL AVERAGES

Arithmetic Mean (X)

When calculated from a frequency distribution, the arithmetic mean ($\bar{X}$) is in effect a weighted average, weighted by the class frequencies. In Table 3-3 the data from Table 3-1 are arranged in a frequency distribution and the arithmetic mean ($\bar{X}$) is calculated.

If the mean were tabulated from the array (Table 3-1), the result would be $39.32. While obviously the mean derived from the array better describes the true mean, the frequency distribution tells how many employees are in each wage range.

Table 3-3   Arithmetic Mean Hourly Wage Rates[a]

1 Classes	2 Frequency (F)	3 Midpoint (X)		4 (2 × 3) Weighted Totals (FX)
$10–$19.99	7	$15		105
$20–$29.99	10	$25		250
$30–$39.99	25	$35		875
$40–$49.99	20	$45		900
$50–$59.99	18	$55	Sum of class	990
	Total = 80		frequencies times } = 3,120	
			midpoints	

$$\bar{X} = \frac{3120}{80} = \$39.00$$

[a] *Source:* hypothetical data.

Geometric Mean (GM)

Where the geometric mean is appropriate to the purposes of the investigation, the average is more efficiently calculated using the logarithmic form. This procedure involves the following steps:

1. convert the class midpoints to their log values;
2. multiply the log values by the class frequency,
3. sum the products of the log-frequencies and divide by the total observations, and
4. convert the log quotient to its antilog.

For the data in Table 3-1 and using the logs in Table 2-4, the geometric mean is calculated in Table 3-4.

Harmonic Mean (1/H)

The harmonic mean $(1/H)$ is calculated by averaging the reciprocals of the midpoints weighted by the class frequencies as follows:

$$\frac{1}{H} = \frac{\Sigma F(1/\bar{X})}{N} \div 1 \tag{3-5}$$

where: X = class midpoint
F = class frequency
N = number of observations

Using the same hourly wage data, the harmonic mean is calculated in Table 3-5.

Table 3-4   Geometric Mean Hourly Wage Rates[a]

1 Classes	2 Frequency (F)	3 Midpoint (X)	4 log X		5 (2 × 4) F log X
$10–$19.99	7	$15	1.1761		8.233
$20–$29.99	10	$25	1.3979		13.979
$30–$39.99	25	$35	1.5441		38.603
$40–$49.99	20	$45	1.6532	Sum of class	33.064
$50–$59.99	18	$55	1.7404	frequencies	31.327
	Total = 80			times logs of midpoints } = 125.206	= 125.206

$$\text{log GM} = \frac{125.206}{80} = 1.565075$$

$$\text{Antilog} = \$36.735$$

[a] *Source:* hypothetical data.

Table 3-5   Harmonic Mean Hourly Wage Rates[a]

1 Midpoint (X)	2 ($1/X$)	3 Frequency (F)	4 (2×3) $F\,(1/X)$
$15	1/15	7	0.4666662
$25	1/25	10	0.4000000
$35	1/35	25	0.7142850
$45	1/45	20	0.4444440
$55	1/55	18	0.3272724

$$\text{Total} = 80 \qquad \left.\begin{array}{l}\text{Sum of reciprocals}\\ \text{times frequencies}\end{array}\right\} = 2.3526676$$

$$\frac{1}{H} = \frac{2.3526676}{80} \div 1$$

$$= \frac{80}{2.3526676}$$

$$= \$34.00$$

[a] *Source:* hypothetical data.

The harmonic mean of $34 assumes each employee earns the identical *total* dollars. Thus, if the eighty employees earned a *total* of $8,000 during a workday ($100 per employee), the hours worked would total 235.29, as calculated from the average hourly wage, $34. By contrast, the arithmetic mean would give an incorrect solution: $39 × 235.29 = $9,176.31. Review the discussion of the harmonic mean in Chapter 2.

POSITIONAL AVERAGES

Unlike their counterparts for ungrouped data, positional averages are not precisely identified in a frequency distribution. We must *estimate* because we cannot actually locate the median and mode of a frequency distribution. Moreover, in a frequency distribution, estimation of the positional averages assumes the frequencies are evenly distributed within each class—a rare phenomenon in practice.

Median (Md)

The median (Md) is estimated by dividing the total observations (N) by 2 in order to locate the median class; the median is estimated by interpolation using the cumulative frequencies within the median class. The formulation is

$$\text{Md} = L + \left(\frac{N/2 - CF_p}{F_m}\right) K \qquad (3\text{-}6)$$

where: L = lower limit of median class

$N/2$ = one-half the total frequencies (this locates the median class)

CF_p = cumulative frequencies for class immediately preceding the median class

F_m = number of frequencies in the median class

K = class interval

Continuing to use the hourly wage rate data from Table 3-1, the median is estimated in Table 3-6.

Recall from Chapter 2 that the median splits the array of data so that 50 percent of the items lie above and below the median. Using the raw data in Table 3-1, the true median of the array is $39.50, the average of the 40th and 41st observations. Again we see the loss of precision when data are grouped in frequency distributions.

Mode (Mo)

In a frequency distribution, the modal class is that containing the largest number of frequencies. The mode is then estimated by interpolating from the midpoint within the modal class. Specifically,

$$Mo = L + \left(\frac{\Delta_1}{\Delta_1 + \Delta_2}\right) K \qquad (3\text{-}7)$$

Table 3-6 Median Average Hourly Wage Rates[a]

1 Classes	2 Frequency (F)	3 Cumulative Frequencies (CF)
$10–$19.99	7	7
$20–$29.99	10	17
$30–$39.99	25	Median class → 42
$40–$49.99	20	62
$50–$59.99	18	80

$$\text{Median class} = \frac{N}{2} = \frac{80}{2} = 40$$

$$Md = \$30 + \left(\frac{80/2 - 17}{25}\right) 10$$

$$= 30 + \left(\frac{23}{25}\right) 10$$

$$= \$39.20$$

[a] *Source:* hypothetical data.

where: L = lower limit of modal class

Δ_1 = difference between frequencies of premodal class and modal class

Δ_2 = difference between frequencies of post-modal class and modal class

K = class interval of modal class

Referring back to Table 3-3, the modal class is $30–$39.99, with 25 frequencies. Therefore,

$$Mo = \$30 + \left(\frac{25 - 10}{(25 - 10) + (25 - 20)} \right) 10$$

$$= 30 + \left(\frac{15}{15 + 5} \right) 10 \qquad (3\text{-}8)$$

$$= \$37.50$$

CUMULATIVE AND RELATIVE FREQUENCY DISTRIBUTIONS

Arranging data cumulatively in the distribution allows analysis of the data above and below certain target levels of interest. For example, management may ask: "How many employees earn wages of less than $50 hourly?" To accommodate this request, the statistician would construct a frequency distribution showing summary information of wages with "less than" class limits or, as a corollary, "more than" class limits.

A "less than" cumulative frequency distribution is illustrated from the hourly wage rates in Table 3-1. The distribution is designed so that the frequencies are added, starting from the top of the distribution, and show values less than or equal to the upper class limit.

Table 3-7 shows at a glance that sixty-two employees earn less than $50 hourly wage rate, seven earn less than $20, and so forth.

**Table 3-7   "Less Than" Cumulative Frequency Distribution
Hourly Wage Rates**[a]

1 Classes	2 Frequency (F)	3 "Less Than" Upper Class Limit
$10–$19.99	7 ⎤	7
$20–$29.99	10	17
$30–$39.99	25 ⎬ Add	42
$40–$49.99	20	62
$50–$59.99	18 ⎦	80

[a] *Source:* hypothetical data.

Table 3-8 "More Than" Cumulative Frequency Distribution Hourly Wage Data[a]

1 Classes	2 Frequency (F)		3 "More Than" Lower Class Limit
$10–$19.99	7		80
$20–$29.99	10		73
$30–$39.99	25	Add	63
$40–$49.99	20		38
$50–$59.99	18		18

[a] *Source:* hypothetical data.

Conversely, adding frequencies from the bottom of the distribution displays information on wages "over" the value of the lower class limits (see Table 3-8).

Table 3-8 shows that only eighteen employees earn $50 or more, sixty-three earn $30 or more, and so forth.

Relative frequency distributions utilize percentages rather than absolute frequencies. Class frequencies are expressed as a percent of total frequencies. Relative frequency distributions are invaluable in comparison studies, particularly where total frequencies differ.

Assume management requires analysis of hourly wage rates for employees in two other offices as a comparison to the eighty employees referred to in Table 3-1. The situation calls for a relative frequency distribution (Table 3-9).

The total number of employees differs in each branch office thereby vitiating absolute comparisons. However, the relative distribution based upon 100 percent indicates more than 22 percent of main office

Table 3-9 Relative Frequency Distribution Hourly Wage Rates for Three Offices[a]

Values	Main Office		Eastern Branch		Western Branch	
	F	Percent	F	Percent	F	Percent
$10–$19.99	7	8.7	9	13.9	9	18.0
$20–$29.99	10	12.5	12	18.5	11	22.0
$30–$39.99	25	31.3	22	33.8	15	30.0
$40–$49.99	20	25.0	16	24.6	10	20.0
$50–$59.99	18	22.5	6	9.2	5	10.0
	80	100.0	65	100.0	50	100.0

[a] *Source:* hypothetical data.

employees earn $50 and up hourly compensation but only 9.2 and 10 percent, respectively, earn more than $50 in the Eastern and Western branches.

MEASURING VARIABILITY FOR GROUPED DATA

Similar to ungrouped data, variability of individual values in a data series can be measured for frequency distributions. Although techniques for computation of the range, quartile, average, and standard deviations are somewhat different for grouped data, the methodologies bear resemblance to those for ungrouped data and have the same business applications and limitations. Greatest emphasis is still placed on the standard deviation because of its importance as a common measure of business risk.

Range

If the range of a frequency distribution is required, it is a simple matter to take the difference between the value of the lower class limit of the smallest class and the upper class limit of the highest class (rounded to the nearest dollar). This is illustrated for hourly wage data for eighty employees (see Table 3-10). The range is equal to $60 - $10, or $50.

Quartile Deviation (QD)

The quartile deviation is measured in a manner analogous to determining the median. Frequencies are cumulated to locate the classes where the quartile midpoint values fall. The formulation to calculate the first and third quartiles is

$$Q_1 = L + \left(\frac{N/4 - CF}{F}\right) K$$

$$Q_3 = L + \left(\frac{3N/4 - CF}{F}\right) K$$

(3-9)

where: Q_1 = first quartile
Q_3 = third quartile
L = lower limit of quartile class
CF = cumulative frequency in class prior to quartile class
F = frequency of the applicable quartile class
K = size of class interval in applicable quartile class
N = number of observations in the series

**Table 3-10   Range Deviation
Hourly Wage Rates**[a]

Classes[b]
$10 –$19.99
$20 –$29.99
$30 –$39.99   Range: $60 − $10 = $50
$40 –$49.99
$50 –$59.99
$60

[a] *Source:* hypothetical data.
[b] See discussion of class intervals on page 37.

In employing hourly wage data the calculation for quartile deviations (Q_1 and Q_3) is given in Table 3-11.

There are eighty employees, and therefore one-fourth, or twenty, are below the first quartile, since Q_1 is the value at the end of (80/4). Or, if seventeen employees earn less than $30 hourly wage and forty-two employees earn less than $40, Q_1 must fall in the $30–$39.99 class. A parallel analysis can be drawn for Q_3, which falls in the $40–$49.99 class, that is, Q_3 is the value at the end of (240/4), or the sixtieth employee.

Table 3-11   Quartile Deviations Hourly Wage Data[a]

1 Classes	2 Frequency	3 Cumulative Frequency
$10–$19.99	7	7
$20–$29.99	10	17
$30–$39.99	25	42 ← Q_1 = $31.20
$40–$49.99	20	62 ← Q_3 = $49.00
$50–$59.99	18	80
	Total = 80	

$$Q_1 = \$30 + \left(\frac{80/4 - 17}{25}\right) 10 = \$31.20$$

$$Q_3 = \$40 + \left(\frac{240/4 - 42}{20}\right) 10 = \$49.00$$

Substituting into the equation (Table 2-11)

$$QD = \frac{\$49.00 - \$31.20}{2} = \$8.90$$

[a] *Source:* hypothetical data.

Table 3-12 Mean Absolute Deviation Hourly Wage Data[a]

1 Classes	2 Frequency (F)	3 Midpoint (X)	4 (X − X̄) Deviations (d)	5 (2 × 4) Fd
$10–$19.99	7	$15	−$24	$168
$20–$29.99	10	$25	−$14	$140
$30–$39.99	25	$35	−$ 4	$100
$40–$49.99	20	$45	+$ 6	$120
$50–$59.99	18	$55	+$16	$288
	Total = 80			$816 (signs ignored)

Sum of class frequencies times deviations } = $816 (signs ignored)

$$\text{MAD} = \frac{\$816}{80} = \$10.2$$

X̄ = $39.00 (Table 3-3)

[a] Source: hypothetical data.

46

Mean Absolute Deviation (MAD)

In a frequency distribution, the calculation of the mean absolute deviation uses the midpoints of each class. Deviations of the midpoints from the mean (or median) are multiplied (weighted) by the frequencies. The products are summed and divided by the number of frequencies. The MAD is used in our illustration for hourly wages in Table 3-12.

If the median of $35 is used as the typical average from which to calculate deviations from the midpoint the result for the mean absolute deviation is $10.0 for hourly wages of eighty employees.

Standard Deviation (σ)

In the case of grouped data, σ remains the most common measure of dispersion. However, the deviations of the midpoints are calculated only from the arithmetic mean. The procedure involves the following steps:

1. Calculate the arithmetic average ($\bar{X}$).
2. Calculate the deviations of the midpoints from the arithmetic average (d).
3. Square the deviations (d^2).
4. Multiply the squared deviations by the class frequency (Fd^2).
5. Sum the products and take the square root.

The standard deviation for the hourly wage data is calculated in Table 3-13.

CHARACTERISTICS OF FREQUENCY DISTRIBUTION

The shape of a frequency distribution is a most important concept in statistics. The concentration of frequencies determines shape and conveys important information concerning the array of data and/or the population from which the array was derived. In classifying frequency distributions by shape, the *normal curve* (Figure 3-1A) occupies the center of the stage. It has the following characteristics:

1. It is bell shaped and symmetrical.
2. The mean, median, and mode of the distribution are equal.
3. The location of any individual observation in the distribution can be determined.

Where in our hourly data (Table 3-1) is the $34 wage located? Answer:

$$\frac{X - \bar{X}}{\sigma} = \frac{\$34 - \$39}{\$12.104} = -0.413 \qquad (3\text{-}10)$$

Table 3-13 Standard Deviation Hourly Wage Data[a]

1 Classes	2 Frequency (F)	3 Midpoint (X)	4 ($X - \overline{X}$) Deviation (d)	5 (4 × 4) d^2	6 (2 × 5) Fd^2
$10–$19.99	7	$15	–$24	$576	$ 4,032
$20–$29.99	10	$25	–$14	$196	$ 1,960
$30–$39.99	25	$35	–$ 4	$ 16	$ 400
$40–$49.99	20	$45	+$ 6	$ 36	$ 720
$50–$59.99	18	$55	+$16	$256	$ 4,608
	Total = 80				= $11,720

$\left.\begin{array}{l}\text{Sum of class}\\\text{frequencies times}\\\text{squared deviations}\end{array}\right\}$

$$\sigma = \sqrt{\dfrac{\$11,720}{80}}$$
$$= \sqrt{\$146.5}$$
$$= \$12.104$$

$\overline{X} = \$39.00$

[a] *Source:* hypothetical data.

Figure 3-1A   Normal Curve

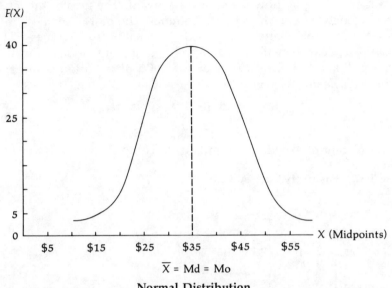

$$\overline{X} = Md = Mo$$

Normal Distribution

Classes	Frequency (F)	Midpoints (X)	Weighted Total (FX)
$10–$19.99	5	$15	$ 75
$20–$29.99	25	$25	$ 625
$30–$39.99	40	$35	$1,400
$40–$49.99	25	$45	$1,125
$50–$59.99	5	$55	$ 275
Total = 100			Σ FX $3,500

$$\overline{X} = \frac{\$3,500}{100} = \$35.00$$

$$Md = \$30 + \left(\frac{100/2 - 30}{40}\right) 10 = \$35.00$$

$$Mo = \$30 + \left(\frac{40 - 25}{(40 - 25) + (40 - 25)}\right) 10 = \$35.00$$

The $34 hourly rate is located less than one standard deviation from the mean.

When a distribution departs from the normal shape, it is said to be *skewed*. Skewness is the tendency of the data to tail off toward high or low values. Where the frequencies concentrate in the lower values and tail off toward the higher values, the distribution is *positively skewed* (Figure 3-1B). If the frequencies concentrate in the higher values and tail off toward the lower values, the distribution is *negatively skewed* (Figure 3-1C).

When the series is skewed, the mean pulls off to the right or left of the mode, depending on how the series is skewed. The greater the *relative* difference between the mean and the mode, the more skewness in the series; the less the relative difference, the smaller the skewness. Thus, in the presence of skewness, the mean, median, and mode of the distribution pull apart. The *relative* skewness of a distribution is measured by the *coefficient of skewness* (S):

$$S = \frac{3(\bar{X} - Md)}{\sigma} \qquad\qquad (3\text{-}11)$$

The coefficient of skewness permits us to compare one series with an-

Figure 3-1B Positively Skewed Curve

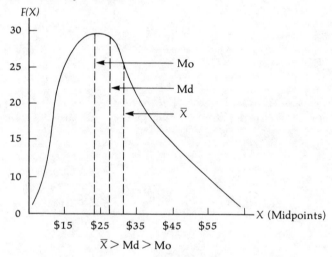

$$\bar{X} > Md > Mo$$

Positively Skewed Distribution

Classes	Frequencies (F)	Midpoints (X)	Weighted Total (FX)
$10–$19.99	25	$15	$375
$20–$29.99	30	$25	$750
$30–$39.99	20	$35	$700
$40–$49.99	15	$45	$675
$50–$59.99	10	$55	$550
Total = 100			Σ FX $3,050

$$\bar{X} = \frac{\$3,050}{100} = \$30.50$$

$$Md = \$20 + \left(\frac{100/2 - 25}{30}\right)10 = \$28.33$$

$$Mo = \$20 + \left(\frac{30 - 25}{(30 - 25) + (30 - 20)}\right)10 = \$23.33$$

Figure 3-1C   Negatively Skewed Curve

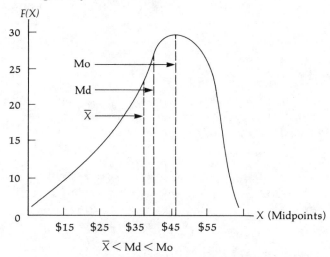

$$\bar{X} < Md < Mo$$

Negatively Skewed Distribution

Classes	Frequencies (F)	Midpoints (X)	Weighted Total (FX)
$10–$19.99	10	$15	$ 150
$20–$29.99	15	$25	$ 375
$30–$39.99	20	$35	$ 700
$40–$49.99	30	$45	$1,350
$50–$59.99	25	$55	$1,375
Total = 100			Σ FX $3,950

$$\bar{X} = \frac{\$3,950}{100} = \$39.50$$

$$Md = \$40 + \left(\frac{100/2 - 45}{30}\right)10 = \$41.66$$

$$Mo = \$40 + \left(\frac{30 - 20}{(30 - 20) + (30 - 25)}\right)10 = \$46.67$$

other and measure their relative departure from symmetry. For our hourly rate (using Tables 3-3, 3-6, and 3-13), the coefficient of skewness is

$$S = \frac{3(\$39 - \$39.20)}{\$12.104} \tag{3-12}$$

$$= \frac{-0.60}{\$12.104}$$

$$= -0.0495, \text{ or } -0.05 \text{ rounded}$$

In positive skewness, $\bar{X} >$ Md $>$ Mo; in negative skewness, $\bar{X} <$ Md $<$ Mo. The hourly wage rate distribution shows a slight negative skewness.

SUMMARY

We have seen again that different types of averages applied to the same data can yield quite different results. In the case of our hourly wage data, we found the following:

$$
\begin{aligned}
\text{Arithmetic mean } (\bar{X}) &= \$39.00 \\
\text{Geometric mean (GM)} &= \$36.74 \\
\text{Harmonic mean } (1/H) &= \$34.00 \\
\text{Median (Md)} &= \$39.20 \\
\text{Mode (Mo)} &= \$37.50
\end{aligned}
$$

The measures of dispersion were as follows:

$$
\begin{aligned}
\text{Range} &= \$50.00 \\
\text{Quartile deviation (QD)} &= \ \ \$8.90 \\
\text{Mean absolute deviation (MAD)} &= \$10.20 \\
\text{Standard deviation } (\sigma) &= \$12.104
\end{aligned}
$$

Each of these averages is valid, subject to the nature of the data and the objectives of the investigation. It behooves the manager using averages in decision making to know the type of average presented and its advantages and limitations. The following questions are also worth posing with respect to frequency distributions:

1. Do the class intervals and the number of classes adequately profile the data or are important characteristics of the data lost in the grouping adopted?
2. Does the frequency distribution approximate the normal curve or is it positively or negatively skewed?
3. If the data are skewed, the mean, median, and mode diverge. Which average was selected to typify the distribution and why?
4. Is the average derived from a relative frequency distribution to facilitate comparison with other pertinent information?
5. Was a cumulative frequency distribution developed as accompanying information?
6. Which measures of dispersion were applied to evaluate the average? Range? Quartiles? Mean absolute deviation? Standard deviation?

7. Which average was used as the basis for measuring dispersion? Mean or median?
8. Will extreme values in the series unduly influence the average and the measure of dispersion?

Averages are so widely used that they are considered to be simple things. Quite the opposite. Averaging data requires some expertise. Only the unsophisticated will accept an average without question.

SECTION III
Is it Probable?

chapter 4

Probabilities in Business Decisions

Some managers recoil from the explicit use of probabilities when faced with a business decision to choose between alternative courses of action. (The same executive may assiduously seek out the point spread on the Sunday afternoon football games before joining the office pool or before contributing to the "improvement of the breed" at the Saturday races.) Yet it is "probably" true to assert that in making certain decisions, managers have in mind a set of probabilities, subjectively or objectively estimated, as to the likelihood of the outcomes. Indeed, probability data are simply a bridge between our limited knowledge and the real environment, that is, a way of reasoning about the environment in the absence of complete information. Probabilities provide the means by which a certain amount of order may be derived from a natural state of uncertainty by specifying the degree of confidence that we may place in the occurrence of some event. However, where probabilities are explicitly incorporated into the decision process, there are "rules of the game" with which the manager should have a basic familiarity to weigh intelligently his expectations and risks.

CONCEPT OF PROBABILITY

A probability is a quantitative value expressed as a ratio. Formally, a probability is defined as follows:

$$\frac{A}{N} = \frac{A}{A + B} \tag{4-1}$$

where: A = the number of successes
B = the number of failures
N = the number of events

If Stage Door Johnny is touted at $3:2$ to win the Kentucky Derby, using equation 4-1, we can see that the odds makers are, in effect, saying he has a 60 percent probability of winning:

$$\frac{3}{3 + 2} = \frac{3}{5} = 0.60$$

Probability indicates the proportion of times that a given event can be *expected* to occur in *a number of attempts*. Running against the same field in repeated races, Stage Door Johnny could be *expected* to win 60 percent of the time. The probability of an event that cannot happen under any circumstances is zero; if the occurrence is certain, the probability is one.

As with other disciplines, there exists in probability studies different schools of thought concerning the measurement and application of probabilities.

Classical Probabilities

Since much of probability theory had its origin in games of chance, the first method of measuring probabilities developed from gambling situations. Classical probability treats *equally probable* events, that is, the probability of a head coming up in the toss of a *fair* coin [1/(1 + 1) = 50%], the probability of tossing a one in the role of a *fair* die [1/(1 + 5) = 16.7%], or the probability of choosing a red marble from a jar of seven reds and three green marbles [7/(7 + 3) = 70%].

The terms *fair* or *true* merely infer that the coin or the die is not biased or loaded toward a given result. Hence, if all possible outcomes are known along with the number of outcomes designated as success, no coin need be tossed or die rolled in order to determine the probabilities. The probabilities are derived *a priori*, without experiment, by deductive reasoning.

Because of the restrictive nature of these assumptions, classical probability has few business applications. However, it does not lack remunerative potential. Card counters at the blackjack table practice classical probability theory.

Empirical Probabilities or the Relative Frequency Concept

Here the probabilities emanate from a large number of repeated experiments or, over the long run, under uniform or stable conditions. Mortality tables illustrate the notion. Medical studies to test the efficacy of a given drug also yield a set of empirical probabilities on the success factor in utilizing the drug. However, the experimentation to determine the relative frequency of success, unlike classical theory, yields only an approximation of the true probability. Some residual error factor remains.

Subjective Probabilities

As the term implies, subjective probability refers to the degree of belief or the degree of confidence placed in the occurrence of an event by a particular individual based upon the evidence available. The evidence may consist of qualitative or quantitative information. Hence, the method permits the assignment of probabilities to phenomena for which there may be no objective data.

Obviously, the empirical and subjective concepts have greater applicability to business decision making, and we shall return to them later.

CLASSIFYING EVENTS

An *event* represents one outcome of a given activity: the result of a coin toss or throwing of a die or, in a business context, selecting a unit of output to test for quality control. An *experiment* refers to the process that results in different possible outcomes or observations. In determining probabilities events can be characterized as (1) independent, (2) dependent, (3) compound, and (4) mutually exclusive.

Independent Events

If the outcome of one event (A) does not determine or condition the outcome of another event (B), the two are independent. For example, if a restaurant chain were considering the opening of new units in widely separated locations where the cash flow from one unit could not influence the cash flow of the other unit, the two events, A and B, would be independent.

Dependent Events

Dependency exists when one event or outcome depends upon or is affected by the occurrence of some other event. For example, in capital budgeting, the acceptance of project B may depend upon the prior acceptance of project A.

Compound Events

These represent combined outcomes either by union [$P(A \cup B)$] or intersection [$P(A \cap B)$]. As we shall illustrate later, the probability of a compound outcome depends on the probabilities for the separate events, A and B.

Mutually Exclusive Events

The outcomes are mutually exclusive if they cannot occur simultaneously, that is, one event precludes the other. Capital budgeting constraints, for example, may dictate that the manager choose location A or B for the new restaurant. Statisticians would say the probability of A and B occurring together is 0, that is $P(A \cap B) = 0$. One or the other project may be undertaken at a later date but for the present the outcomes of the analysis are mutually exclusive.

The concepts of indepedence and mutual exclusivity are very important in statistical decision making. Most decisions employing probability distributions require an initial classification of the events as independent or dependent and/or mutually exclusive. In this respect, the reader will note that dependent events need not be mutually exclusive, but mutually exclusive events must be dependent since by definition the decision on one determines the decision on the other.

TYPES OF PROBABILITY

In many experiments, it is convenient to add, multiply, or otherwise manipulate events based upon the preceding classification in order to answer probability questions formulated from the analysis. The manipulative process generates several types of probabilities.

Marginal Probability

The term refers to the probability of a given outcome, that is, the probability of A, denoted $P(A)$, or the probability of B, $P(B)$. For example, in a business forecast, what is the probability of sales amounting to $100,000?

Conditional Probabilities

Denoted by $P(A/B)$, conditional probabilities relate to the probability of A occurring given B. [When the events are independent $P(A/B) = P(A)$—see equation (4-8).] In the introduction of a new product, especially for the early years, the cash flow of the second fiscal year may depend upon the cash flow of the first fiscal year and so on for successive years. If the Edsel had good cash flows in its initial years, it might still grace the nation's highways! But, chronological order is not necessarily implied in conditional probability.

Joint Probabilities

These relate to compound events, the probability of A and B both occurring.

THE RULES OF THE GAME

The 100 Percent Rule

The sum of the probabilities of all possible outcomes in an experiment must equal 100 percent.

By way of illustration, assume the manager of the restaurant must choose between two locations, A and B. The cash flows at each location are necessarily mutually exclusive. Also within each project the inter-period cash flows are independent, that is, cash flows in period one do not influence the cash flows in period two. The data on location A includes:

Required investment (I)	$200,000
Life of project (N)	10 years
Discount rate applied to project (R)	12%
Net Annual Operating Cash Flows:	

Annual Cash Flow Outcomes	Probability[1]
$ 10,000	0.10
$ 30,000	0.15
$ 70,000	0.50
$ 90,000	0.15
$100,000	0.10
Total probabilities	1.00

Note that the forecast of project A's cash flows has been prepared as a probability distribution. What is the annual cash flow most likely to be realized in the long run at location A? Each cash flow event—$10,000, $30,000, and so forth—is mutually exclusive. The outcome in any period cannot both be $10,000 and $90,000. Assuming market research has reasonably identified the range of outcomes for location A, Table 4-1 indicates an expected annual cash flow of $64,000.

The expected value, therefore, is a weighted average of the cash flows by their respective probabilities. It designates the best bet in repeated trials over the long run. Thus, the manager projects that on the average over the next ten years at location A the cash flow would approximate $64,000 per period.

Discounting the expected value, $64,000, for 10 years at 12 percent yields an *Expected Present Value* [E(PV)] of $361,600. Subtracting the investment of $200,000 leaves an *Expected Net-Present Value* [E(NPV)] of $161,600 from location A. This form of analysis is quite common in evaluating capital projects, that is, long-term asset management.

[1] Although probability of a given event can never exceed one and thus, strictly speaking, a zero before the decimal point is not necessary, for both ease of reading and consistency with other decimal figures in this text, a zero will precede decimal throughout text.

Table 4-1   Expected Cash Flow Location A^a

(1) Annual Cash Flow	(2) Probability	3 (2 × 1) Expected Cash Flow
$10,000	0.10	$ 1,000
$30,000	0.15	$ 4,500
$70,000	0.50	$35,000
$90,000	0.15	$13,500
$100,000	0.10	$10,000
Expected annual cash flow		$64,000

^{a} *Source:* hypothetical data.

The Addition Rule

If two outcomes are mutually exclusive (one precludes the other), the probability of either event is simply the sum of the probability of A plus the probability of B: $P(A \cup B) = P(A) + P(B)$. A contingency table will illustrate the point. Suppose we have hypothetical data on the high and low yields on Boeing and General Motors stock and the number of times these levels were jointly accomplished.

Table 4-2 tells us the number of times General Motors and Boeing hit their low yields jointly, that is, 30. Or when General Motors hit its low of 15 percent, how many times did Boeing hit its high of 25 percent? Answer, 25 times.

Table 4-2 can be converted into a set of probabilities by dividing the number of events in each box by the total number of events: 30/185, 70/185, and so forth (Table 4-3).

Table 4-3, alternatively, could be cast as a table of marginal probabilities (Table 4-4). The reader will also observe that the probabilities in the body of Table 4-3 (0.16, 0.14, 0.38, and 0.32) are joint probabilities.

The addition rule is applicable whenever we are interested in the probability that any one of several mutually exclusive events will occur.

Table 4-2   Contingency Table^a

Boeing / General Motors	Yields 15%	Yields 25%	Total Events
15%	30	70	100
25%	25	60	85
Total Events	55	130	185

^{a} *Source:* hypothetical data.

Table 4-3   Probability Table[a]

Boeing \ General Motors Yields	15%	25%	Marginal Probabilities
15%	0.16	0.38	0.54
25%	0.14	0.32	0.46
Marginal Probabilities	0.30	0.70	1.00 (Total)

[a] *Source:* hypothetical data.

Using Table 4-3, what is the probability of both stocks jointly achieving their high *or* low yields? The probability of both stocks jointly hitting either their high or low yields is the sum of the probabilities

$$P(A \cup B) = P(A) + P(B)$$
$$= 0.16 + 0.32 \qquad (4\text{-}2)$$
$$= 0.48$$

Or, using Table 4-4, what is the probability of General Motors stock hitting its high *or* low yield?

$$P(A \cup B) = P(A) + P(B)$$
$$= 0.30 + 0.70 \qquad (4\text{-}3)$$
$$= 1.00$$

What is the probability of Boeing hitting its high *and* low yield? Answer: 0. The events are mutually exclusive, therefore, $P(A \cup B) = 0$.

Conversely, if the events are not mutually exclusive but are independent, the expression becomes

$$P(A \cup B) = P(A) + P(B) - P(A \cap B) \qquad (4\text{-}4)$$

In this case, the addition rule tells us to add the probability of event A to probability of event B and substract the probability of the intersection

Table 4-4   Marginal Probability Distribution of Boeing and General Motors High and Low Yields[a]

	General Motors	Boeing
15%	0.30	0.54
25%	0.70	0.46
	1.00	1.00

[a] *Source:* hypothetical data.

of A and B for it has been counted twice, both in $P(A)$ and in $P(B)$. What is the probability of either Boeing or General Motors reaching its high yield? From Table 4-3, the probability of both companies achieving their high yields is 0.32. From Table 4-4, the probability of Boeing reaching its high yield is 0.46; for General Motors, the figure is 0.70. Therefore,

$$P(A \cup B) = 0.46 + 0.70 - 0.32 \qquad (4\text{-}5)$$
$$= 0.84$$

There is, accordingly, an 84 percent probability that one or the other security will make its highest yield.

The Multiplication Rule

The multiplication rule may be used to obtain the joint probability of the successive or simultaneous occurrence of two or more independent events. Thus, the probability of A and B $[P(A \cap B)]$ equals the probability of $A[P(A)]$ times the probability of B $[P(B)]$:

$$P(A \cap B) = P(A)P(B) \qquad (4\text{-}6)$$

From Table 4-4, what is the probability of both stocks showing their high yields? Answer,

$$P(A \cap B) = 0.46 \times 0.70 \qquad (4\text{-}7)$$

The joint probability of both outcomes is 32 percent, as per Table 4-3.

The Conditional Probability Rule

What is the probability of Boeing (A) reaching its high yield if General Motors (B) has reached its high yield? The events are independent.

$$P(A/B) = \frac{P(A \cap B)}{P(B)} = \frac{P(A)\ P(B)}{P(B)}$$
$$= \frac{0.46 \times 0.70}{0.70}$$
$$= \frac{0.32}{0.70} \qquad (4\text{-}8)$$
$$= 0.46$$

The process, of course, can be reversed. What is the probability of B given that A has occurred?

$$P(B/A) = \frac{P(A \cap B)}{P(A)} \qquad (4\text{-}9)$$

In our case,

$$P(B/A) = \frac{0.46 \times 0.70}{0.46}$$

$$= \frac{0.32}{0.46}$$

$$= 0.70$$

(4-10)

In both cases above, it can be seen that, because two events are independent, $P(A/B) = P(A)$ and $P(B/A) = P(B)$, as was stated earlier p (60).

The illustration in Table 4-5 uses hypothetical cash flows to integrate several of the types of probabilities defined above.

In period 1, the probabilities—0.60 and 0.40—are *marginal probabilities*. For periods 2 and 3, the probabilities are *conditional*; that is, in period 2, there exists a 50 percent chance of having a cash flow of $20 if the cash flow in period 1 is $20. Or, if the cash flow in period 2 is $40, there is a 20 percent probability of attaining a cash flow of $60 in period 3. What is the probability of attaining a total cash flow of $60 for series 1

Table 4-5   Dependent Cash Flows

Period 1		Period 2		Period 3		Series	P_j	C_j	P_jC_j
P_1	C_1	$P_2\|P_1$	C_2	$P_3\|P_2$	C_3				
				0.60	$ 20	1	0.180	$ 60.	$ 10.80
		.50	$20	0.30	30	2	0.090	70.	6.30
				0.10	40	3	0.030	80.	2.40
				0.50	30	4	0.090	90.	8.10
.60	$20	.30	40	0.30	40	5	0.054	100.	5.40
				0.20	60	6	0.036	120.	4.32
				0.50	60	7	0.060	140.	8.40
		.20	60	0.40	70	8	0.048	150.	7.20
				0.10	80	9	0.012	160.	1.92
				0.30	50	10	0.036	170.	6.12
		.30	50	0.40	60	11	0.048	180.	8.64
				0.30	70	12	0.036	190.	6.84
				0.40	60	13	0.080	210.	16.80
.40	70	.50	80	0.50	80	14	0.100	230.	23.00
				0.10	100	15	0.020	250.	5.00
				0.30	80	16	0.024	250.	6.00
		.20	100	0.50	100	17	0.040	270.	10.80
				0.20	150	18·	0.016	320.	5.12
							TOTAL: 1.000		$143.16

in Table 4-5? Answer: The product of $0.60 \times 0.50 \times 0.60 = 0.18$—an 18 percent chance of a cash flow total of $60. This is a *joint probability*.

The possible outcomes within each period are *mutually exclusive*. The sum of the probabilities for any set of outcomes is always 100 percent. Multiplying the *joint probabilities* by the related total cash flow and summing gives the *expected cash flow* ($143.16) for the three periods. Obviously, the illustration is pertinent to any type of analysis where cash flows of one period (year, quarter, month, and so forth) depend upon the cash flow of the previous period, that is, a situation of *dependent events*.

OTHER ILLUSTRATIONS

Portfolio Management

In constructing a portfolio, the investor is concerned with the return and risk on his selections. Generally, investors expect the assumption of greater risk to be accompanied by higher returns. In a portfolio, risk will depend upon the *covariance* of returns on the securities comprising the portfolio, that is, the way the returns on the securities move in the same or opposite directions as the market fluctuates. Thus, the investor can distinguish between the following:

1. *Positive covariance*. Comparing the returns on two securities— A and B—when the return on A exceeds the expected return on A and the return on B also exceeds the expected return on B, a positive covariance exists. The opposite condition would result when the returns on A and B decline. In sum, the returns on A and B move together or are affected similarly by movements in the market. High positive covariance among the securities in a portfolio intensifies risk.
2. *Negative covariance*. If when the return on A exceeds its expected return, the return on B tends to fall below its expected return, a negative covariance exists. The returns on the two securities tend to move in opposite directions, that is, are oppositely affected by movements in the economy. Negative covariance tends to minimize risk.

Suppose an investor is preparing to purchase two securities A and B with the following characteristics:

	A	B
Expected Return [$E(R)$]	0.104	0.149
Standard deviation of the expected return (σ)	0.37	0.149

Table 4-6   Contingency Table of Security Returns $(R)^a$

B \ A	0.08	0.10	0.12	0.14	0.16	Total Events
0.08	10	15	10	20	8	63
0.10	15	20	25	30	10	100
0.12	20	30	35	45	15	145
0.14	10	10	25	40	10	95
0.16	5	5	10	22	10	52
Total events	60	80	105	157	53	455

^{a} *Source:* hypothetical data.

The investor wishes to calculate his expected return $[E(R_p)]$ and risk (σ_p) if the portfolio is composed of securities A and B only and if equal amounts are invested in each security.[2]

We first convert the contingency table (Table 4-6) into a table of marginal and joint probabilities and substitute the deviations of the returns from their expected return in the column headings (Table 4-7).

The covariance between two paired securities is the algebraic sum of the products of their paired deviations and the related joint probabilities: $\Sigma P_{AB}\, d_A d_B$, as in Table 4-8.

Observe that the covariance may be positive or negative.

Since the investor is committing an equal amount of funds to the portfolio, the weights (X_A and X_B) in the portfolio are the same, or, 0.5. The standard deviation of the portfolio (σ_p) is taken to measure the risk

Table 4-7   Probability Table of Deviations (d)
From Expected Return^a

B \ A	-0.024	-0.004	$+0.016$	$+0.036$	$+0.056$	Marginal Probabilities
			$[R - E(R_A)]$			
-0.069	0.022	0.033	0.022	0.044	0.017	0.138
-0.049	0.033	0.044	0.055	0.066	0.022	0.220
-0.029	0.044	0.066	0.077	0.099	0.033	0.319
-0.009	0.022	0.022	0.055	0.088	0.022	0.209
-0.011	0.011	0.011	0.022	0.048	0.022	0.114
Marginal Probabilities	0.132	0.176	0.231	0.345	0.116	1.00 Total

(Left margin label for B rows: $[R - E(R_B)]$)

^{a} *Source:* hypothetical data.

[2] Recall from Chapters 2 and 3 that risk is measured by the standard deviation.

Table 4-8   Covariance of Securities A and B^a

1 $[R_A - E(R_A)]$	$\times$	2 $[R_B - E(R_B)]$	$=$	3 $d_A d_B$	$\times$	4 P_{AB}	$=$	5 $P_A d_A d_B$
−0.024		−0.069		+0.00166		0.022		+0.0000365
−0.004		−0.069		+0.00028		0.033		+0.0000092
+0.016		−0.069		−0.00110		0.022		−0.0000243
+0.036		−0.069		−0.00248		0.044		−0.0001091
+0.056		−0.069		−0.00386		0.017		−0.0000656
−0.024		−0.049		+0.00118		0.033		+0.0000389
−0.004		−0.049		+0.00020		0.044		+0.0000088
+0.016		−0.049		−0.00078		0.055		−0.0000430
+0.036		−0.049		−0.00176		0.066		−0.0001162
+0.056		−0.049		−0.00274		0.022		−0.0000603
−0.024		−0.029		+0.00070		0.044		+0.0000308
−0.004		−0.029		+0.00012		0.066		+0.0000079
+0.016		−0.029		−0.00046		0.077		−0.0000354
+0.036		−0.029		−0.00104		0.099		−0.0001033
+0.056		−0.029		−0.00162		0.033		−0.0000535
−0.024		−0.009		+0.00022		0.022		+0.0000048
−0.004		−0.009		+0.00004		0.022		+0.0000009
+0.016		−0.009		−0.00014		0.055		−0.0000077
+0.036		−0.009		−0.00032		0.088		−0.0000282
+0.056		−0.009		−0.00050		0.022		−0.0000110
−0.024		+0.011		−0.00026		0.011		−0.0000029
−0.004		+0.011		−0.00004		0.011		−0.0000004
+0.016		+0.011		+0.00018		0.022		+0.0000040
+0.036		+0.011		+0.00040		0.048		+0.0000192
+0.056		+0.011		+0.00062		0.022		+0.0000136
Sum of probabilities						1.00		
covariance (A,B)								−0.0004859

^{a} *Source:* hypothetical data.

associated with the investment. Therefore,

$$\sigma_p = \sqrt{X_A^2 \sigma_A^2 + X_B^2 \sigma_B^2 + 2(X_A)(X_B)(\sigma_{AB})}$$

$$= \sqrt{(0.5^2)(0.37^2) + (0.5^2)(0.149^2) + 2(0.5)(0.5)(-0.004859)}$$

$$= \sqrt{(0.25)(0.1369) + (0.25)(0.0222) - 0.000243} \qquad (4\text{-}11)$$

$$= \sqrt{0.034225 + 0.00555 - 0.000243}$$

$$= \sqrt{0.0395320}$$

$$= 0.1988$$

To calculate the expected return on the portfolio $[E(R_p)]$ we multiply each expected return by the weight and then add them:

$$E(R_p) = E(R_A)(X_A) + E(R_B)(X_B)$$
$$= (0.104)(0.5) + (0.149)(0.5)$$
$$= 0.052 + 0.075$$
$$= 0.127$$

The investor can anticipate an expected return of 12.7 percent on the portfolio, subject to a standard deviation of 19.88 percent, resulting in a range of -7.2 to 32.6 percent. The use of covariance is quite common in modern portfolio theory. Manifestly, as the number of securities in the portfolio increases, the calculations become rather cumbersome. Hence, the work is done by computers and/or by use of shortcut methods. However, the theory is basically the same.

Inventory Management

Safety stock

The occurrence of an inventory stock-out represents a loss of potential profit for the firm. To hedge against this contingency, management may maintain a safety stock of inventory at a level to cover delays in inventory deliveries. Conversely, the carrying of a safety stock adds to the cost of inventory management. The question therefore becomes, What is the optimal quantity of safety stock that will balance the loss potential of a stock-out and the additional expenses of a larger inventory? Probabilities have a part to play in the solution.

As an example, assume a firm has a stock-out cost of $4 per unit, inventory carrying costs of $6 per unit, and the firm reorders inventory whenever the level drops to 500 units. Hence, if subsequent demand exceeds 500 units, a stock-out occurs and deliveries are late. The pattern of subsequent demand, based upon past experience, is described in Table 4-9 and the loss potential from a stock-out in Table 4-10.

The optimal safety stock level (200 units) is the strategy that results in the minimum combination of the cost of carrying the safety stock inventory and the cost of a stock-out (see Table 4-11).

Table 4-9 Probability of Stock-out at 500 Unit Inventory Level[a]

Subsequent Demand	Probability	Size of Safety Stock	Percentage of Time Having Stock-outs
500 units	0.74	0	0.26 (1.00 − 0.74)
600 units	0.15	100	0.11 (1.00 − 0.89)
700 units	0.07	200	0.04 (1.00 − 0.96)
800 units	0.03	300	0.01 (1.00 − 0.99)
900 units	0.01	400	0.00 (1.00 − 1.00)
	1.00		

[a] *Source:* hypothetical data.

Table 4-10 Stock-out Costs[a]

1 Assumed Safety Stock	2 Subsequent Demand (Units)	3 Short Fall (Units)	4 Stock-out Cost per Unit ($)	5 Probability	6 Number of Times May Occur During Year	7 (3 × 4 × 5 × 6) Annual Expected Stock-out Cost ($)
0	500	0	4	0.74	6	0
	600	100	4	0.15	6	360
	700	200	4	0.07	6	336
	800	300	4	0.03	6	216
	900	400	4	0.01	6	96
						$1008
100	500	0	4	0.74	6	0
	600	0	4	0.15	6	0
	700	100	4	0.07	6	168
	800	200	4	0.03	6	144
	900	300	4	0.01	6	72
						$384
200	500	0	4	0.74	6	0
	600	0	4	0.15	6	0
	700	0	4	0.07	6	0
	800	100	4	0.03	6	72
	900	200	4	0.01	6	48
						$120
300	500	0	4	0.74	6	0
	600	0	4	0.15	6	0
	700	0	4	0.07	6	0
	800	0	4	0.03	6	0
	900	100	4	0.01	6	24
						$24
400	500	0	4	0.74	6	0
	600	0	4	0.15	6	0
	700	0	4	0.07	6	0
	800	0	4	0.03	6	0
	900	0	4	0.01	6	0
						0

[a] Source: hypothetical data.

Table 4-11   Optimal Safety Stock[a]

1 Safety Stock Strategies	2 Cost of Safety Stock per Unit	3 (1 × 2) Cost of Safety Stock	4 Expected Stock-out Costs	5 (3 + 4) Optimal Safety Stock Strategy
0	$2	$ 0	$1,008	$1,008
100	$2	$200	$ 384	$ 584
200	$2	$400	$ 120	$ 520
300	$2	$600	$ 24	$ 624
400	$2	$800	$ 0	$ 800

[a] *Source:* hypothetical data.

Inventory Composition

A firm has the following inventory of TV sets:

Portable, color (PC)	100 units
Portable, black and white (PB)	200 units
Console, color (FC)	150 units
Console, black and white (FB)	550 units
Total	1000

If a buyer purchases a portable set, what is the *conditional probability* that it is a color set? That it is a black and white set? What are the joint probabilities of the purchase of a color portable or black and white console?

The relative frequency of each type of portable in relation to total inventory is

$$P(PC) = \frac{100}{1000} = 0.1$$

$$P(PB) = \frac{200}{1000} = 0.2 \tag{4-12}$$

and the relative frequency of a portable in relation to total inventory is

$$P(P) = \frac{300}{1000} = 0.3 \tag{4-13}$$

We are now ready to calculate the conditional probabilities.[3] Using equation (4-9) and substituting the values from equations (4-12) and

[3] Since $P(PC)$, $P(PB)$, and $P(P)$ are not independent events, the multiplication rule does not hold. However, examination shows that $P(PC \cap P) = P(PC)$ and $P(PB \cap P) = P(B)$, because the only way to both buy a color portable *and* a portable is to buy a color portable. The same logic holds for buying both a black and white portable *and* a portable.

(4-13) we have

$$P(PC/P) = \frac{P(PC \cap P)}{P(P)} = \frac{P(PC)}{P(P)} = \frac{0.1}{0.3} = 0.33$$

$$P(PB/P) = \frac{P(PB \cap P)}{P(P)} = \frac{P(PB)}{P(P)} = \frac{0.2}{0.3} = 0.67$$

(4-14)

The joint probability of buying a color portable or a black and white console is the sum of their individual probabilities, as they are mutually exclusive events. The probability of a black and white console being purchased is

$$P(FB) = \frac{550}{1000} = 0.55$$

(4-15)

To this we add the probability of a color portable being bought, already calculated in equation (4-12):

$$P(PC \cup FB) = P(PC) + P(FB)$$
$$= 0.1 + 0.55 = 0.65$$

(4-16)

Quality Control

A production line turns out 300 voltage regulators per day in 50-unit batches. Based upon past experience, ten of the regulators will be defective. What is the probability of any given batch containing two defective units $[P(A_1)$ and $P(A_2)]$?

The two events (A_1 and A_2) are not independent because if the first occurs (A_1) this affects the probability that the second event (A_2) will occur. Specifically, if A_1 occurs, then a defective regulator was chosen, leaving 49 regulators, of which 9 are likely to be defective. Thus the probability of a second defective unit in the batch depends upon the prior selection, that is, a case of conditional probability. Therefore,

$$P(A) = P(A_1) \, P(A_2 A_1)$$
$$= \frac{10}{50} \times \frac{9}{49}$$
$$= 0.037$$

(4-17)

The plant runs a 3.7 percent chance that in any batch there will be two defective regulators.

Decision Trees

In assigning probabilities to a business problem, it is first necessary to identify all possible outcomes. In this task, a decision tree can provide a technique for structuring pertinent information about the problem at hand. A decision tree portrays in sequence the alternative outcomes

Table 4-12   Company Performance Over Business Cycle[a]

State of the Economy (S)	Company X	Earnings per Share (R) Company Y	Company Z
Recession	$1.50	$0.75	$0.20
Depression	$0.50	$0.40	−$0.80
Revival	$0.75	$0.60	−$0.20
Prosperity	$2.00	$1.00	$1.00
The probabilities associated with each state of the economy are:			
Recession	0.25		
Depression	0.15		
Revival	0.20		
Prosperity	0.40		
	1.00		

[a] *Source:* hypothetical data.

and possible (or probable) states of nature (the economy or other external environment).

For example, a firm may be contemplating diversification of its product line and considers a takeover bid to one of three possible targets. In the process of investigation, the acquiring company works up data on the target companies performance over the course of several business cycles (Table 4-12). Figure 4-1 sets up a decision tree that graphs the outcomes using expected values. These indicate that over the course of a typical business cycle Company X will produce the highest average earnings per share. The earnings per share of the acquiring company over the term of the business cycle could be compared to company X to see if greater stability of earnings would result from the combination.

Cumulative Probabilities

Frequently in business situations the manager will wish to ascertain the probability of reaching or exceeding some goal. The purpose can be served by a cumulative probability distribution based upon the additive rule. What is the probability of an annual growth rate of 9.9% or less? Table 4-13 gives the answer: 65%.

WHERE DO THE PROBABILITIES COME FROM?

One can demonstrate the manipulation of assumed probabilities and by contrived examples the potential usefulness of probabilistic data in business decision making. It is quite another task to elucidate convincingly the derivation of the assigned probabilities. Classical theory excepted, the latter is most often the source of business resistance to the use of probabilities. Businessmen may regard the probability of this or

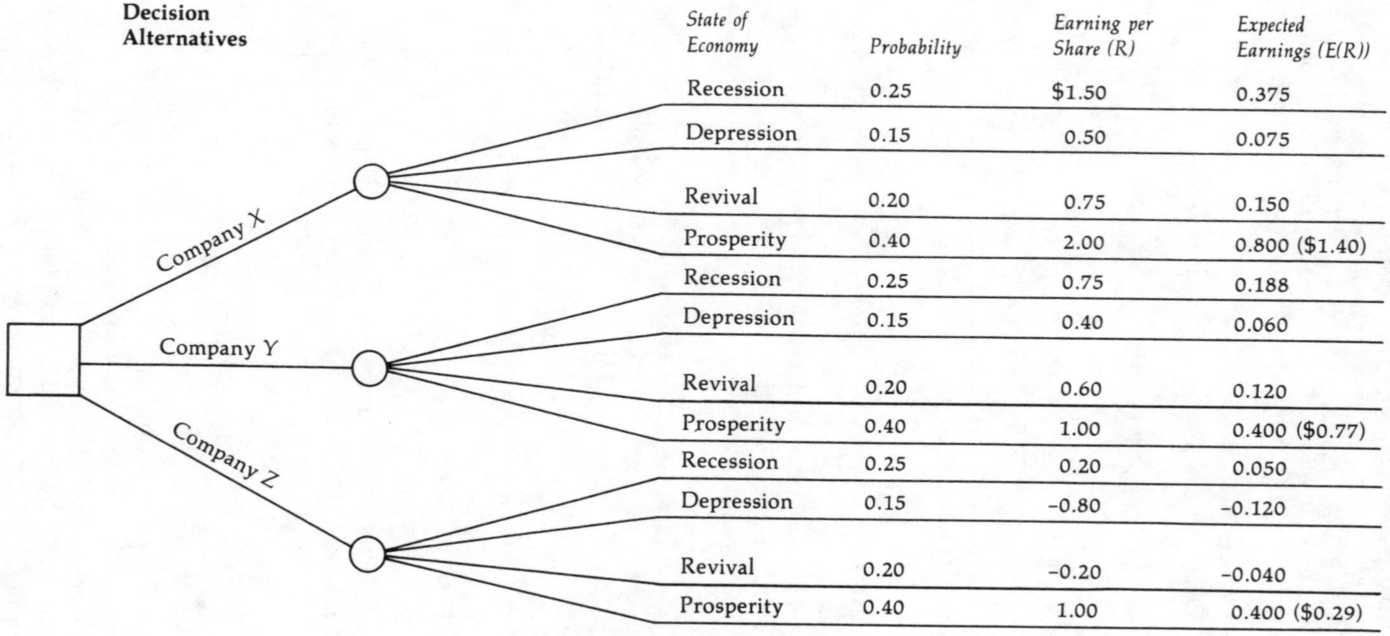

Decision
Alternatives

State of Economy	Probability	Earning per Share (R)	Expected Earnings (E(R))
Recession	0.25	$1.50	0.375
Depression	0.15	0.50	0.075
Revival	0.20	0.75	0.150
Prosperity	0.40	2.00	0.800 ($1.40)
Recession	0.25	0.75	0.188
Depression	0.15	0.40	0.060
Revival	0.20	0.60	0.120
Prosperity	0.40	1.00	0.400 ($0.77)
Recession	0.25	0.20	0.050
Depression	0.15	-0.80	-0.120
Revival	0.20	-0.20	-0.040
Prosperity	0.40	1.00	0.400 ($0.29)

Company X
Company Y
Company Z

Expected Earnings per Share
$$E(Rx) = \$1.40$$
$$E(Ry) = .77$$
$$E(Rz) = .29$$

Figure 4-1 Decision Tree of Expected Earnings per Share

74

Table 4-13 Annual Rental Growth Rate[a]

Growth Rate (%)	Relative Frequency	Cumulative Probabilities
8.0– 8.4	0.05	0.05
8.5– 8.9	0.10	0.15
9.0– 9.4	0.10	0.25
9.5– 9.9	0.40	0.65
10.0–10.4	0.20	0.85
10.5–10.9	0.05	0.90
11.0–11.4	0.05	0.95
11.5–11.9	0.05	1.00

[a] *Source:* hypothetical data.

that event as soft data in the nature of a "guestimate." Indeed, the term "equally likely" may have no more than an intuitive foundation when referring to possible outcomes. All the same, if aggregated into a probability distribution, discrete probabilities become weights in determining expected value, which is the most likely value of the variable in the long run and a pertinent input to the decision making process.

In assigning probabilities, however, it is useful to restate two basic rules: (a) all possible outcomes or events in a given situation must be identified so that the sum of the probabilities satisfies the 100 percent rule; (b) the probability assigned to any one event can never be less than zero nor more than one. A zero probability implies the outcome is impossible; a probability of one implies the outcome is certain. These rules suggest the graphing of a probability tree (Figure 4-1) to assure that all bases have been touched.

As we have seen in the discussion of schools of thought in probability theory, probabilities can be derived from experience or from experimental data. Hence, in Table 4-2, the highs and lows of Boeing and General Motors stocks could have been counted for some relevant time period and based upon the distribution of observations the probabilities calculated. The underlying assumption of the distribution states that the empirical relationship between the variables displayed will hold for the future. The stated probabilities are *objectively* derived from historical data. The probabilities discussed in Chapters 8 and 9—"Time Series" and "Correlation"—fall into this category. Sampling data can also provide the basis for a statement of objective probabilities. The life insurance industry, for example, establishes mortality tables by observing how many males and females of a given age die within a year based upon a sample of 100,000.

Unfortunately in many instances historical data may be either unavailable or not relevant to capital budgeting or the introduction of new products. Subjective probabilities might fill the need in these cases.

Subjective probabilities, by contrast, are derived from the estimates of experienced managers using quantitative or qualitative information. Unlike objective probability, there is no way to check on a single subjective estimate to determine its accuracy. However, managers can be trained in making probability estimates and supervisors can maintain a record on their previous performance. This will generally show that some managers are chronic optimists, always overestimating outcomes. In time, higher management will be able to adjust the estimates to allow for the propensities of the estimators.

There are three prerequisite elements in developing subjective estimates: (a) a single objective criterion must be defined for choosing between outcomes; for example, select the outcome which maximizes profit or minimizes cost; (b) all possible outcomes must be specified; and (c) the most experienced managers must be used.

A statistician who uses subjective probabilities is called a Bayesian statistician and the Bayesian method affords another approach to computing conditional probability. To illustrate Bayes' theorem, suppose we have two events, A and B, and the probability of B is greater than 0. Therefore, the conditional probability of A given the probability of B becomes

$$P(A_1|B) = \frac{P(A_1 \cap B)}{P(B)} = \frac{P(A_1)\ P(B|A_1)}{P(A_1)\ P(B|A_1) + P(A_2)\ P(B|A_2)} \qquad (4.18)$$

where

1. The probabilities of $P(A_1)$ and $P(A_2)$ are termed the *prior probabilities* of event A_1 and its complement A_2.
2. The computed probability, $P(A_1|B)$, is referred to as the *posterior probability* of event A, given the presence of B.
3. The probability of the intersection of events A and B [$P(A_1 \cap B)$] is the *joint probability* of events A and B.
4. The divisor, $P(B)$, is the *unconditional* or the *marginal probability* of event B.

Bayes' concept in effect disaggregates the conditional probability $P(A_1|B) = P(A_1 \cap B)/P(B)$ into smaller elements $P(A_1)\ P(B|A_1)/[P(A_1)\ P(B|A_1) + P(A_2)\ P(B|A_2)]$. The process weights prior information with experimental evidence. Subjective prior probabilities are assigned reflecting the degree of belief by managers according to their intuition and present quantitative knowledge. The prior probabilities are then revised as appropriate empirical data surfaces.

Suppose a corporation introduces an aptitude test in the selection of sales people. Past experience, before the introduction of the test, shows that 65 percent of all applicants received a classification of satisfactory when on the job [$P(A_1)$] and 35 percent were unsatisfactory [$P(A_2)$].

These are *prior* probabilities. Before the introduction of the test, if management selected a random applicant, the personnel department might state that the selection has a 65 percent chance of succeeding on the job.

After the introduction of the test, new data shows that 80 percent of the satisfactory group passed the test $[P(B|A_1)]$ and 30 percent of the unsatisfactory group passed the test $[P(B|A_2)]$. These constitute *posterior probabilities* or *revised probabilities*, for they find their source in new data. Therefore, given the revised data base, what is the probability that an applicant would be a satisfactory salesperson after achieving a passing grade on the aptitude test? Applying equation (4-18),

$$P(A_1|B) = \frac{(0.65)(0.80)}{(0.65)(0.80) + (0.35)(0.30)} = 0.83 \qquad (4\text{-}19)$$

If the company accepts applicants without the test, the probability of success for the random applicant is 65 percent. If the company accepts only applicants who pass the test, the probability of a successful choice rises to 83 percent.

The Bayesian theorem offers a technique for using subjective probability estimates of experienced managers and then refining the estimates as additional evidence becomes available. It also raises the question of whether the cost of administering the test is worth the increase in the degree of confidence that can now be placed in the selection process.

SUMMARY

The potential usefulness of probabilities to managers runs the gamut of business decisions—the management of liquidity (cash and marketable securities), accounts receivable and inventory management, capital budgeting and long term asset management, sales or expense forecasting—in short, any situation where knowledge of the environment is incomplete thereby generating uncertainty and risk.

While others may analyze and render reports on the preferred course of action, managers are paid to "bite the bullet." Hence, the recipient of a staff report based upon the use of probabilistic data must himself decide the degree of confidence he can place in the recommendations. The manager can satisfy himself on this score by posing fundamental questions aimed at the assumptions of the analysis:

1. What are the sources of uncertainty which warrant the use of probabilities?
2. Are there other sources of uncertainty overlooked in the report?
3. Have all possible outcomes or scenarios been identified before assigning probabilities?

4. Are the outcomes independent? Dependent? Mutually exclusive?
5. What kinds of probability are employed? Marginal or unconditional probabilities? Conditional probabilities? Joint probabilities? Bayesian statistics?
6. How were the probabilities determined? From the past experience of the firm? From the subjective estimates of the supervisors concerned with the problem? If the latter, what is their
   prior track record in assessing probable outcomes?
7. How sensitive are the recommendations to changes in the
   probability distribution?
8. If expected values were used, did the report include the accompanying standard deviations as measures of the degree of confidence in the averages or to set up a range of fluctuation for the
   likely outcomes?

chapter 5

Probability Distributions

An absolute frequency distribution shows the number of observations, based upon a sample or complete enumeration, grouped into defined classes. By contrast, a *probability distribution* is in the nature of a relative frequency distribution. *It deals with all possible values of a random variable and their probabilities of occurrence.*

Probability distributions play a key role in managerial statistics because they assist the investigator in assessing the characteristics of a population based upon a sample. The particular probability distribution chosen for the analysis depends upon the type of sample, the size of the sample vis-a-vis the population, the assumptions made about the underlying population, and so forth. A word of caution is appropriate, however. While probability distributions assist management in estimating the likelihood of outcomes that occur randomly or by chance, they do not allow predictions of specific outcomes with certainty. The statistician cannot predict with complete certainty that sales demand will equal twenty units but he can prognosticate the likelihood that demand will amount to twenty units, thirty units, and so on. Recall from Chapter 1, statistics does not treat the behavior of a single item but relies on the stability of mass data.

RANDOM VARIABLES

Business decisions are made in an environment of uncertainty. Cyclical, seasonal, trend, and random factors combine to shape the course of business activity. Common stock prices, monthly inventory levels, cash balances, interest rates can all vary significantly from expectations. If changes in a business statistic emanate in chance factors, the statistic is a random variable. When the statistician assigns probabilities to all possible values or changes in value of a random variable, whether determined by objective data or subjective considerations, the result is

Table 5-1 Probability Distribution
Changes in Common Stock Prices[a]

Changes in Common Stock Prices (X)	Probability $P(X)$
−$3	0.02
−$2	0.09
−$1	0.25
0 (no change)	0.28
+$1	0.25
+$2	0.09
+$3	0.02
	$\Sigma P(X) = \overline{1.00}$

[a] *Source:* hypothetical data.

termed a probability distribution. For example, changes in common stock prices are widely believed to appear randomly in the market (see Table 5-1).

TYPES OF DISTRIBUTIONS

Probability distributions are classified into two major categories— discrete or continuous. The distributions can be *univariate*, dealing with one variable, or *multivariate*, dealing with more than one variable. Our interest concentrates on univariate distributions for discrete and continuous variables.

Discrete variables can assume only finite values, that is, countable integers representing whole units. The data consist of discontinuous values, for example, the number of automobiles produced in the United States by year. Integers are the unit of measurement—it is not possible to produce $1/2$ a car. Discrete probability distributions of major importance are the *binomial, hypergeometric,* and *Poisson* distributions.

A continuous random variable can assume any numerical value within a specific range. Units may be divided into fractions of any size so that a continuous flow of measurements with infinitely minute gradations is possible. Examples include height, weight, time, length, and temperature. The number of possible values between 1 and 2 miles is infinite if you consider a large number of decimal places. Even smaller units of measurement touch each other in a continuous flow of values. Since values cannot be specifically enumerated with related probabilities (as a practical matter), a curve is used to represent the continuous probability distribution. The *normal curve* is the most prominent of the continuous distributions. Other continuous distributions include the *t-distribution*, *F-distribution*, and *Chi-square*.[1]

DISCRETE PROBABILITY DISTRIBUTIONS

Binomial Distribution

Although probability distributions can be subjective, and probabilities assigned to each value by judgmental methods, the binomial by comparison is a theoretical distribution, determined mathematically.

In general, the binomial is used to estimate the probability that a particular outcome will occur a given number of times out of a total number of trials. Suppose a firm experiences a 10 percent delinquency rate on accounts receivable. If five customer accounts are randomly sampled, what is the probability that one account of the five will be delinquent? The occurrence of a delinquent account is labeled "success"; the absence of a delinquent account represents "failure."

Assumptions of Binomial Distribution

Similar to all quantitative techniques used in managerial situations, the business problem under investigation must conform to the assumptions of the model. The assumptions of the binomial model include the following:

1. There are only two possible mutually exclusive outcomes on each trial. These are termed success or failure; good or defective; accepted or rejected; yes or no; and so forth. The probability of a success in the above example is 10 percent, while the probability of a failure is 90 percent.
2. Each trial or observation is performed independently. That is, the outcome of any trial does not influence the outcome of subsequent trials.
3. The probability of the possible outcomes remains constant for each repeated trial. For instance, the probability of the firm's delinquency rate is determined as 10 percent. This probability remains the same for each trial in the five accounts drawn. It also infers the probability of a nondelinquency customer account remains at 90 percent from trial to trial. The sum of the probabilities of the two outcomes must total 1.
4. Items drawn are replaced in the population after each trial. Thus, if a delinquent account is replaced in the population after it is selected in a sample, it is again subject to selection and

---

[1] Chi-square is often written χ^2.

consequently the probability of drawing it again remains the same. On the other hand, for all practical purposes, where the sample size is small relative to the population, the probability of drawing a delinquent account will vary only slightly without replacement.

Formulation of Binomial Distribution

Symbolically, for the binomial distribution, the two possible outcomes of a random event are designated:

p = probability that a successful event (x) will appear in a single trial or draw;

$q = (1 - p)$ = probability that a successful event (x) will *not* occur in a single trial or draw.

To determine the values of p or q, it is necessary to know the number of ways in which successes and failures can occur in a specified number of trials (n). This is obtained from the *binomial coefficient:*

$$\binom{n}{x} \tag{5-1}$$

where: n = the number of trials; and
x = the number of times a successful outcome will occur.

For the accounts receivable example, the binomial coefficient is calculated to be

$$\binom{5}{1} = 5 \tag{5-2}$$

That is, the number of possible combinations of an event where 5 accounts are randomly selected with the probability of 1 delinquent account is

$$
\left.\begin{array}{l}
\text{D N N N N} \\
\text{N D N N N} \\
\text{N N D N N} \\
\text{N N N D N} \\
\text{N N N N D}
\end{array}\right\}
\qquad
\begin{array}{l}
\text{D = delinquent account;} \\
\text{N = nondelinquent account.}
\end{array}
$$

Table 5-2 shows the binomial coefficients for various combinations of n and x, that is, the number of ways a delinquent account can be drawn from n trials. In four trials, one successful trial will appear in four possible combinations; in fourteen trials, three successful trials can appear in 364 combinations.

The formulation for determining the probability of a designated number of successes $P(X)$ in n trials equals the number of possible com-

Table 5-2   Binomial Coefficients $\binom{N}{X}$ (Selected Numbers)

n	$\binom{n}{0}$	$\binom{n}{1}$	$\binom{n}{2}$	$\binom{n}{3}$
0	1			
1	1	1		
2	1	2	1	
3	1	3	3	1
4	1	4	6	4
5	1	5	10	10
6	1	6	15	20
7	1	7	21	35
8	1	8	28	56
9	1	9	36	84
10	1	10	45	120
11	1	11	55	165
12	1	12	66	220
13	1	13	78	286
14	1	14	91	364
15	1	15	105	455
20	1	20	190	1140

binations of the event multiplied by the probability of success and failure:

$$P(X) = \binom{n}{x}(p)^x(1 - p)^{n-x} \qquad (5\text{-}3)$$

Reverting to the accounts receivable illustration, the probability of drawing one delinquent account in five trials is

$$\begin{aligned}
P(1) &= \binom{5}{1}(0.10)^1(1 - 0.10)^{5-1} \\
&= 5(0.10)(0.90)^4 \\
&= 0.5(0.6561) \\
&= 0.32805, \text{ or } 0.33 \text{ rounded}
\end{aligned} \qquad (5\text{-}4)$$

There exists a 33% probability that one delinquent account will be drawn in five trials.

Table 5-3 Calculation of Binomial Probabilities Delinquent Accounts[a]

1 Number of X Values from 5 Trials	2 Possible Combinations[b]	3 Number of Combinations	4 Probability of Events[c]
5 out of 5	D D D D D	1	$(0.10)^5 (0.90)^0 = \underline{0.00001}$
4 out of 5	D D D D N		$(0.10)^4 (0.90)^1 = 0.00009$
	D D D N D		$(0.10)^4 (0.90)^1 = 0.00009$
	D D N D D	5	$(0.10)^4 (0.90)^1 = 0.00009$
	D N D D D		$(0.10)^4 (0.90)^1 = 0.00009$
	N D D D D		$(0.10)^4 (0.90)^1 = \underline{0.00009}$
			0.00045
3 out of 5	D D D N N		$(0.10)^3 (0.90)^2 = 0.00081$
	N N D D D		$(0.10)^3 (0.90)^2 = 0.00081$
	D N D N D		$(0.10)^3 (0.90)^2 = 0.00081$
	N D N D D		$(0.10)^3 (0.90)^2 = 0.00081$
	D N N D D	10	$(0.10)^3 (0.90)^2 = 0.00081$
	N D D D N		$(0.10)^3 (0.90)^2 = 0.00081$
	N D D N D		$(0.10)^3 (0.90)^2 = 0.00081$
	D D N N D		$(0.10)^3 (0.90)^2 = 0.00081$
	D D N D N		$(0.10)^3 (0.90)^2 = 0.00081$
	D N D D N		$(0.10)^3 (0.90)^2 = \underline{0.00081}$
			0.00810
2 out of 5	D D N N N		$(0.10)^2 (0.90)^3 = 0.00729$
	N N N D D		$(0.10)^2 (0.90)^3 = 0.00729$
	D N N N D		$(0.10)^2 (0.90)^3 = 0.00729$
	N D N D N		$(0.10)^2 (0.90)^3 = 0.00729$
	D N D N N	10	$(0.10)^2 (0.90)^3 = 0.00729$
	N D D N N		$(0.10)^2 (0.90)^3 = 0.00729$
	N D N N D		$(0.10)^2 (0.90)^3 = 0.00729$
	N N D N D		$(0.10)^2 (0.90)^3 = 0.00729$
	D N N D N		$(0.10)^2 (0.90)^3 = 0.00729$
	N N D D N		$(0.10)^2 (0.90)^3 = \underline{0.00729}$
			0.07290
1 out of 5	N N N N D		$(0.10)^1 (0.90)^4 = 0.06561$
	D N N N N		$(0.10)^1 (0.90)^4 = 0.06561$
	N D N N N	5	$(0.10)^1 (0.90)^4 = 0.06561$
	N N D N N		$(0.10)^1 (0.90)^4 = 0.06561$
	N N N D N		$(0.10)^1 (0.90)^4 = \underline{0.06561}$
			0.32805
0 out of 5	N N N N N	1	$(0.10)^0 (0.90)^5 = 0.59049$

[a] *Source:* hypothetical data.
[b] D = delinquent account (success); N = nondelinquent account (failure).
[c] Any number raised to the zero power is equal to one, that is, $(0.90)^0 = 1$.

Binomial Probability Distribution

Suppose management needs a probability distribution for the number of delinquent accounts—one that covers all possible values of X (delinquent accounts) out of a given number of observations (n). Table 5-3 calculates all possible values of X (0, 1, 2, 3, and so forth) and the probability of each event out of n number of trials for the accounts receivable problem. Table 5-4 summarizes the outcomes of Table 5-3.

When using the binomial distribution it should constantly be remembered that the probabilities remain the same from trial to trial—in the accounts receivable illustration: the probability of delinquent accounts is always 10 percent and the probability of nondelinquent accounts is always 90 percent. Hence, for any given value of the random variable (delinquent accounts), each outcome has the same probability of occurrence. Also, to reiterate, a random variable takes on different values because of the chance factors at work in the sampling process. Therefore, the outcome of a trial (selecting an item as part of a sample) is often termed a random or stochastic process.

Binomial Probability Tables

Manifestly, when the number of trials (n) is large, the procedure for setting up a binomial probability distribution becomes quite tedious due to the number of possible combinations, p and q, involved. Standard probability tables are fortunately available to provide ready answers, for example, Table 5-5. These show all possible values of X and their corresponding probability for a given number of trials.

For example, management experience indicates that 20 percent of customers pay cash for purchases. Out of the next fifteen customers, what is the probability that five customers will pay cash? From Table

Table 5-4 Binomial Probability Distribution Delinquent Accounts[a]

1 Number[b] of Delinquent Accounts (X)	2 Probability P(X)
5	0.00001
4	0.00045
3	0.00810
2	0.07290
1	0.32805
0	0.59049
	$\Sigma P(X) = 1.00000$

[a] Source: hypothetical data.
[b] Based upon 5-item sample.

Table 5-5 Binomial Probability Distribution[a]—Values of Probability $P(X; n, P) = {}_nn_X \cdot P^X \cdot Q^{n-X}$

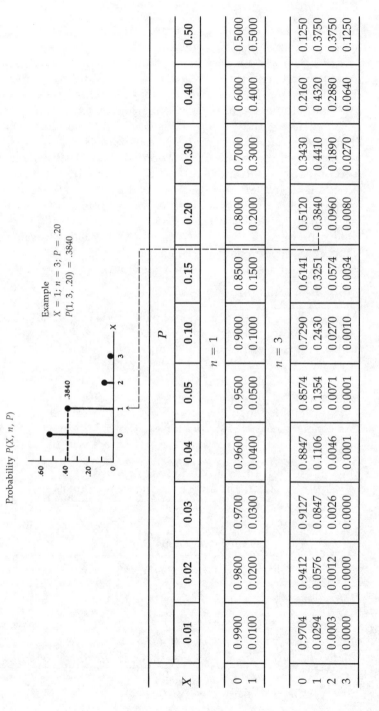

Example
$X = 1$; $n = 3$; $P = .20$
$P(1, 3, .20) = .3840$

X	0.01	0.02	0.03	0.04	0.05	0.10	0.15	0.20	0.30	0.40	0.50
							$n = 1$				
0	0.9900	0.9800	0.9700	0.9600	0.9500	0.9000	0.8500	0.8000	0.7000	0.6000	0.5000
1	0.0100	0.0200	0.0300	0.0400	0.0500	0.1000	0.1500	0.2000	0.3000	0.4000	0.5000
							$n = 3$				
0	0.9704	0.9412	0.9127	0.8847	0.8574	0.7290	0.6141	0.5120	0.3430	0.2160	0.1250
1	0.0294	0.0576	0.0847	0.1106	0.1354	0.2430	0.3251	0.3840	0.4410	0.4320	0.3750
2	0.0003	0.0012	0.0026	0.0046	0.0071	0.0270	0.0574	0.0960	0.1890	0.2880	0.3750
3	0.0000	0.0000	0.0000	0.0001	0.0001	0.0010	0.0034	0.0080	0.0270	0.0640	0.1250

$n = 5$

x											
0	0.9510	0.9039	0.8587	0.8154	0.7738	0.5905	0.4437	0.3277	0.1681	0.0778	0.0312
1	0.0480	0.0922	0.1328	0.1699	0.2036	0.3280	0.3915	0.4096	0.3602	0.2592	0.1562
2	0.0010	0.0038	0.0082	0.0142	0.0214	0.0729	0.1382	0.2048	0.3087	0.3456	0.3125
3	0.0000	0.0001	0.0003	0.0006	0.0011	0.0081	0.0244	0.0512	0.1323	0.2304	0.3125
4	0.0000	0.0000	0.0000	0.0000	0.0000	0.0004	0.0022	0.0064	0.0284	0.0768	0.1562
5	0.0000	0.0000	0.0000	0.0000	0.0000	0.0000	0.0001	0.0003	0.0024	0.0102	0.0312

$n = 15$

x											
0	0.8601	0.7386	0.6333	0.5421	0.4633	0.2059	0.0874	0.0352	0.0047	0.0005	0.0000
1	0.1303	0.2261	0.2938	0.3388	0.3658	0.3432	0.2312	0.1319	0.0305	0.0047	0.0005
2	0.0092	0.0323	0.0636	0.0988	0.1348	0.2669	0.2856	0.2309	0.0916	0.0219	0.0032
3	0.0004	0.0029	0.0085	0.0178	0.0307	0.1285	0.2184	0.2501	0.1700	0.0634	0.0139
4	0.0000	0.0002	0.0008	0.0022	0.0049	0.0428	0.1156	0.1876	0.2186	0.1268	0.0417
5	0.0000	0.0000	0.0001	0.0002	0.0006	0.0105	0.0449	0.1032	0.2061	0.1859	0.0916

$n = 20$

x											
0	0.8179	0.6676	0.5438	0.4420	0.3585	0.1216	0.0388	0.0115	0.0008	0.0000	0.0000
1	0.1652	0.2725	0.3364	0.3683	0.3774	0.2702	0.1368	0.0576	0.0068	0.0005	0.0000
2	0.0159	0.0528	0.0988	0.1458	0.1887	0.2852	0.2293	0.1369	0.0278	0.0031	0.0002
3	0.0010	0.0065	0.0183	0.0364	0.0596	0.1901	0.2428	0.2054	0.0716	0.0123	0.0011
4	0.0000	0.0006	0.0024	0.0065	0.0133	0.0898	0.1821	0.2182	0.1304	0.0350	0.0046

Source: Stephen P. Shao, *Statistics for Business and Economics*, 2nd ed. Columbus, Ohio: Charles E. Merrill Publishing Co. 1972. Partial table and illustrations.

5-5, $n = 15$, $p = 0.20$, and $x = 5$. Answer: 0.1032, or 10.3% probability. For speed and ease of calculation use the tables.

If this be so, why bother with an extended discussion on the derivation of the binomial tables? It must be stressed that unless the manager grasps the notion underlying the construction of the tables, he will never know whether they are rightly or wrongly applied in a given case.

Binomial Distribution as a Proportion

Table 5-3 can be converted to proportions by dividing X by n (Table 5-6).

The probability of scoring four successes in five trials is only 0.00045 but the probability of zero percent successes after five trials rises to 59 percent.

Cumulative Binomial Distribution

Twenty percent of the firm's customers pay cash. If twenty customers are randomly selected, what is the probability that fewer than five will pay cash? From Table 5-5, where $p = 0.20$ and $n = 20$, the following probabilities are obtained:

$$\begin{array}{ll} 0 \text{ will pay cash} = & 0.0115 \\ 1 \text{ will pay cash} = & 0.0576 \\ 2 \text{ will pay cash} = & 0.1369 \\ 3 \text{ will pay cash} = & 0.2054 \\ 4 \text{ will pay cash} = & \underline{0.2182} \\ \text{Total} = & 0.6296 \end{array}$$

The probability that less than five customers pay cash approximates 63 percent.

Table 5-6   Binomial Probability Distribution of Proportion Delinquent Accounts [a]

1 Number [b] of Delinquent Accounts (X)	2 Proportion $X/5$	3 Probability $P(X)$
5	5/5 = 1.00	0.00001
4	4/5 = 0.80	0.00045
3	3/5 = 0.60	0.00810
2	2/5 = 0.40	0.07290
1	1/5 = 0.20	0.32805
0	0/5 = 0.00	0.59049
		$\Sigma P(X) = \overline{1.00000}$

[a] *Source:* hypothetical data.
[b] Based upon 5-item sample.

Mean and Standard Deviation of the Binomial Distribution

The mean and standard deviation of the binomial distribution is calculated in the normal fashion. Using data from Table 5-4, we construct Table 5-7.

The shape of the binomial distribution depends upon the values of p and q. If $p = q$, the binomial will graph as a symmetrical curve. If $p \neq q$, the curve will tail off toward high or low values. In any event, as n increases (approaches infinity) the degree of skewness drops sharply, and the binomial blends into the normal curve.

The binomial distribution presumes knowledge of the population parameters, p and q. With this information, the formulation for computing the mean or expected value and standard deviation can be shortened. In the interest of clarity, we shall use the symbol μ to refer to the mean of discrete and continuous probability distributions, and reserve $(\bar{X})$ for other calculations of the mean. Accordingly, the mean (μ) of the binomial can be restated as

$$\mu = np \qquad \qquad (5\text{-}5)$$

Thus, for the delinquent accounts problem

$$\mu = 5(0.10) = 0.50$$

the same answer produced in Table 5-7, column 3. The mean of the probability distribution also represents the Expected Value $[E(V)]$ of the distribution.

Similarly, the standard deviation (σ) of the binomial can be restated as

$$\begin{aligned}
\sigma &= \sqrt{np\,(1-p)} \\
&= \sqrt{(5)(0.10)(0.90)} \qquad (5\text{-}6) \\
&= \sqrt{0.450} \\
&= 0.6708
\end{aligned}$$

Again this matches the result calculated in Table 5-7.

In business situations, many times the population parameters will not be known and must be estimated from sample data. However, once the estimates are derived, knowing the random variable is binomially distributed provides valuable input to test the goodness of the estimate.

Hypergeometric Distributions

The hypergeometric distribution substitutes for the binomial distribution when the items drawn in the sampling process do not reappear —are not replaced—in the population. Subject to this constraint, the distribution, similar to the binomial, deals with the probability of success $[P(X)]$ in n trials of a random variable.

Table 5-7 Mean and Standard Deviation for Binomial Distribution: Delinquent Accounts Sample[a]

1 Number[b] of Accounts (X)	2 Probability P(X)	3 (1 × 2) [XP(X)]	4 [X − ΣXP(X)] Deviations (d)	5 (4 × 4) d²	6 (2 × 5) Pd²
0	0.59049	0	−0.50045	0.250450	0.1478882
1	0.32805	0.32805	+0.50045	0.250450	0.0821600
2	0.07290	0.14580	+1.50045	2.251350	0.1641230
3	0.00810	0.02430	+2.50045	6.252250	0.0506430
4	0.00045	0.00180	+3.50045	12.253150	0.0055140
5	0.00001	0.00005	+4.50045	20.254050	0.0002030
	$\Sigma P(X) = 1.00000$	$\Sigma XP(X) = 0.49955$			$\Sigma Pd^2 = 0.4505312$ ≈ 0.45

Mean or approximately $0.50 = \dfrac{\Sigma XP(X)}{\Sigma P(X)} = \dfrac{0.49955}{1} \approx .50000$

Standard deviation $(\sigma) = \sqrt{\dfrac{\Sigma Pd^2}{\Sigma P(X)}} = \sqrt{\dfrac{0.45}{1}} = 0.6708$

[a] Source: hypothetical data.
[b] Based upon sample of 5 items.

Assumptions of Hypergeometric Distribution

The following assumptions underlie the hypergeometric distribution:

1. A finite population, that is, a population fixed in size, is assumed.
2. Since each item sampled is not returned to the population and cannot be selected again, the size of the population changes as the sampling process proceeds.
3. Although the number of trials in the sample remains constant, if the size of the population changes with each trial, then the probability of success changes from trial to trial.
4. The outcomes of a single trial are mutually exclusive—either success or failure. However, since the probabilities of success (or failure) vary from trial to trial, the trials are dependent. The outcome of one trial effects the outcome of subsequent trials. By contrast, in the binomial distribution, the outcomes are mutually exclusive and the trials are independent.

Formulation of the Hypergeometric Distribution

The probability of success $[P(X)]$ in the hypergeometric equals

$$P(X) = \frac{\binom{a}{x} \times \binom{b}{n-x}}{\binom{a+b}{n}} \tag{5-7}$$

where: a = number of successes in the population
   b = number of failures in the population
   n = number of trials
   x = number of possible successes in a sample of n trials

Assume that out of twenty customers, fifteen purchase on credit and five pay cash. What is the probability that in a sample of three customers, all will pay cash?

$$P(X) = \frac{\binom{5}{3} \times \binom{15}{3-3}}{\binom{20}{3}} \tag{5-8}$$

We now use the binomial coefficient in Table 5-2:

$$P(X) = \frac{10 \times 1}{1140} \tag{5-9}$$

$$\approx 0.008$$

There is an approximately 0.008 probability that the three trials in the sample will all constitute cash customers.

The same procedure can be used to calculate the probability of two successes out of three trials, one out of three, and zero out of three.

Hypergeometric Probability Distribution

The probabilities for all possible outcomes for three trials are summarized in Table 5-8.

The population comprises 25 percent cash customers and 75 percent credit customers (5/20 and 15/20, respectively). What is the probability of securing three cash customers in three picks? Recall each outcome depends on the previous results. Thus, assuming three successful picks, the probabilities change successively for the items are not replaced. Hence,

$$\frac{5}{20} \times \frac{4}{19} \times \frac{3}{18} = (0.25)(0.2105263)(0.1666666)$$

$$= 0.0087719$$

the same answer found in equation (5-9). What is the probability of drawing no cash customers out of three trials? Again the probabilities change with each trial:

$$\frac{15}{20} \times \frac{14}{19} \times \frac{13}{18} = (0.75)(0.7368421)(0.722222)$$

$$= 0.3991227, \text{ or } 0.399$$

which is the same answer as would be found using equation (5-7). Between the two extremes of the distribution, the probabilities vary

Table 5-8   Hypergeometric Probability Distribution Cash Customers[a]

1 Number of Cash Customers (X)	2 Probability P(X)
0	0.399
1	0.461
2	0.132
3	0.008
	$\Sigma P(X) = 1.000$

[a] Source: hypothetical data.
[b] Based upon 3-item sample.

Table 5-9 Mean and Standard Deviation for Hypergeometric Distribution: Customer Cash Purchases[a]

1 Number of Cash Customers $P(X)$	2 Probability $P(X)$	3 (1×2) $[XP(X)]$	4 $[X - \Sigma XP(X)]$ Deviations d	5 (4×4) d^2	6 (2×5) Pd^2
0	0.399	0.000	−0.749	0.561001	0.2238393
1	0.461	0.461	+0.251	0.063001	0.0290434
2	0.132	0.264	+1.251	1.565001	0.2065800
3	0.008	0.024	+2.251	5.067001	0.0405360
$\Sigma P(X) = 1.000$		$\Sigma XP(X) = 0.749$			$\Sigma Pd^2 = 0.4999987$

$$\mu = \frac{\Sigma XP(X)}{\Sigma P(X)} = \frac{0.749}{1} = 0.749, \text{ or } 0.75$$

or

$$\mu = np = (3)(0.25) = 0.75$$

and

$$\sigma = \sqrt{\Sigma Pd^2} = \sqrt{0.4999987} = 0.707$$

or

$$\sigma = \sqrt{n(p)(1 - p)\,\frac{N - n}{N - 1}} = \sqrt{(3)(0.25)(1 - 0.25)\,\frac{20 - 3}{20 - 1}}$$

$$= \sqrt{(0.562)(0.894)}$$

$$= \sqrt{0.502}$$

$$= 0.709$$

[a] *Source:* hypothetical data.

with the number of possible combinations of success and failure which can constitute a trial.

Mean and Standard Deviation

The calculation of the mean (μ) or expected value for the hypergeometric is similar to the binomial. The standard deviation (σ) differs somewhat in that the formulation contains a correction factor for the finite population.

Obviously the binomial and hypergeometric distributions bear a considerable similarity. In fact where the sample size is small in relation to population, the differences from using either distribution are quite insignificant. Thus, the binomial is often used in practice even when the hypergeometric actually applies. Only when n increases in size in relation to the population do significant differences result from using one rather than the other. The lack of replacement in the hypergeometric has a lesser impact if n is relatively small.

Poisson Distribution

The Poisson applies to situations where the number of trials in a sample is very large and the probability of success on any one trial is very small. Events occur over a continuum of time or space, for example, the number of defects per mile of telephone cable, the number of minicomputers sold per day, the number of telephone calls per minute on a switchboard, the number of misprints per page in a book, and so forth. This differs from the preceding distributions which predicted the likelihood of success in a given number of trials.

Assumptions of the Poisson Distribution

The assumptions of the Poisson largely match those of the binomial:

1. The events are independent. The number of defects per measurement does not depend on events in other intervals of measurement or other areas.
2. The probability of occurrence remains constant along the continuum of time or space. If four units of demand represents the average rate of occurrence per day, eight units apply to a 2-day interval. The average specified is in constant proportion to the length of time and space.
3. It assumes that p (the probability of success) and n (the number of trials) are unknown. The Poisson will not tell us the percentage of defects along a continuum, only the number of defects per interval. To wit, the percentage of defects per mile of telephone cable is not calculable, only the number of defects is determinable.

Formulation of the Poisson Distribution

The key to the construction of the Poisson Distribution lies in the average number of successes for the specified time or space. The Poisson formulation becomes:

$$P(X|\mu) = \frac{\mu^x}{X!} e^{-\mu} \qquad (5\text{-}10)$$

where: $P(X|\mu)$ = the probability of a stated number of successful events (X) given the average number of occurrences per interval of time or space (μ)

μ = the average number of occurrences or events per interval

e = a constant equal to 2.718281824 . . ., the number base of the natural system of logarithms

x = number of successful occurrences or events

$!$ = the factorial of X

The factorial of a number equals the product of the integer multiplied by all the lower integers; thus the factorial of 5 (5!) is $5 \times 4 \times 3 \times 2 \times 1$ = 120. The factorial of zero (0!) is defined as 1. Table 5-10 gives the factorials of numbers 0 to 15, which will save time in computing Poisson probabilities.

   Similarly, Table 5-11 calculates $e^{-\mu}$ for selected values of μ running from 0 to 9.9.

Table 5-10   Factorials

n	$n!$
0	1
1	1
2	2
3	6
4	24
5	120
6	720
7	5,040
8	40,320
9	362,880
10	3,628,800
11	39,916,800
12	479,001,600
13	6,227,020,800
14	87,178,291,200
15	1,307,674,368,000

Table 5-11   Values of $e^{-\mu}$ (Selected Numbers)[a]

μ	$e^{-\mu}$	μ	$e^{-\mu}$	μ	$e^{-\mu}$	μ	$e^{-\mu}$
0.0	1.000	2.5	0.082	5.0	0.0067	9.5	0.00008
0.1	0.905	2.6	0.074	5.1	0.0061	9.6	0.00007
0.2	0.819	2.7	0.067	5.2	0.0055	9.7	0.00006
0.3	0.741	2.8	0.061	5.3	0.0050	9.8	0.00006
0.4	0.670	2.9	0.055	5.4	0.0045	9.9	0.00005

[a] *Source:* Stephen P. Shao, *Statistics for Business and Economics,* 2nd ed. Columbus, Ohio: Charles E. Merrill Publishing Company, 1972.

Assume that management's analysis of inventory turnover shows that average sales demand for a minicomputer is five per day. Management wishes to know the probability of zero sales on any randomly selected day. Using equation (5-10),

$$P(0|5) = \frac{5^0}{0!} \times 2.718281824^{-5} \qquad (5\text{-}11)$$

From Table 5-10, 0! = 1, from Table 5-11, $2.718281824^{-5} = 0.0067$, and from your calculator, $5^0 = 1$. Therefore,

$$P(0|5) = \frac{1}{1} \times 0.0067 \qquad (5\text{-}12)$$

$$= 0.0067$$

The probability of zero sales on any randomly chosen day is approximately $2/3$ of 1 percent.

Suppose management wished to know the probability of selling four units in any randomly selected day:

$$P(4|5) = \frac{5^4}{4!} \times 2.718281824^{-5} \qquad (5\text{-}13)$$

From Table 5-10, 4! = 24, from Table 5-11, $2.718281824^{-5} = .0067$, and from your calculator, $5^4 = 625$. Accordingly,

$$P(4|5) = \frac{625}{24} \times 0.0067 = 0.174479, \text{ or } 0.1745 \qquad (5\text{-}14)$$

Poisson Probability Distribution

The complete probability distribution of the daily demand for minicomputers (see Table 5-12) can be calculated using equation (5-12) or taken directly from published tables (for example, Table 5-13) found in most all statistical handbooks.

Table 5-12 Poisson Probability Distribution Daily Sales Demand of Mini-Computers[a]

Demand Mini-Computers (X)	Probability P(X)	Expected Value XP(X)
0	0.0067	0.0000
1	0.0337	0.0337
2	0.0842	0.1684
3	0.1404	0.4212
4	0.1755	0.7020
5	0.1755	0.8775
6	0.1462	0.8772
7	0.1044	0.7308
8	0.0653	0.5224
9	0.0363	0.3267
10	0.0181	0.1810
11	0.0082	0.0090
12	0.0034	0.0041
13	0.0013	0.0017
14	0.0005	0.0007
15	0.0002	0.0003
	1.0000	4.8567

[a] *Source:* hypothetical data.

The slight discrepancy in the probabilities obtained from equation (5-10) and the published tables results from rounding differences in the $e^{-\mu}$ factor.

Cumulative Poisson Probability Distributions

These show the probability of the number of successes less than or more than a given value of X. In determining cumulative probabilities, the addition rule is used for mutually exclusive events.

By way of illustration, management needs to know the probability of the daily sales demand for fewer than three computers. This is expressed as

$$P(X < 3 | \mu = 5.0) = P(X = 2) + P(X = 1) + P(X = 0) \quad (5\text{-}15)$$

where (from Table 5-13):

$$P(X = 0) = 0.0067$$
$$P(X = 1) = 0.0337$$
$$P(X = 2) = \underline{0.0842}$$
$$0.1246$$

Therefore, the probability of selling fewer than three computers on any randomly selected day is about 12.5 percent.

Table 5-13 Poisson Probability Distribution[a]**—Values of $P(X) =$**
$$\frac{\mu^x \cdot e^{-\mu}}{X!}$$ **(Selected Numbers)**

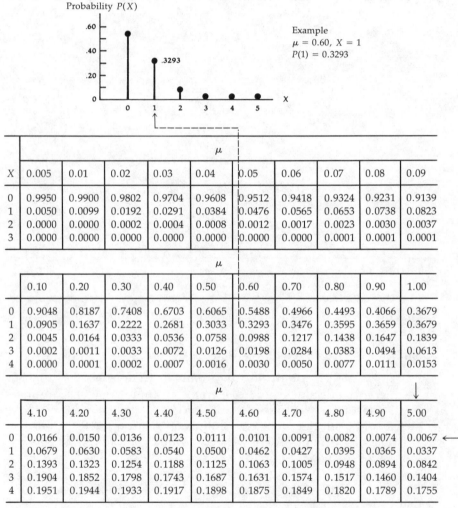

Probability $P(X)$

Example
$\mu = 0.60$, $X = 1$
$P(1) = 0.3293$

X	0.005	0.01	0.02	0.03	0.04	0.05	0.06	0.07	0.08	0.09
0	0.9950	0.9900	0.9802	0.9704	0.9608	0.9512	0.9418	0.9324	0.9231	0.9139
1	0.0050	0.0099	0.0192	0.0291	0.0384	0.0476	0.0565	0.0653	0.0738	0.0823
2	0.0000	0.0000	0.0002	0.0004	0.0008	0.0012	0.0017	0.0023	0.0030	0.0037
3	0.0000	0.0000	0.0000	0.0000	0.0000	0.0000	0.0000	0.0001	0.0001	0.0001

μ

	0.10	0.20	0.30	0.40	0.50	0.60	0.70	0.80	0.90	1.00
0	0.9048	0.8187	0.7408	0.6703	0.6065	0.5488	0.4966	0.4493	0.4066	0.3679
1	0.0905	0.1637	0.2222	0.2681	0.3033	0.3293	0.3476	0.3595	0.3659	0.3679
2	0.0045	0.0164	0.0333	0.0536	0.0758	0.0988	0.1217	0.1438	0.1647	0.1839
3	0.0002	0.0011	0.0033	0.0072	0.0126	0.0198	0.0284	0.0383	0.0494	0.0613
4	0.0000	0.0001	0.0002	0.0007	0.0016	0.0030	0.0050	0.0077	0.0111	0.0153

μ

	4.10	4.20	4.30	4.40	4.50	4.60	4.70	4.80	4.90	5.00
0	0.0166	0.0150	0.0136	0.0123	0.0111	0.0101	0.0091	0.0082	0.0074	0.0067 ←
1	0.0679	0.0630	0.0583	0.0540	0.0500	0.0462	0.0427	0.0395	0.0365	0.0337
2	0.1393	0.1323	0.1254	0.1188	0.1125	0.1063	0.1005	0.0948	0.0894	0.0842
3	0.1904	0.1852	0.1798	0.1743	0.1687	0.1631	0.1574	0.1517	0.1460	0.1404
4	0.1951	0.1944	0.1933	0.1917	0.1898	0.1875	0.1849	0.1820	0.1789	0.1755

[a] *Source:* Stephen P. Shao, *Statistics for Business and Economics*, 2nd ed. Columbus, Ohio: Charles E. Merrill Publishing Co. 1972. Partial table and illustration.

Mean and Standard Deviation of the Poisson

The mean and standard deviation of the Poisson can be determined in a manner similar to the binomial (see Table 5-7). However, it is mathematically possible to show that the mean of the Poisson distribution is simply the expected value of X, or $\Sigma XP(X)$ from Table 5-12. Thus,

$$\mu = \Sigma XP(X) = 4.8567 \qquad (5\text{-}16)$$

for the mini-computers problem. The standard deviation becomes

$$\sigma = \sqrt{\mu}$$
$$= \sqrt{4.8567} \qquad (5\text{-}17)$$
$$= 2.204$$

CONTINUOUS PROBABILITY DISTRIBUTIONS

When compared to discrete distributions of a random variable, a continuous distribution has an infinite number of values so that the probability a random value will equal a specific value of (X) cannot be determined. Common continuous variables include weight, volume, time, and distance. However, it is possible to determine the probability that the random variable will assume a value between stated intervals (between two points). Also, the distribution of a continuous random variable can resemble the now familiar configurations: positive or negative skewness; bimodal, or normal (symmetrical).

Normal Distribution

As noted previously, a normal curve is a symmetrical or bell-shaped design. *The actual shape depends upon the dispersion of values from the mean of the distribution.* Values close to the mean form a peaked distribution; values widely dispersed from the mean form a flatter, spread out distribution. Consequently, *the normal curve is completely defined if the population mean (μ) and the standard deviation (σ) are known.* With the values of μ and σ available, the mathematical equation for the curve permits the calculation of the height of the curve for each point and the area under the curve between any two points on the X axis.

A normal distribution with $\mu = 0$ and $\sigma = 1$ is termed a *standard normal distribution*. The area under the curve divides into three standard deviations from the mean (Figure 5-1) as follows:

$\mu \pm 1\sigma = 68.27\%$ of the area under the curve;
$\mu \pm 2\sigma s = 95.45\%$ of the area under the curve; and
$\mu \pm 3\sigma s = 99.73\%$ of the area under the curve.

In the standard normal distribution, the mean, median, and mode are equal to zero.

Study Figure 5-1. The values of the random variable are displayed on the X axis in terms of deviations from the mean and the probabilities on the Y axis. The probabilities of different values for the random variable

Figure 5-1   Standard Normal Distribution

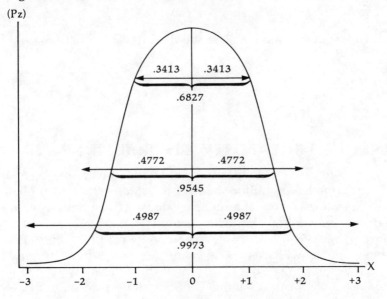

$$x \text{ axis} = \sigma \text{ units}$$
$$\mu = 0 \text{ and } \sigma = 1$$

If $x = 1\sigma$, $Z = \dfrac{1 - 0}{1} = 1$. From Table 5-14, $Z = 1$ converts to 0.3413 or

34.13%

If $x = 2\sigma s$, $Z = \dfrac{(2 \times 1) - 0}{1} = 2$. From Table 5-14, $Z = 2$ converts to

0.4772 or 47.72%

If $x = 3\sigma s$, $Z = \dfrac{(3 \times 1) - 0}{1} = 3$. From Table 5-14, $Z = 3$ converts to

0.4987 or 49.87%

of a normal distribution in standardized form or otherwise are derived
by applying the formula:

$$Z = \frac{X - \mu}{\sigma} \tag{5-18}$$

where: X = value of a normal random variable,
   μ = mean value of a normal random variable,
   σ = standard deviation of the normal random variable, and
   Z = number of standard deviations that a given value of
   random variable is from the mean.

Applying the Normal Distribution

Assume management has determined sales demand follows a normal distribution. Expected sales or mean sales are 200,000 (μ) units, and the standard deviation calculated from expected sales is 10,000 units (σ). Since only by coincidence will actual sales match estimated sales precisely, management needs to know the "confidence level" they can place in these estimates of the underlying population. Hence, the company requests the following information:

1. The probability that sales will attain levels between 200,000 units and 220,000 units.
2. The probability that sales will surpass 210,000 units.
3. The probability that sales will fall below 185,000 units.

Answer to 1. The following values are given:

$$X = 220,000 \text{ sales units}$$
$$\mu = 200,000 \text{ sales units}$$
$$\sigma = 10,000 \text{ sales units}$$

Then, using equation (5-18),

$$Z = \frac{220,000 - 200,000}{10,000} \qquad (5\text{-}19)$$
$$= +2.0$$

From the standardized normal distribution (Table 5-14) row 2.0 and column 0.00, the probability that sales will attain a level between 200,000 and 220,000 units equals 0.4772, or 48 percent.

Answer to 2.

$$X = 210,000 \text{ sales units}$$
$$\mu = 200,000 \text{ sales units}$$
$$\sigma = 10,000 \text{ sales units}$$

Thus

$$Z = \frac{210,000 - 200,000}{10,000} \qquad (5\text{-}20)$$
$$= +1.0$$

A Z value of $+1$ has a probability of 0.3413. This is the probability of something falling *between* the mean and one standard deviation away. Since we are interested here in sales *exceeding* 210,000 units, that is, surpassing 1σ, we must subtract 0.3413 from the sum of the probabilities in the right side of the distribution total, 0.5000. Hence, 0.5000 − 0.3413 = 0.1587, or there exists a 15.87 percent probability of sales exceeding 210,000 units.

To reiterate, the right side (or plus side) of the standardized normal

Table 5-14   Table of Standard Normal Distribution: Areas of the Normal Curve Between Maximum Ordinate and Ordinate at Z

*z[a]	0.00	0.01	0.02	0.03	0.04	0.05	0.06	0.07	0.08	0.09
0.0	0.0000	0.0040	0.0080	0.0120	0.0160	0.0199	0.0239	0.0279	0.0319	0.0359
0.1	0.0398	0.0438	0.0478	0.0517	0.0557	0.0596	0.0636	0.0675	0.0714	0.0753
0.2	0.0793	0.0832	0.0871	0.0910	0.0948	0.0987	0.1026	0.1064	0.1103	0.1141
0.3	0.1179	0.1217	0.1255	0.1293	0.1331	0.1368	0.1406	0.1443	0.1480	0.1517
0.4	0.1554	0.1591	0.1628	0.1664	0.1700	0.1736	0.1772	0.1808	0.1844	0.1879
0.5	0.1915	0.1950	0.1985	0.2019	0.2054	0.2088	0.2123	0.2157	0.2190	0.2224
0.6	0.2257	0.2291	0.2324	0.2357	0.2389	0.2422	0.2454	0.2486	0.2517	0.2549
0.7	0.2580	0.2611	0.2642	0.2673	0.2704	0.2734	0.2764	0.2794	0.2823	0.2852
0.8	0.2881	0.2910	0.2939	0.2967	0.2995	0.3023	0.3051	0.3078	0.3106	0.3133
0.9	0.3159	0.3186	0.3212	0.3238	0.3264	0.3289	0.3315	0.3340	0.3365	0.3389
1.0	0.3413	0.3438	0.3461	0.3485	0.3508	0.3531	0.3554	0.3577	0.3599	0.3621
1.1	0.3643	0.3665	0.3686	0.3708	0.3729	0.3749	0.3770	0.3790	0.3810	0.3830
1.2	0.3849	0.3869	0.3888	0.3907	0.3925	0.3944	0.3962	0.3980	0.3997	0.4015
1.3	0.4032	0.4049	0.4066	0.4082	0.4099	0.4115	0.4131	0.4147	0.4162	0.4177
1.4	0.4192	0.4207	0.4222	0.4236	0.4251	0.4265	0.4279	0.4292	0.4306	0.4319
1.5	0.4332	0.4345	0.4357	0.4370	0.4382	0.4394	0.4406	0.4418	0.4429	0.4441
1.6	0.4452	0.4463	0.4474	0.4484	0.4495	0.4505	0.4515	0.4525	0.4535	0.4545
1.7	0.4554	0.4564	0.4573	0.4582	0.4591	0.4599	0.4608	0.4616	0.4625	0.4633
1.8	0.4641	0.4649	0.4656	0.4664	0.4671	0.4678	0.4686	0.4693	0.4699	0.4706
1.9	0.4713	0.4719	0.4726	0.4732	0.4738	0.4744	0.4750	0.4756	0.4761	0.4767
2.0	0.4772	0.4778	0.4783	0.4788	0.4793	0.4798	0.4803	0.4808	0.4812	0.4817
2.1	0.4821	0.4826	0.4830	0.4834	0.4838	0.4842	0.4846	0.4850	0.4854	0.4857
2.2	0.4861	0.4864	0.4868	0.4871	0.4875	0.4878	0.4881	0.4884	0.4887	0.4890
2.3	0.4893	0.4896	0.4898	0.4901	0.4904	0.4906	0.4909	0.4911	0.4913	0.4916
2.4	0.4918	0.4920	0.4922	0.4925	0.4927	0.4929	0.4931	0.4932	0.4934	0.4936
2.5	0.4938	0.4940	0.4941	0.4943	0.4945	0.4946	0.4948	0.4949	0.4951	0.4952
2.6	0.4953	0.4955	0.4956	0.4957	0.4959	0.4960	0.4961	0.4962	0.4963	0.4964
2.7	0.4965	0.4966	0.4967	0.4968	0.4969	0.4970	0.4971	0.4972	0.4973	0.4974
2.8	0.4974	0.4975	0.4976	0.4977	0.4977	0.4978	0.4979	0.4979	0.4980	0.4981
2.9	0.4981	0.4982	0.4982	0.4983	0.4984	0.4984	0.4985	0.4985	0.4986	0.4986
3.0	0.4987	0.4987	0.4987	0.4988	0.4988	0.4989	0.4989	0.4989	0.4990	0.4990

$$^a Z = \frac{X - \mu}{\sigma}$$

distribution contains 50 percent of the values. As management wants to know the probability for the interval or area above 210,000, then 0.3413, the area from the mean (μ) to (X)—200,000 to 210,000—is subtracted from the total area of 0.5000 on the right side of the normal curve to obtain the remaining area, which gives us the probability of sales exceeding 210,000 units, that is 15.87 percent.

Answer to 3.

$$X = 185,000 \text{ sales units}$$
$$\mu = 200,000 \text{ sales units}$$
$$\sigma = 10,000 \text{ sales units}$$

Thus

$$Z = \frac{185,000 - 200,000}{10,000} \qquad (5\text{-}21)$$
$$= -1.5$$

The Z value of -1.5 standard deviations marks an area to the left of the mean encompassing 0.4332 of the values. Since the left side of the normal curve contains .5000 of the values and the area from the mean to -1.5 standard deviations contains 0.4332 of the values, the remaining area is obtained by performing the following subtraction:

$$0.5000 - 0.4332 = 0.0668, \text{ or } 6.68 \text{ percent}$$

This is the probability that sales will fall below 185,000 units.

Other variations are also possible, for example, the probability of estimated sales occurring *between* 185,000 and 205,000 units is calculated as follows:

$$X = 185,000 \text{ and } 205,000 \text{ sales units}$$
$$\mu = 200,000 \text{ sales units}$$
$$\sigma = 10,000 \text{ sales units}$$

Therefore,

$$Z = \frac{185,000 - 200,000}{10,000} = -1.5$$
$$\qquad (5\text{-}22)$$
$$Z = \frac{205,000 - 200,000}{10,000} = +0.50$$

From Table 5-14,

$$-1.5 = 0.4332$$
$$+0.50 = \underline{0.1915}$$
$$.6247$$

Because one value of Z is positive and another negative, the areas between the two equals the sum of the probabilities. Hence, the probability of sales occurring between 185,000 and 205,000 units is 62.47 percent.

Assumptions of the Normal Distribution

The normal distribution ranks as perhaps the most important distribution in statistics. It assumes that the underlying population from which a sample is taken comprises values of a random variable that is normally distributed. Based upon this assumption, inferences can be made from a sample concerning characteristics of the population. For example, in the preceding illustrations, the normal distribution allowed us to make inferences about various sales levels.

Although the normal curve portrays the distribution of a continuous random variable, many discrete random variables demonstrate characteristics that permit comparison with the normal distribution. Note also the distribution of a particular random variable may have a mean (μ) and standard deviation (σ) of any amount and yet be adjusted to the standard normal distribution to derive related probabilities. It is only necessary that the former meet the mathematical criteria of a normal distribution.

Student's t-Distribution

The t-distribution applies to the analysis of samples taken from the population of a normally distributed random variable. If the population random variable (X) is normally distributed, then the sample mean ($\bar{X}$) will be normally distributed and the t-distribution assumes a symmetrical configuration. Thus far, the same could be said of the normal curve.

However, if we do not know the standard deviation of the population (σ) and must rely on the sample standard deviation (σ_s) for an estimate, an element of added uncertainty enters the picture. Recall in using the normal curve, we knew the population mean (μ) and standard devia-

Table 5-15   Student's t-Distribution (Selected Numbers)

Degrees of Freedom	Probability						
	0.50	0.30	0.20	0.10	0.05	0.02	0.01
1	1.000	1.963	3.078	6.314	12.706	31.821	63.657
2	0.816	1.386	1.886	2.920	4.303	6.965	9.925
3	0.765	1.250	1.638	2.353	3.182	4.541	5.841
⟨:⟩	⟨:⟩	⟨:⟩	⟨:⟩	⟨:⟩	⟨:⟩	⟨:⟩	⟨:⟩
7	0.711	1.119	1.415	1.895	2.365	2.998	3.499
12	0.695	1.083	1.356	1.782	2.179	2.681	3.055
13	0.694	1.079	1.350	1.771	2.160	2.650	3.012
14	0.692	1.076	1.345	1.761	2.145	2.624	2.977
15	0.691	1.074	1.341	1.753	2.131	2.602	2.947
⟨:⟩	⟨:⟩	⟨:⟩	⟨:⟩	⟨:⟩	⟨:⟩	⟨:⟩	⟨:⟩
23	0.685	1.060	1.319	1.714	2.069	2.500	2.807
24	0.685	1.059	1.318	1.711	2.064	2.492	2.797
25	0.684	1.058	1.316	1.708	2.060	2.485	2.787
⟨:⟩	⟨:⟩	⟨:⟩	⟨:⟩	⟨:⟩	⟨:⟩	⟨:⟩	⟨:⟩
120	0.677	1.041	1.289	1.658	1.980	2.358	2.617
∞	0.674	1.036	1.282	1.645	1.960	2.326	2.576

tion (σ). The smaller the sample size (n), the greater the uncertainty and the distribution becomes more spread out (flatter or less peaked). Consequently, the t-distribution is symmetrical but slightly flatter than the standardized normal distribution.

The flatness of the t-distribution, it follows, increases as n (sample size) decreases. Since the estimated population standard deviation (σ) depends upon the sample standard deviation (σ_s), the t-distribution statistic changes value with the *degrees of freedom* (df) in the sample. The latter term, used in correcting sampling errors, equals $n - 1$. The formulation of the value of t becomes

$$t = \frac{\bar{X} - \mu}{\sigma_s/\sqrt{n}} \qquad (5\text{-}23)$$

where: $\bar{X}$ = the mean of the sample
μ = the mean of the population
n = size of the sample
σ_s = sample standard deviation of the sample

Applying the t-Statistic

Assume a manufacturer wishes to test the durability of aircraft shock absorbers. Based on experience, the average shock absorber lasts 100 hours. A sample of 25 is drawn from a production run. The sample has a mean durability of 95 hours and a standard deviation of 10 hours. The manufacturer has no field data on the standard deviation but desires to know whether the mean of the sample (95) differs significantly from the mean of the population (100). Applying equation (5-23),

$$\begin{aligned} t &= \frac{95 - 100}{10/\sqrt{25}} \\ &= \frac{-5}{10/5} \\ &= \frac{-5}{2} \\ &= -2.5 \end{aligned} \qquad (5\text{-}24)$$

The t-Distribution

The t-distribution is not a single distribution but a family of distributions. There is a different distribution for each degree of freedom. When the number of degrees is small, say less than 30, the variation from the normal distribution takes on marked significance. As the degrees of freedom increases—reach 100 and approach infinity—the t-distribution merges into the normal distribution. Table 5-15 displays certain values of the t-distribution.

To use Table 5-15, read down the first column for the appropriate degrees of freedom. In the shock absorber illustration, there are 24 degrees of freedom ($n - 1 = 25 - 1$). Read across to a desired level of probability, say 5 percent. If $df = 24$ and the probability level is 0.05, $t = 2.064$. Since the computed value of t [equation (5-24)] is -2.5, the investigator could tell management there exists a significant difference between the sample mean and the population mean. In making this statement, the investigator runs a 5 percent chance of error. To summarize:

What is tested? Answer: The average durability of the shock absorbers is 100 hours.

Criterion for decision? Answer: Reject the statement if the computed value of t (-2.5) is greater than $+2.064$ or less than -2.064, that is, if $t > +2.064$ or $t < -2.064$.

Possibility of error? Answer: At the selected level of probability the investigator has a 95 percent likelihood of a correct estimate and a 5 percent chance of error.

Generally, the t-distribution applies to the evaluation of small samples, 30 or fewer items in the sample.

Chi-Square (χ^2) Distribution

The t-distribution told us that the mean durability of shock absorbers was not 100 hours. It did not enable us to estimate the standard deviation (σ) of the population or the variance (σ^2) of the population. Chi-square, on the other hand, permits the investigator to set up an interval containing the population variance (σ^2) for a given level of probability. The interval derives from the sample variance (σ_s^2) and like the t-distribution depends upon the degrees of freedom. Table 5-16 gives the values of chi-square.

The confidence interval formulation for the population variance is defined by

$$\frac{(n - 1)\sigma_s^2}{X_{U;\, n-1}^2} \leq \sigma^2 \leq \frac{(n - 1)\sigma_s^2}{X_{L;\, n-1}^2} \tag{5-25}$$

where: $n - 1$ = degrees of freedom

σ_s^2 = sample variance, or the sample standard deviation squared

σ^2 = population variance, or the standard deviation of the population squared

X_U^2 and X_L^2 = upper and lower limits of the confidence interval based upon the chosen level of probability (values are taken from Table 5-16).

Using the data in the shock absorber illustration, assume management would be content with a 90 percent confidence interval for the standard

Table 5-16   Chi-Square Distribution (Selected Numbers)[a]

Left Side

df \ α	0.001	0.005	0.010	0.025	0.050	0.100
1	0.000	0.000	0.000	0.001	0.004	0.016
2	0.002	0.010	0.020	0.051	0.103	0.211
3	0.024	0.072	0.115	0.216	0.352	0.584
4	0.091	0.207	0.297	0.484	0.711	1.06
5	0.210	0.412	0.554	0.831	1.15	1.61
24	8.08	9.89	10.9	12.4	13.8	15.7

Right Side

df \ α	0.100	0.050	0.025	0.010	0.005	0.001
1	2.71	3.84	5.02	6.63	7.88	10.8
2	4.61	5.99	7.38	9.21	10.6	13.8
3	6.25	7.81	9.35	11.3	12.8	16.3
4	7.78	9.49	11.1	13.3	14.9	18.5
5	9.24	11.1	12.8	15.1	16.7	20.5
24	33.2	36.4	39.4	43.0	45.6	51.2

[a] *Source:* R. A. Fisher and F. Yates, *Statistical Tables for Biological, Agricultural and Medical Research.* Biometrika, Vol. 32 pp. 187–191, published by Oliver & Boyd, Edinburgh.

deviation of the population. This lops off 5 percent of the values from both ends of the distribution, as indicated in Figure 5-2. Then from Table 5-16.

$$X_U^2; \; n - 1 = 36.4$$
$$X_L^2; \; n - 1 = 13.8$$

Therefore

$$\frac{(25 - 1)10^2}{36.4} \leq \sigma^2 \leq \frac{(25 - 1)10^2}{13.8}$$

$$\frac{2400}{13.8} \leq \sigma^2 \leq \frac{2400}{36.4} \qquad (5\text{-}26)$$

$$173.91 \leq \sigma^2 \leq 65.93$$

Based upon the sample variance of 100 ($\sigma_s = 10$ and $\sigma_s^2 = 100$), the investigator could give management 90 percent assurance that the population variance lies between 65.93 hours and 173.91 hours. Or taking the square roots of 65.93 and 173.91, respectively, the standard deviation of the population falls between 8.11 hours and 13.18 hours.

Figure 5-2   Chi-Square Distribution, 90 Percent Confidence Interval (note: chi-square is non-symmetrical; the distribution is skewed to the right)

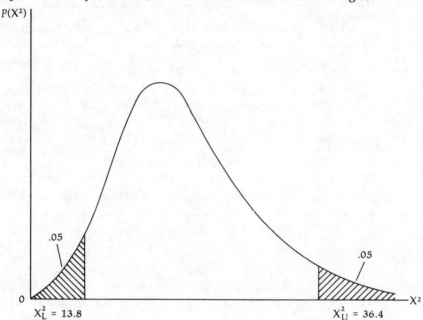

SUMMARY

Construction of probability distributions lies in the province of the specialist rather than a line manager. Yet probability distributions constitute an integral part of the sampling process that strives to make generalizations about the characteristics of populations or larger masses of data. The decision maker at any level of the management hierarchy who uses sample data cannot avoid, therefore, the responsibility of developing some insight into the validity of his information.

In particular, where the specialist uses a statistical model (or distribution) to draw inferences about the population, the manager must realize that models rest upon assumptions and these assumptions should reflect real-world phenomena. If they do not, the question arises as to whether the departure is sufficiently serious to render the model inapplicable. This question rests with the manager for experience in a given field contributes much to the judgment on the appropriateness of the model.

Recall the assumptions underlying some or all of the statistical models described above:

1. The population comprises values of a random variable.
2. The variable is discrete or continuous.

3. The random variable is normally distributed.
4. The sample observations are independent or dependent.
5. The mean and the standard deviation of the population are known.
6. The mean is known but the standard deviation can only be inferred from the sample.
7. The size of the sample relates to the selection of a statistical model.

SECTION IV
Sampling

chapter 6

Designing a Sample

Decisions regarding the implementation of many managerial policies are dependent on the input of sample data. Examples include market research on the introduction of new products, establishing selling prices and credit terms, selection and training of personnel, and quality control. Public accountants utilize sampling techniques as a normal routine of auditing. In these and other cases, sampling is preferred over a complete enumeration of the population either because the latter is too costly or impossible to secure.

A sample de facto constitutes a carefully defined, partial enumeration of the population to obtain data from which to make inferences about the characteristics of the population. Properly constructed and executed, it represents a microcosm of the population. In this respect, noted in Chapter 1, inferences about the characteristics of the population derive only from random samples.

PRINCIPLES OF SAMPLING

The rationale for making inferences about a population on the basis of sample data rests upon certain statistical principles.

Central Limit Theorem

Perhaps the most important theorem in statistics, the central limit theorem states that as the size of the sample increases, *regardless of the shape of the population (normal, positively skewed, or negatively skewed)*, the sampling distribution of the mean will approach the normal curve. Corollaries to the central limit theorem are given below:

1. If all possible random samples were drawn from a population and the mean of each sample computed ($\bar{X}$), the mean of the distribution of sample means ($\bar{X}$ values) would equal the population mean (μ).
2. As the size of the samples increases, the distribution of sample means ($\bar{X}$ values) taken from skewed populations approaches the normal curve.

3. The distribution of sample means ($\overline{X}$ values) drawn from a normally distributed population will be normally distributed.

Tchebycheff's Theorem

The probability that a random variable (X) will differ from its mean ($\overline{X}$) by more than a given number of standard deviations equals $1/h^2$, where h is the number of deviations. That is, whether the distribution is normal or skewed, the probability that X will have a value outside the interval $\mu \pm h\sigma$ can be no more than $1/h^2$. What is the probability of X differing from its mean $\overline{X}$ by more than 2 standard deviations? Answer: $1/h^2 = 1/4 = 0.25$.

Conversely, what is the probability that X will lie *within* the range of the population mean (μ) plus or minus 2 standard deviations? Answer: $1 - 0.25 = 0.75$. That is, the probability that X will lie within the defined range is 75 percent.

Law of Large Numbers

For a large number of trials, the probability that the sample proportion of successes will differ by more than an arbitrarily small constant from the true probability of success on a given trial is very nearly zero. The larger the number of trials, the smaller is this probability.

TYPES OF RANDOM SAMPLES

Simple Random Samples

Every item in the population has the same chance of being selected. If the sample were to consist of restaurants in New York City, every restaurant in the defined area would have the same probability of being drawn into the sample. A random sample should satisfy the following tests:

1. The population defined must relate to the objectives of the study. If the study proposes to investigate the *annual* dollar amounts of delinquent receivables, a random sample of six month's accounts is inappropriate.
2. Define the sample unit or element, that is, the individual item in the population. In the study of delinquent receivables, the individual account represents the sampling unit.
3. Any item drawn from the sample must be included. When randomly selected, it cannot be excluded and another element substituted.
4. Every possible combination of sampling units must have an

equal probability of inclusion in the sample. If items intentionally or inadvertently have a zero probability of inclusion, the sample ceases to be randomized.

When the sample design meets these criteria, the selection of sample elements is objective and the sampling error—that is, the difference between the sample results and the results obtainable from a complete enumeration—can be measured. Sampling errors occur because of the partial enumeration of the population and the random nature of the selection. Nonsampling errors can also contribute to variations between sample results and the true characteristics of the population. These are not a result of the random nature of the sample but have their roots in faulty techniques of data collection, misinterpretation of data, and so forth.

Stratified Random Sample

This type of sample divides the population into strata or subgroups that share a common characteristic. For example, in sampling restaurants in New York City, we might subdivide the population by location, by union and nonunion organization, and/or by number of personnel. A random sample is taken within each subgroup. The size of the subgroup samples depends on the proportionate representation of the subgroups in the total population. Suppose 20 percent of the restaurants were nonunion shops, then 20 percent of the sample items would be drawn from this category.

Stratified random sampling has several advantages:

1. It is a useful technique in dealing with heterogeneous and highly skewed populations. In these situations, while the subgroups may exhibit common features, the differences between the subgroups may prove quite extensive.
2. It may result in a more representative sample by allowing consciously for the representation of extreme values.
3. When each subgroup is homogeneous, the stratified sample can reduce the costs of sampling selection and minimize the sampling error.

On the other hand, if the population is normally distributed, stratified sampling is not appropriate.

Cluster Sampling

After dividing the population into clusters, a random sample is taken within each cluster. For example, suppose a survey of taxable wages paid for covered employment in the United States were desired. Cluster sampling would involve first drawing a simple random sample of *counties* in the United States and then taking a simple random sample of taxable wages within each cluster or county chosen.

The preceding illustration is termed a two-stage cluster sample. If all taxable wages in the selected counties were surveyed, the procedure would become a single-stage cluster sample.

Unlike stratified sampling, efficiency in cluster sampling presumes differences among the elements within each cluster but looks to greater homogeneity among the clusters. However, in practice the criterion is difficult to obtain because like elements tend to cluster together. Hence, cluster sampling will usually result in a greater sampling error than a comparable stratified sample. Conversely, in area sampling—involving regions, counties, states, and the like—cluster sampling may be more cost effective than stratified sampling, especially when a complete listing of the population is not available.

Systematic Sampling

The method consists of calculating an interval, termed the Kth item, and systematically selecting items for the sample based upon the size of the Kth item interval. The concept is best understood by illustration. Assume management decides to sample 100 delinquent accounts (n) from a population of 7000 accounts (N) numbered from 1001 to 8000. The procedure of systematic sampling involves the following steps:

1. Set up the Kth item interval by the ratio N/n in the present case 7000/100, or 70.
2. From a table of random numbers (discussed later) select a random number between 0 and 70 to obtain the starting point of the sample. If the randomly selected number were, say, 10, the first account in the sample would be 1011 (1001 + 10); the second account in the sample would be 1081 (1011 + 70); and so forth to the completion of the sample.

Systematic sampling not only has the advantage of simplicity but the sequential listing of sampled items it provides may be useful to management. The arrangement of the sampled items in an orderly manner may lead to a more representative sample than the simple random technique. Thus, a systematic sample of a company payroll arrayed from the lowest to the highest payment will better portray the payroll profile because the selection of every Kth item tends to ensure representation for each payroll category from the lowest to the highest.

On the negative side, the application of systematic sampling requires that the investigator look carefully at the population. If some predetermined pattern runs through the population and impacts on the characteristics under study, the systematic sample could produce biased results. If, for example, every Kth item sampled happens to be a foremen's salary, the average wage based upon the systematic sample will not accurately describe the profile of the payroll. The investigator in this instance needs to redefine the population under study.

NONRANDOM SAMPLES

Unlike the random methods, nonrandom samples do not conform to a probability design but depend upon other criteria, such as judgment and convenience. Although in certain situations they are useful nonrandom samples do not offer a valid basis for enunciating generalizations about population characteristics.

Judgment Sampling

Judgment sampling relies on the expertise of specialists to select sample units from a population about which they are knowledgable. The specialist makes a judgment as to the *typical* item in the population without reference to the probabilities governing selection. Judgment sampling is cost efficient when samples are small and items not easily located. However, the results lack objectivity, since precision depends on the expert's interpretation of the data and level of judgment.

Convenience Sampling

Sometimes referred to as chunk sampling, convenience sampling involves pinpointing a segment of a population from which to draw sample data, based on accessibility but not necessarily representativeness. For example, using a published mailing directory to select sample units. The advantage of convenience is counter balanced by the loss of objectivity. The probabilities are unknown and the method of selection lacks the quality of randomness.

ASSUMING RANDOM SELECTION

Table of Random Numbers

The Table of Random Numbers (Table 6-1) provides a technique for the selection of items in a random sample. To illustrate its use, assume a random sample of 50 accounts is required from a population of 1000 accounts, numbered from 1001 to 2000. The random selection of accounts proceeds as follows:

1. Relate each item (account) in the population to a specific number in Table 6-1. (Many company records are prenumbered, thereby simplifying the problem.)
2. Determine the range of numbers to be sampled and the number

Table 6-1   Random Number Table (Selected Numbers)[a]

48611	62866	33963	14045	79451	04934	45576
78812	03509	78673	73181	29973	18664	04555
19472	63971	37271	31445	49019	49405	46925
51266	11569	08697	91120	64156	40365	74297
55806	96275	26130	47949	14877	69594	83041
77527	81360	18180	97421	55541	90275	18213
77680	58788	33016	61173	93049	04694	43534
15404	96554	88265	34537	38526	67924	40474
14045	22917	60718	66487	46346	30949	03173
68376	43918	77653	04127	69930	43283	35766

[a] *Source:* John E. Freund, *Statistics—A First Course,* 2nd ed., Englewood Cliffs, NJ: Prentice-Hall, 1976.

of digits to use in table 6-1. In the present example, the numbers range from 1001 to 2000 and the series consists of four digit numbers.

3. Determine the starting point from which to begin the selection process. Some practitioners use the dart board method: others take a blind stab from any page from a complete table of random members.

4. Determine a route for using Table 6-1, such as choosing numbers vertically or horizontally, and consistently adhere to the predetermined order of selection, beginning with the starting point selected previously. It is not appropriate to skip around in the selection process.

5. Discard random numbers that fall outside the range of established numbers to be sampled, like #4861 in this example, and duplicate numbers which sometimes appear. In place of the latter, select the next usable number. The process of selecting random numbers continues until the sample is complete.

6. Select accounts from the company records with numbers corresponding to the list of numbers established from Table 6-1. These accounts selected now constitute the sample.

Computer Terminals

Another technique employed to assure random samples is the use of computer terminals or computer time-sharing programs. Here, programs for the selection of random numbers are provided. Use of computer terminals has the obvious advantages of saving time and improving accuracy. An ancillary benefit is the ability to store the information for permanent record or documentation. Again, each element of the population must have assigned specific numbers for identification.

Again, the range of numbers for the population must correspond to the random numbers generated by the computer. In this way duplicate numbers or inappropriate numbers (those outside the established range of numbers) are discarded automatically. Hence, similar to the "manual" operation by use of the Table 6-1, the computer must be given the instructions on the range of numbers (lowest to highest) in the population, the quantity of random numbers needed, and the starting point. In addition, instructions to the computer are needed for arrangement of selected random numbers in numerical sequence to facilitate finding corresponding company records.

PLANNING THE SAMPLING EXPERIMENT

Planning the sampling experiment comprises a sequence of steps before samples can be drawn and estimates made about population parameters. Although estimation constitutes the ultimate objective of sampling, the outcome of the estimation process depends predominantly on the validity of the sample data inputs to the statistical models employed. To ensure the quality of the sample data, planning the sampling experiment necessitates careful attention to the following:

1. Defining the sampling problem.
2. Defining the characteristics of the population or universe under study.
3. Conducting a pilot study.
4. Determining the sample size.
5. Selecting the sampling method and drawing the sampled elements.
6. Estimating the population characteristics from the sample.
7. Testing the sampling results for significance.

Defining the Sampling Problem

Management is responsible for defining the nature of the problem for investigation, that is, stating the universe or population to be surveyed. Precise definition is vital if the sample data is to conform to the objectives of the study. The *universe* or *population* includes all items that fall within the framework of statistical investigation. If a study of the average life of a lot of 600 television tubes is required, the population consists of the number of hours of use for all the 600 tubes in the lot.

Population Characteristics

Management also must define the population characteristics or parameters to be estimated. The population parameter for the televison tubes in the above example is the *average* number of hours of use for the 600 tubes. Descriptive measures—such as averages, standard deviations, proportions, probabilities, and the like—are termed *statistics* if derived from a sample and *parameters* if derived from a population.

Pilot Study

Frequently, the situation indicates the need for a pilot study to evaluate the feasibility of the proposed sample. Such a preliminary investigation may expose deficiencies in the population concept and in the definition of the problem. By the same token, it may provide tentative estimates of sample statistics.

Sample Size

The sample size affects the reliability of the study and consequently the attainment of management's objectives. The sample size depends on (a) the degree of precision, or reliability required by management and (b) the level of probability for the required precision. For instance, management might specify a 90 percent probability that the sample average of television tubes will fall within a range of the population mean plus/minus 50 hours. In all cases, however, greater degrees of precision and higher probability confidence levels imply larger sample sizes.

Selecting the Sample Method

Depending upon the objectives of management and the outcome of the pilot study, the investigator will settle upon one of the random or nonrandom sampling techniques discussed earlier.

Estimation

Statistical estimation or inference means making a decision about a population *parameter*—a mean, standard deviation, probability, and the like—from sample statistics where the sample is representative of the population. Estimation may be in the form of a *point estimate* or *interval estimate*.

Point Estimation

A point estimate designates a single figure to identify a population parameter. For example, a sample of 25 common stock prices may specify an average price of $45 dollars. The Dow Jones Average measures overall market movements based on the price changes in 65 stocks. It is fair to say that only by coincidence will either point estimate hit the true market average and the estimates tell us nothing about the dispersion around the averages or the level of confidence that can be placed in the estimates.

Interval Estimation

The interval estimate at least alerts management to the risks inherent in point estimates. The interval estimate will state that on the basis of a particular type of sample and confidence level the population parameter has a given probability of falling within a particular range. For example, in the stock price illustration above, management might have been told there exists a 95 percent probability that the true average will lie in a range of $42–$47. Or, using Tchebycheff's Theorem, that the probability the average price ($45) will lie outside the range of the population mean plus/minus 2 standard deviations is 25 percent.

The following case study will summarize the discussion up to this point on planning a sampling experiment.

Case Study

Sampling Problem

Mini-Computer, Inc. plans to revise its credit policy and management of bad debts after review of the total amount of delinquent accounts. The population under study is the dollar amount of delinquent accounts located in the central credit office of corporate headquarters.

Population Characteristics

Management requires an estimate of the population parameters covering (a) average dollar amount of delinquent accounts, (b) standard deviation of the average dollar amount per delinquent accounts, (c) the proportion of delinquent accounts that will prove uncollectible, and (d) the total dollar amount tied up in uncollectible accounts. Interval estimates will suffice for the specified characteristics, assuming a 95 percent confidence level that the true population of delinquent accounts will fall within the interval estimates.

Pilot Study. Management waives a pilot study since the population is clearly defined and the data readily available at the central office. Furthermore, refinements necessary to clarify the sampling problem or population characteristics are not anticipated.

Sample Size. Management's objectives will determine the size of the sample required. Management will accept an estimate of the *average* dollar amount per delinquent account which will fall into a range of the true population mean (μ) plus/minus $2,000 at a 95 percent confidence level. In this respect, previous studies as well as experience indicates the population has a standard deviation of $10,204. Accepting this datum, the formulation for the minimum sample size necessary to estimate the average dollar amount per delinquent account becomes:

$$n = \left(\frac{Z\sigma}{E}\right)^2 \qquad\qquad (6\text{-}1)$$

where: n = required sample size

        Z = confidence level—at the 95% confidence level, Z = 1.96
          (Table 5-14)

        σ = standard deviation of population, \$10,204, and

        E = error factor: plus/minus \$2,000

Therefore,

$$n = \left(\frac{1.96 \times \$10,204}{\$2,000}\right)^2$$

$$= \left(\frac{20,000}{2,000}\right)^2 \tag{6-2}$$

$$= (10)^2$$

$$= 100$$

The minimum required sample size to estimate the average dollar amount per delinquent account is 100, given the error factor of \$2,000 and the 95 percent confidence level desired.

Sample Method. The simple random sample meets the needs of the situation. Each account has a four digit designation arranged numerically in the file from 1001 to 8000. Using Table 6-1 to select sample items, the starting point for selection is the top of the fourth column, following a route down the column to the last number and returning to the top of the fifth column, downward again, until 100 items are selected. The following represents a partial list of random numbers:

1. 1404
2. 7318
3. 3144
4. 9112 ← discard
5. 4794
6. 9742 ← discard
7. 6117
8. 3453
9. 6649
10. 0412 ← discard

Only numbers ranging from 1001 to 8000 qualify for inclusion in the sample. Number 9112 is discarded and replaced by the next usable number, that is, 4794. The same consideration applies to numbers 9742 and 0412 which also lie outside the range of delinquent account numbers. Similarly any duplicate numbers are discarded and replaced by the next usable number.

Select Sample Items. Delinquent accounts with numbers corresponding to those selected from Table 6-1 are pulled. These comprise the sample.

Estimation of Population Parameters from Sample Data

The objective of this penultimate step in the sample plan is the use of the sample statistics—sample mean and standard deviation, in particular—to estimate the true population mean (μ) and standard deviation (σ) as well as other parameters useful to management. Estimation depends on the theorems described above (page 113) and assumes the sample statistics result from a random sample.

The specifics of estimation, not the concept, vary with the size of the sample.

Large Sample. Management requests an estimate of the average dollar amount per delinquent account. Assuming a large sample of 100 items, the dollar amounts of the selected accounts are summed and divided by the sample size (n). Let us posit an average of $150,000 per account. In any event, the sample average is a random variable since it can assume different values, depending on the selection of items drawn for the sample.

$\overline{X}$ represents the mean of a particular random sample. If a large number of random samples were taken and the mean of each sample calculated, the distribution of sample means ($\overline{X}$ values) would plot as a normal curve. Accordingly, the expected value of the distribution of sample means [$E(\overline{X})$] approximates the true population mean (μ).

The sample standard deviation (σ_s) is also an estimator of the population standard deviation when the latter is unknown. Using the sample standard deviation to estimate the standard deviation of the population and assuming a sample standard deviation of $5,000, the standard deviation (or error) of the distribution of sample means (σ) is denoted by

$$\sigma = \frac{\sigma_s}{\sqrt{n}}$$

$$= \frac{\$5,000}{\sqrt{100}} \tag{6-3}$$

$$= \$500$$

Since the sample statistics ($\overline{X}$ and σ_s) are used to secure *estimates* of the population parameters (μ and σ), management must allow for some variation in the data. Preferably, management could employ a range within which the true population parameters would be likely to fall if accompanied by some indication of the probability that the stipulated range will contain the population parameters. The interval estimate for the population mean of delinquent accounts at a 95 percent probability level takes the form

$$\overline{X} \pm Z(\sigma) \tag{6-4}$$

where: $\bar{X}$ = the sample mean, \$150,000
        σ = the standard error of the distribution of sample means, \$500
        Z = 1.96 from Table 5-14—the area containing 95% of the cases

Therefore the confidence interval (C.I.)

$$\begin{aligned} \text{C.I.} &= \$150,000 \pm 1.96 \,(\$500) \\ &= \$150,000 \pm \$980 \\ \text{Range} &= \$149,020 \text{ to } \$150,980 \end{aligned} \qquad (6\text{-}5)$$

Management can have 95 percent confidence that the true population average will fall within the described interval.

Small Sample. Because of the Central Limit Theorem, when the sample is large ($n \geq 30$) the sampling distribution of mean tends to conform to the normal curve. When the sample is small ($n < 30$), however, and the population standard deviation unknown, estimation resorts to the t-distribution. For example, using the same value for sample deviation as above but reducing the sample size to $n = 25$,

$$\sigma = \frac{\sigma_s}{\sqrt{n}} = \frac{\$5,000}{\sqrt{25}} = \$1,000 \qquad (6\text{-}6)$$

(Comparison with equation (6-3) will show that the standard error of the distribution of sample means is doubled when the sample size is reduced from 100 to 25.) We are now ready to replace Z in equation (6-4) with t in order to determine our confidence interval:

$$\bar{X} \pm t(\sigma) \qquad (6\text{-}7)$$

where: $\bar{X}$ = \$150,000
        σ = \$1,000
        t = 2.064 from t-distribution (Table 5-15) for the 95% confidence level based upon $n - 1$ (=24) degrees of freedom

We now have

$$\begin{aligned} \text{C.I.} &= \$150,000 \pm 2.064\,(\$1,000) \\ &= \$150,000 \pm \$2,064 \\ \text{Range} &= \$147,936 \text{ to } \$152,064 \end{aligned} \qquad (6\text{-}8)$$

The confidence interval here is considerably wider than that of equation (6-5). This is due to the doubling in the value of σ noted above.

A further possibility remains: if the sample size is small ($n < 30$) and the population skews positively or negatively, then neither the t-distribution nor normal distribution apply when determining confidence levels for the mean. In this case, we resort to Tchebycheff's Theorem to demonstrate the probability of obtaining a sample mean which falls within h standard errors from the population (μ).

$$\text{Degree of confidence} = 1 - \frac{1}{h^2} \tag{6-9}$$

For the 95% confidence level, we substitute 0.95 on the left-hand side of equation (6-9) and solve for h:

$$0.95 = 1 - \frac{1}{h^2}$$

$$0.05 = \frac{1}{h^2}$$

$$0.05\ h^2 = 1 \tag{6-10}$$
$$h^2 = 20$$
$$h = \sqrt{20}$$
$$h = 4.47 \text{ standard deviations}$$

We obtain the interval estimate by replacing t with h in equation (6-7) so that:

$$\bar{X} \pm h\ (\sigma) = \$150{,}000 \pm 4.47\ (\$1{,}000)$$
$$= \$150{,}000 \pm \$4{,}470 \tag{6-11}$$
$$\text{Range} = \$145{,}530 \text{ to } \$154{,}470$$

Estimation of Proportion

To determine the interval estimate for uncollectibles as a percent of total delinquent accounts necessitates a sample of adequate size. Size depends on the level of precision and the probability of precision specified by management. Assume management seeks a 95 percent confidence limit so that the estimate of sampling error will not exceed 0.05. The sample proportion ($\bar{p}$) of uncollectibles averages 10 percent but the population proportion remains uncertain. The sample size (n) for the required proportion equals:

$$n = \frac{Z^2\ (\bar{p})(1 - \bar{p})}{E^2} \tag{6-12}$$

where: $Z = 1.96$ (95 percent confidence coefficient) from the normal distribution (Table 5-14)
$\bar{p}$ = proportion of uncollectibles = 0.10
$1 - \bar{p}$ = proportion collected on delinquent accounts (1 − 0.10 = 0.90)
E = error factor = .05

Therefore

$$n = \frac{(1.96)^2(0.10)(0.90)}{(0.05)^2} \tag{6-13}$$

$$= 139$$

The estimate for the confidence interval relating to the population proportion is formulated by

$$\bar{p} \pm Z(\sigma_{\bar{p}}) \tag{6-14}$$

where $\sigma_{\bar{p}}$, the standard error of $\bar{p}$, is

$$\sigma_{\bar{p}} = \sqrt{\frac{\bar{p}(1 - \bar{p})}{n}} = \sqrt{\frac{(0.10)(0.90)}{139}}$$

$$= 0.0254 \tag{6.15}$$

Substituting in equation (6-14)

$$\begin{aligned}\bar{p} \pm Z(\sigma_{\bar{p}}) &= 0.10 \pm 1.96 \ (0.0254) \\ &= 0.10 \pm 0.0500 \\ &= 0.050 \text{ to } 0.1500\end{aligned} \tag{6-16}$$

Therefore, the population proportion of uncollectible accounts is estimated to be included in the interval 5.0 to 15.0 percent of delinquent accounts with a probability of 95 percent.

Total Value of Uncollectible Accounts

To obtain an interval estimate of the total dollar value of uncollectible accounts, multiply the interval limits of the sample mean by the total number of uncollectible accounts in the population (N). Assuming $N = 7,000$ and the proportion of uncollectible accounts is 10 percent, the interval estimate of the total dollar value of uncollectible accounts at the 95 percent confidence level amounts to:

$$\bar{p}N[\bar{X} \pm Z(\sigma)] \tag{6-17}$$

Hence, given that

$$\bar{p}(N) = 0.10(7,000) = 700$$

and

$$(\bar{X} \pm Z(\sigma)) = \$150,000 \pm \$980 \text{ (Equation 6-5)}$$

then

$$\text{C.I.} = 700 \ (\$150,000 \pm \$980)$$
$$\text{Range} = \$104,300,000 \text{ to } \$105,700,000$$

The above values are, of course, based on the fact that the original sample included more than thirty elements. As discussed earlier, when dealing with small ($n < 30$) or small skewed samples, the t or h statistic, respectively, is used. In these cases, t or h would be substituted for Z in equation 6-17.

The confidence interval estimates for the average dollar amount per *delinquent* account varies with sample size as follows:

> For small samples ($n \geq 30$): \$149,020–\$150,980   (6-5)
> For small samples ($n < 30$): \$147,936–\$152,064   (6-8)
> For small samples and a nonnormally distributed population:
> \$145,530–\$154,470   (6-11)
> For the proportion of *uncollectibles:* $0.05 - 0.15$
> For large samples, the total dollar value of uncollectible accounts:
> \$104,300,000 to \$105,700,000   (6-17)

The final step in a sample experiment involves testing the significance of sample statistics. Termed "hypothesis testing," it forms the subject matter of the next chapter.

SUMMARY

In one form or another and at almost all organizational levels, managers rely on sample data in decision making. Admittedly, sampling is a technique few managers directly supervise; most assign it to the province of the expert. Yet to use data and not have a rudimentary knowledge of its validity places the manager in a potentially vulnerable position. The manager must attempt to gain some perspective on the development of sample data used by him. The following questions may prove germane to this end:

1. How has the investigator defined the population to be sampled? Is the population assumed to be normally distributed or skewed? Is the population so defined relevant to the decisions to be taken? Or will the sample provide the appropriate data for the particular decision?
2. As a corollary, are the sampling objectives properly defined and the sampling experiment properly structured to achieve these objectives?
3. What are the population parameters of interest to management?
4. What type of sample is to be conducted? Simple random sample? Stratified random sample? And so forth. Will the particular sample type capture the population characteristics under study? Are there hidden biases in the sample?
5. Was a pilot study conducted to test the sampling design, to sharpen definitions of the population characteristics subject to survey, and/or to obtain tentative data on population parameters?
6. How were the elements included in the sample selected in order to assure randomness? By computer? By using a table of random numbers?

7. What size sample is appropriate to the degree of precision required by the question at hand? A larger sample properly conducted offers higher-quality results. However, a sample must
   be cost effective and management should not spend for a degree of precision not required in order to make the proper decision.
8. As a corollary, what level of precision is necessitated by the situation? A 95 percent level of precision tells the manager that a
   particular range of values has a 95 percent probability of containing the true population parameter needed for the decision.
   Or, on the other hand, there exists a 5 percent chance of error,
   that is, that the true value of the population parameter will fall
   outside the range. Management defines the level of precision.

chapter 7

Testing the Evidence

The dictionary defines a hypothesis as something *assumed* to be true for the purpose of testing its soundness or uncovering new evidence. In managerial statistics, hypothesis testing deals with methods that guide management in deciding whether to accept or reject a hypothesis about a population based on sample information. It is a form of *statistical inference* insofar as sample results are the basis for accepting or rejecting claims about parameters, such as the mean, standard deviation, or proportions of populations.

For example, in the course of business, management frequently makes assumptions about the number of defective items per production run or the average operating life of a product or the average household income in a service area, or the average cash flow from capital investment, and so on. To verify these assumptions, samples may be taken. If the differences between the sample results and the assumptions made about the population are deemed statistically significant (too large to be due to chance), then the hypothesis concerning the population is questionable. On the other hand, if the differences are slight (due to chance or random factors), the sample results support the assumptions about the population.

FORMAT OF HYPOTHESIS TESTING

Null Hypothesis

The null hypothesis is a statement or claim concerning the value of a population parameter (an assumption) that management will accept or reject after evaluating sample information. The term "null" infers there is no difference (it nullifies differences) between management's statement about the parameter and the true value of the parameter. The null hypothesis is rejected only if sample results are so different from the hypothesized value that the probability of such a difference occurring by chance is very low or insignificant. The procedure also allows the investigator to determine the probability of incorrectly rejecting a true hypothesis.

The null hypothesis (H_0) is always accompanied by an alternative hypothesis (H_A). For example, management might assume the average sales of product X at \$140,000, that is, the assumed population mean (μ). The alternative hypothesis states this is not the case. Hence,

$$\text{Null hypothesis} \qquad H_0: \mu = \$140,000$$
$$\text{Alternative hypothesis } H_A: \mu \neq \$140,000$$

The investigator will test the assumed population mean ($\mu = \$140,000$) against the sample mean ($\bar{X}$). If a population proportion (P) were tested, the appropriate sample statistic is the sample proportion ($\bar{p}$). Or the standard deviation of the population (σ) against the standard deviation of the sample (σ_s).

Types of Errors

The acceptance or rejection of a hypothesis is not without pitfalls. Actually, a statistical hypothesis represents an assumption made about the distribution of a *random variable*. As we have seen, the means ($\bar{X}$) of successive random samples drawn from the same population differ one from the other due to random factors. It follows, therefore, that any decision rule based on sample information is subject to error. Given the nature of the null hypothesis statement, two types of errors appear in hypothesis testing.

Type I Error

A Type I error rejects the null hypothesis (H_0) when it is correct or true. When a Type I error occurs, the wrong action is taken only if the null hypothesis is rejected.

Type II Error

This decision errs in accepting the null hypothesis (H_0) when it is false. When a Type II error occurs, wrong action is taken only when management does not reject the null hypothesis. Possible outcomes of the decision to accept or reject the null hypothesis, illustrated in Table 7-1, show that management can accept a true null hypothesis when it is correct or accept it when it is incorrect; conversely they may reject the null hypothesis when it is correct or reject it when it is incorrect.

Note it is always the null hypothesis that is being tested against the alternative hypothesis. *Note* also that management must first formulate a hypothesis about the population based upon experience, knowledge,

Table 7-1   Type I and Type II Errors

States of Nature / Action	Null Hypothesis	
	Correct H_0	Incorrect H_0
Reject H_0	Type I error (wrong action)	Correct Action
Accept H_0	Correct action	Type II error (wrong action)

or theory. The sample follows the formulation of the hypothesis, not vice-versa. If the latter were so—if a sample were taken in order to formulate the hypothesis—the investigator would end up testing one random sample against another in order to find a significant difference. The procedure defies logic.

Level of Significance

The level of significance refers to the specified probability for making a Type I error: rejecting the null hypothesis when it is correct. For Type I errors, the level of significance is designated by α (alpha). Typically, the level of significance is set at 0.01 or 0.05. For example, if management set the level of significance for α at 0.05 and H_0 were rejected, the possibility of a wrong decision is 5 percent. In the long run, the outcome of repeated samples would cause rejection of a true null hypothesis 5 percent of the time; alternatively in the long run, the sample data would justify accepting the true null hypothesis 95 percent of the time.

The probability of committing a Type II error is designated by beta (β). Table 7-2 can be modified to show the relationship between alpha and beta. A Type I error can be made only when the null hypothesis is incorrectly rejected; a Type II error can be made only when the null hypothesis is incorrectly accepted. If the level of significance, therefore, is set to reduce the probability of a Type I error (rejecting H_0 when it is

Table 7-2   Probabilities of Types I and II Errors

States of Nature / Action	Null Hypothesis	
	Correct H_0	Incorrect H_0
Reject H_0	α	$1 - \beta$
Accept H_0	$1 - \alpha$	β
Total	1.00	1.00

true), the probability of a Type II (not rejecting H_0 when it is false) is increased.

Who should chose the level of significance? Since the level of significance determines the risk of wrongly accepting or rejecting the null hypothesis, the burden falls upon the decision maker. Rationally, the decision maker must assess where the most adverse consequences arise. From making a Type I error? Or a Type II error? If the greater loss would result from a Type I error, then management should specify α at 0.01 or less. Here the Type II error represents a lower concern. In the opposite situation where making a Type I error is less costly, the decision maker should specify α at 0.05 or higher. In any event, for a sample of a given size (n), the larger the α, the smaller the β will be. The higher the probability of committing a Type I error, the smaller is the probability of committing a Type II error. Only a complete enumeration of the population can completely remove the possibility of error.

Standard Error of the Mean

An important statistic in hypothesis testing is the standard error of the mean which estimates the standard deviation of the universe (σ). Recall once again that if we drew a series of random samples from a universe, each sample would differ from every other sample due to random influences. However, if the means of these samples were plotted, they would form a normal bell-shaped curve. Therefore, *the true mean of the universe (μ) may be taken to be a certain value lying in the middle of a distribution of means of samples selected randomly from an homogeneous universe*. How then do we measure the standard deviation of this distribution of sample means? Or, what is the standard error of a series of means computed from random samples drawn from a single homogeneous population.

However, as a practical matter, we do not have a large number of sample means ($\bar{X}$) and sample standard deviations (σ_s). We do have, in most cases, a single sample mean and standard deviation. Hence, it is necessary to estimate from a single sample statistic the magnitude of the standard error[1] of a large group of sample means. This can be done quite easily.

Standard Error of the Mean

Large Samples. Assume that management has taken a 100-item random sample of sales commissions. The average commission earnings per salesmen is $50,000 ($\bar{X}$), with a standard deviation of $15,000 ($\sigma_s$). How is the standard deviation (σ) of the population estimated?

---

[1] Note that standard error and standard deviation of the sampling distribution can be, and are, used interchangeably.

$$\sigma = \frac{\sigma_s}{\sqrt{n}} \tag{7-1}$$

where: σ_s = standard deviation of the sample
n = number of items in sample

Therefore,

$$\sigma = \frac{\$15,000}{\sqrt{100}}$$

$$= \frac{\$15,000}{10} \tag{7-2}$$

$$= \$1,500$$

Small Samples.   Assume the same data as above but let $n = 15$. Then

$$\sigma = \frac{\sigma_s}{\sqrt{n}}$$

$$= \frac{\$15,000}{\sqrt{15}} \tag{7-3}$$

$$= \frac{\$15,000}{3.873}$$

$$= \$3,873$$

In deriving the sample standard deviation (σ_s), the denominator is $n - 1$; thus $\sigma_s = \sqrt{\Sigma(X - \bar{X})^2/n - 1}$. On the other hand, the standard deviation of the distribution of means (used in estimating the standard deviation of the population) is calculated by $\sigma_s/\sqrt{n}$ as in expressions 7-1 and 7-3. As a working rule, these formulae can be applied without regard to sample size. However, as illustrated in the following examples of hypothesis testing, a distinction between small samples ($n < 30$) and large samples ($n \geq 30$) is made. For small samples, the testing statistic is taken from the t-distribution in contrast to the normal table used with large samples.

The standard error or deviation of the population has manifold applications in managerial statistics:

1. *As a measure of reliability of* $\bar{X}$. Since the true mean of the population represents a central value in a distribution of means, 68.27 percent of all sample means will fall within 1 σ of this true mean. So our average sales commissions stands a 68.27 percent chance of falling within the range of the true mean (μ) plus or minus one standard deviation, a 95.45 percent chance of falling within $\mu \pm 2\sigma$, and a 99.73 percent chance of falling into the range $\mu \pm 3\sigma$. If, therefore, the standard deviation is small, the

sample mean may be a very good description of the true mean; if large, a poor one.

2. *As an evaluator of the size of the sample.* The reliability of sampling results increases as the square root of the size of the sample increases. If a standard error were not too large in view of the objectives of the sample, a 50-item sample might suffice, but the standard error could be reduced by 50 percent with a 200 item sample.

3. *As an estimator of the true mean.* The problem is to determine whether the sample mean based on the data and a hypothetical mean could both find their places in a given distribution of sample means. The procedure involves setting up the following critical ratio:

$$Z = \frac{\bar{X} - \mu}{\sigma} \tag{7-4}$$

Suppose management had hypothesized that average sales commissions were \$40,000, could this figure be the true mean of the population?

$$Z = \frac{\$50,000 - \$40,000}{\$15,000} \tag{7-5}$$
$$= 0.67$$

Suppose management had further stipulated that its hypothesis be tested at a 5 percent level of significance. Referring to Table 5-14, the Z value at 5 percent is 1.96; that is, $\mu \pm 1.96\sigma$ will define an area under the normal curve containing 95 percent of the items. Since $0.67 < 1.96$, we might assert that management's hypothesis could be correct; that is, \$40,000 could be the true mean. The difference between sample and the hypothesized mean reflects the influence of random elements.

4. *As a component in setting up a confidence interval.* For any given level of significance, a confidence interval (C.I.) between the extremes of the distribution can be calculated as follows:

Level of Significance	Confidence Interval	
0.05	$\bar{X} \pm 1.96\sigma$	
0.01	$\bar{X} \pm 2.58\sigma$	(7-6)

1.96 and 2.58 represent Z values for areas of the normal curve that contain 95 percent and 99 percent of the cases, respectively. In our example, at the 0.05 level of significance, we obtain the following:

$$\begin{aligned} \text{C.I.} &= \$50,000 \pm 1.96 \, (\$15,000) \\ &= \$50,000 \pm \$29,400 \qquad (7\text{-}7) \\ \text{Range} &= \$20,600 \text{ to } \$79,400 \end{aligned}$$

Figure 7-1   Two-Tailed Test, 0.05 Level of Significance

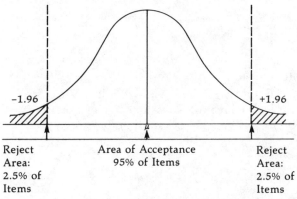

−1.96		+1.96

Reject	Area of Acceptance	Reject
Area:	95% of Items	Area:
2.5% of		2.5% of
Items		Items

The confidence interval identifies a whole series of possible means. Any tested value of the true mean is accepted on the basis of the sample. The 5 percent interval locates the possible true mean in a narrower interval than the 1 percent level of significance. At the 5 percent level of significance, there exists a 95 percent probability (termed, confidence coefficient) that the true mean will lie within the computed interval; at the 1 percent level, the interval is widened so that the confidence coefficient becomes 99 percent. The possibility of error is 5 percent and 1 percent, respectively. (See Figure 7-1.)

TESTING HYPOTHESES

The preceding discussion can now be integrated by a series of examples showing how hypothesis testing can assist decision making. Testing a hypothesis involves six steps:

1. Formulating the hypothesis
2. Specifying the level of significance
3. Selecting the testing statistics
4. Establishing the decision criteria
5. Computing the critical ratio
6. Making a decision

Example 1

Over the past two years, a firm has averaged $300,000 sales per month with a standard deviation of $30,000. Management feels that rising interest rates will reduce average monthly sales. To this end, management has decided to take a random sample of 200 purchasing agents of customer firms. The sample mean projects average monthly sales at $250,000. Does this represent a significant change in the population mean of $300,000?

Formulating the Hypothesis

$$\text{Null hypothesis:} \qquad H_0: \mu = \$300,000$$
$$\text{Alternative hypothesis: } H_A: \mu \neq \$300,000$$

Level of Significance

$\alpha = 0.05$. Management would prefer to minimize the chance of a Type II error (accepting the null hypothesis when it is false). It is less costly to budget the business for a lower level of sales than to set objectives at higher levels and later be forced to scale down operations.

Testing Statistic

$$Z = \frac{\bar{X} - \mu}{\sigma} \tag{7-8}$$

Decision Rule

With $\alpha = 0.05$, reject the null hypothesis (H_0) if $Z > 1.96$ or < -1.96

Computations

1. *Standard error of the estimate:*

$$\sigma = \frac{\$30,000}{\sqrt{200}}$$
$$= \frac{\$30,000}{14.14} \tag{7-9}$$
$$= \$2,122$$

2. *Critical ratio:* Using equations (7-8) and (7-9),

$$Z = \frac{\$250,000 - \$300,000}{\$2,122} \tag{7-10}$$
$$Z = -23.56$$

Making a Decision

Since $-23.56 < -1.96$, the null hypothesis is rejected. The difference of $50,000 cannot be ascribed to random influences or chance. The average monthly sales will decline and management must now deal with the budgetary implications.

Example 2

National statistics show that Americans tend to spend 95¢ out of each dollar of disposal income. The management of a nationally known retail chain of stores feels that its customers spend 92¢ out of each dollar of disposable income. That is, its customers, who come largely from middle income brackets, have a higher propensity to save. It authorizes a random sample to ascertain the facts. The sample of 200 customers indicates an average propensity to spend 97¢ out of each dollar of disposable income. The sample standard deviation is 15¢. What does the sample data tell management?

Formulating the Hypothesis

Null hypothesis: $H_0: \mu = 0.92$
Alternative hypothesis: $H_A: \mu \neq 0.92$

Level of Significance

$\alpha = 0.01$. Management wishes to minimize the chance of a Type I error (rejecting the null hypothesis when it is true). Rejecting a true null hypothesis could require revamping the merchandising policy of the chain and this should not be done lightly. A Type II error (accepting the null hypothesis when it is false) is probably less risky at least in the short term and pending the appearance of further evidence.

Testing Statistic

$$Z = \frac{\bar{X} - \mu}{\sigma} \qquad (7\text{-}11)$$

Decision Rule

With $\alpha = 0.01$, reject the null hypothesis (H_0) if $Z > 2.58$ or < -2.58.

Computations

1. *Standard error of the estimate:*

$$\sigma = \frac{0.15}{\sqrt{200}}$$

$$= \frac{0.15}{14.14} \qquad (7\text{-}12)$$

$$= .011$$

2. *Critical ratio:* Using equations (7-11) and (7-12),

$$Z = \frac{0.97 - 0.92}{0.011} \qquad (7\text{-}13)$$

$$= 4.55$$

Making a Decision

Since $4.55 > 2.58$, the null hypothesis is rejected. Management's customers tend to spend a higher proportion of their disposable income than management believes. The store has an incorrect appreciation of its clientele, which might be highly significant in reviewing its merchandising policies.

If the sample were tested against the national average, then the critical ratio becomes:

$$Z = \frac{0.97 - 0.95}{0.011}$$

(7-14)

$$= 1.82$$

Since $1.82 < 2.58$, we might accept a revised null hypothesis of $\mu = 0.95$. In this case, we would tell management that the propensity to spend by its customers shows no significant difference from the national average. Apparent differences are due to chance factors.

Examples 1 and 2 fall into the category of two-tailed tests. In a two-tailed test, the null hypothesis is rejected if the sample mean falls in either tail of the distribution of sample means. In other words, the two-tailed test looks at variations from the population mean in both directions. Figure 7-1 depicts the areas of acceptance and rejection for a two-tailed test at a 0.05 significance level.

Example 3

The illustration here concerns the comparison of two populations to ascertain if they can in fact be treated as a single population. Suppose a pharmaceutical company has to choose between the introduction of two new drugs dealing with cardiac disease. The company conducts 100-item samples of patients treated with each drug. Patients treated with drug A showed an average decrease in diastolic blood pressure of 22 points, with a standard deviation of 10; those treated with drug B presented an average 30 point drop, with a standard deviation of 12. The company wishes to decide whether there is a significant difference between the two population means to help decide whether to market A or B.

Formulating the Hypothesis

$$\text{Null hypothesis:} \qquad H_0: \mu_A = \mu_B$$
$$\text{Alternative hypothesis: } H_A: \mu_A \neq \mu_B$$

Level of Significance

$\alpha = 0.05$. A Type II error would have graver implications.

Testing Statistic

$$Z = \frac{\bar{X}_A - \bar{X}_B}{\sigma_{\Delta\bar{x}}}$$

(7-15)

Decision Rule

With $\alpha = 0.05$, reject the null hypothesis (H_0) if > 1.96 or < -1.96.

Computations

1. *Standard error of the estimate:*

$$\sigma_{\Delta\bar{x}} = \sqrt{\frac{\sigma_{SA}^2}{n_A} + \frac{\sigma_{SB}^2}{n_B}}$$

$$= \sqrt{\frac{100}{100} + \frac{144}{100}} \tag{7-16}$$

$$= \sqrt{1 + 1.44}$$

$$= 1.56$$

2. *Critical ratio:* Using equations (7-15) and (7-16),

$$Z = \frac{22 - 30}{1.56} \tag{7-17}$$

$$= -5.128$$

Making a Decision

Since $-5.128 < -1.96$, the null hypothesis is rejected. There exists a significant difference between the population means. However, in a sense, this leaves management hanging. If the two drugs cannot be treated as belonging to the same population, which drug is more effective? Reformulating the hypothesis might assist management in this regard:

Null hypothesis: $H_0: \mu_A = \mu_B$
Alternate hypothesis: $H_A: \mu_A < \mu_B$

The revised decision rule is now to reject the null hypothesis (H_0) only if $Z < -1.65$. Again the null hypothesis is rejected and presents a stronger indication that the advantage lies with drug B. The coefficient of variation (V) confirms this suspicion.

$$V = \frac{\sigma_s}{\bar{X}}$$

$$V_A = \frac{10}{22} = 0.45 \tag{7-18}$$

$$V_B = \frac{12}{30} = 0.40$$

Drug B is the more effective medication, having a higher mean score and proportionately lower standard deviation.

The revised second decision rule refers to a left-tail test, that is, the test relates to the left half of the sample distribution of means. Thus, at the 0.05 level of significance, 45 percent of the cases will lie in the accep-

Figure 7-2   Left- and Right-Tailed Tests

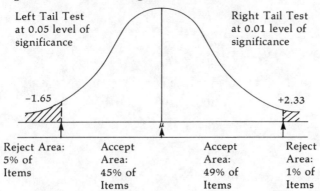

Left Tail Test
at 0.05 level of
significance

Right Tail Test
at 0.01 level of
significance

−1.65

+2.33

Reject Area:
5% of
Items

Accept
Area:
45% of
Items

Accept
Area:
49% of
Items

Reject
Area:
1% of
Items

tance region and 5 percent in the rejection region. The acceptance region includes Z values greater than zero as well as Z values from zero to -1.65. The alternate hypothesis suggests a left-tail test (see Figure 7-2) since the firm is primarily concerned with determining whether drug A is less effective than B.

Example 4

Suppose an airline management were contemplating the purpose of a new transport plane. To be profitable average cruising speed *must exceed* 800 miles per hour. One hundred test runs are made and the aircraft averages 870 miles per hour with a standard deviation of 90 miles. Management has now to evaluate the experiment.

Formulating the Hypothesis

Null hypothesis: H_0: $\mu = 800$
Alternate hypothesis: H_A: $\mu > 800$

Level of Significance

Rejection of H_0, if true, could have dire implications for the airlines profit position. Rejection will lead to purchasing aircraft which must have average speed of 800 mph or more. This suggests setting a low probability against rejecting the null hypothesis when it is true. Accordingly management sets $\alpha = 0.01$.

Testing Statistic

$$Z = \frac{\bar{X} - \mu}{\sigma} \qquad (7\text{-}19)$$

Decision Rule

Reject H_0 if $Z > 2.33$; if less, accept the null hypothesis.

Computations

1. *Standard error of the estimate:*

$$\sigma = \frac{90}{\sqrt{100}} \qquad\qquad (7\text{-}20)$$

$$= 9$$

2. *Critical ratio:* Using equations (7-19) and (7-20),

$$Z = \frac{870 - 800}{9} \qquad\qquad (7\text{-}21)$$

$$= 7.78$$

Making a Decision

Since 7.78 > 2.33, the null hypothesis is rejected; the aircraft will be purchased.

This example illustrates a right-tail test at the 0.01 level of significance. The test relates to the right half of the sample distribution of means. At the 0.01 level of significance, 49 percent of the cases will lie in the acceptance region and 1 percent in the rejection region (see Figure 7-2). The decision to stipulate a left- or right-tailed test depends upon the nature of the problem—the former is applied for alternate hypotheses taking the form $\bar{X} < \mu$; for alternate hypotheses taking the form $\bar{X} > \mu$ a right-tailed test is required.

Example 5

Suppose now management wished to test for significant differences between means of two samples expressed as proportions of their respective populations. For example, as a test of whether a new product line was gaining wider acceptance with the passage of time, the management ran two separate random samples (fifty items) at 6-month intervals. Sample 1 showed that 10 percent of those sampled (P_1) had used the product and sample 2 that 14 percent (P_2) had used the product.

Formulating the Hypothesis

Null hypothesis: $\qquad H_0: \mu_1 = \mu_2$
Alternate hypothesis: $H_A: \mu_1 \neq \mu_2$

Level of Significance

$$\alpha = 0.05.$$

Testing Statistic

$$Z = \frac{P_1 - P_2}{\sigma_{\Delta p}} \qquad\qquad (7\text{-}22)$$

Decision Rule

Reject H_0 if $Z < -1.96$ or > 1.96.

Computations

1. *Standard error of the estimate:* The computation of $\sigma_{\Delta p}$ first requires an estimate of the true population proportion $(\bar{P})$ as follows:

$$\bar{P} = \frac{n_1 p_1 + n_2 p_2}{n_1 + n_2}$$

$$= \frac{(50)(0.10) + 50(0.14)}{50 + 50} \qquad (7\text{-}23)$$

$$= \frac{5 + 7}{100}$$

$$= 0.12$$

then

$$\sigma_{\Delta p} = \sqrt{\bar{P}(1 - \bar{P})\left(\frac{n_1 + n_2}{n_1 n_2}\right)}$$

$$= \sqrt{0.12(1 - 0.12)\left(\frac{50 + 50}{2500}\right)} \qquad (7\text{-}24)$$

$$= \sqrt{0.12(0.88)(0.04)}$$

$$= \sqrt{0.004224}$$

$$= 0.0649923$$

2. *Critical Ratio:* Using equations (7-22)–(7-24)

$$Z = \frac{0.10 - 0.14}{0.0649923} \qquad (7\text{-}25)$$

$$= -0.615 \text{ (rounded)}$$

Making a Decision

Since $-0.615 > -1.96$, the null hypothesis is accepted. There has been no significant change in product acceptance.

Before exploring other illustrations on hypothesis testing, we can state some generalizations concerning the procedures employed in Examples 1–5.

Samples taken from the population were simple random samples.
The samples were large: more than 30 items.
The samples were taken from an homogeneous universe.
The null hypothesis is always tested, not the alternative hy-

pothesis. Techniques are available for testing the alternative hypothesis but these lie beyond the introductory level.

A 0.01 level of significance sets a low probability of committing a Type I error, rejecting the null hypothesis when it is true. A 0.05 level of significance raises the probability of rejecting the null hypothesis when it is true. If rejecting the null hypothesis could lead to a wrong decision involving financial loss to the firm, setting $\alpha = 0.01$ would represent the prudent decision rule. On the other hand, if more damage would result from accepting the null hypothesis when it is false (Type II error), prudence dictates a 0.05 level of significance.

If the alternative hypothesis (H_A) is stated as $\bar{X} > \mu$, a right-tail test is necessary—$Z > 2.33$ at 0.01 level of significance or $Z > 1.65$ at .05 level of significance. If H_A takes the form $\bar{X} < \mu$, a left-tail test is necessary—$Z < -1.65$ at the 0.05 level of significance.

All decision criteria are taken from Table 5-14.

Example 6

Only slight modification in our procedures is required in the hypothesis testing of small samples. A small manufacturer offering credit terms of 2/10, n 30 judges that his average customer pays in 21 days. He decides to sample 15 customers chosen randomly to test this opinion. The sample shows an average time of payment equal to 27 days, with a standard deviation of 8. Does the manufacturer's opinion differ significantly from the sample?

Formulating the Hypothesis

Null hypothesis: H_0: $\mu = 21$ days
Alternative hypothesis: H_A: $\mu \neq 21$ days

Level of Significance

$$\alpha = 0.05.$$

Testing Statistic

$$t = \frac{\bar{X} - \mu}{\sigma} \tag{7-26}$$

Decision Rule

From the t-distribution in Table 5-15, for $n - 1$ degrees of freedom $(15 - 1 = 14)$, reject H_0 if $Z < -2.145$ or $Z > 2.145$.

Computations

1. *Standard error of the estimate:*

$$\sigma = \frac{\sigma^s}{\sqrt{n}} = \frac{8}{\sqrt{15}}$$

$$= \frac{8}{3.873} \tag{7-27}$$

$$= 2.085$$

2. *Critical ratio:* Using equations (7-26) and (7-27)

$$t = \frac{27 - 21}{2.085} \tag{7-28}$$

$$= 2.88$$

Making a Decision

Since $2.88 > 2.145$, the null hypothesis is rejected. The customers are paying at a slower pace than management anticipates.

SUMMARY

The important consideration for a manager to bear in mind when presented with the results of a test for significant differences is that it is always easier to reject a hypothesis than to accept it. The rejection statement is definitive but the acceptance statement is always qualified by the condition "on the basis of the sample." Further evidence from other samples might possibly reverse the decision.

The attitude arises from the structure of the testing methodology. The stipulation of a level of significance by management places the rejection risk directly under control and with a large sample the decision maker can be almost certain of making the correct choice. Moreover, while rejection remains subject to error, the decision to reject rests upon a degree of confidence not associated with the contrary decision to accept the hypothesis.

In all events, a manager presented with this type of analysis will wish to do the following:

1. Explore the quality of the null hypothesis and the alternative hypothesis.
2. Question the size and standard deviation of the sample.
3. Determine if the sample is random and the population homogeneous.
4. Explore the level of significance set in relation to the consequences of a Type I or Type II error for the company.

5. Set up a confidence interval based upon the sample mean and standard error of the estimate to provide a range of possible true values of the mean.
6. Determine from the nature of the decision to be made whether the test should be two-tailed, left-tailed, or right-tailed.
7. Look for further evidence to support acceptance or rejection. Rejection of the null hypothesis should imply automatic acceptance of the alternative hypothesis.

SECTION V
Time and
Association

chapter 8

Time Series Analysis: Dynamic Factors in Business Data

Business does not rest in static equilibrium. It is a dynamic system that moves through time under the influence of long-term trends, seasonal variations, cyclical movements (such as the business cycle, construction cycle, agricultural cycles), and random occurrences in the nature of unforeseen events (war, technological innovations, acts of God, and so forth). The characteristics of these dynamic movements—their duration and amplitude—are naturally sources of interest to managers in both the public and private sectors of the economy. This task falls upon time series analysis.

A time series consists of statistical data that are recorded over successive increments of time (as in Table 8-1). Each time series (y), accordingly, consists of four components:

1. *Secular Trend* (T). The underlying long-term sweep of the data.
2. *Cyclical Component* (C). A series of irregular, wavelike patterns of more than one year's duration that vary in length and amplitude from one cycle to another. Generally, the pattern has exhibited four phases: prosperity, recession, depression, and revival, with each phase leading into the next.
3. *Seasonal Variation* (S). A recurrent pattern of change in demand or production which occurs within a year or shorter time frame.
4. *Irregular Variation* (I). Nonrecurring, sporadic, or random forces that cannot be classified as part of the secular trend, cyclical movement, or seasonal variation.

Table 8-1   Consumer Installment Credit Outstanding 1970–1976[a]

Year	Amount (in billions of dollars)
1970	101.9
1971	111.2
1972	126.8
1973	146.4
1974	155.4
1975	162.2
1976	178.8
1977	185.3

[a] *Source: Statistical Abstract of the United States, 1978.*

MEASURING THE SECULAR TREND (T)

Arithmetic Straight Line Trend

The measure applies to time series that tend to increase (or decrease) by *constant absolute amounts.* A graph of the data in Table 8-1 indicates that a straight line may fairly represent the trend of Consumer Installment credit (Figure 8-1). The Arithmetic Straight Line Trend (Y_c) is defined as

$$Y_c = \alpha + \beta(X) \tag{8-1}$$

where: Y = historical data represented by the time series
          Y_c = calculated values of the trend
          α = the origin of the trend line
          β = the change in Y_c per unit of time
          X = units of time as 0, 1, 2, 3, 4, . . .
          N = number of values in the series
          Σ = summation

To calculate the parameters—α and β—the following normal equations are applied:

$$\Sigma Y = N\alpha + \beta\Sigma X$$
$$\Sigma XY = \alpha\Sigma X + \beta\Sigma X^2 \tag{8-2}$$

     To solve the normal equations (8-2), take the raw data from Table 8-2 and substitute the totals for their formula symbols; for example, $\Sigma X = 28$. Then multiply the first line by a value which will serve to eliminate α; in this case the multiplier is 3.5. Thus

$$1168 = 8\alpha + 28\beta \leftarrow \text{(Multiply by 3.5)}$$
$$4606.5 = 28\alpha + 140\beta$$

Figure 8-1   Arithmetic Straight Line Trend

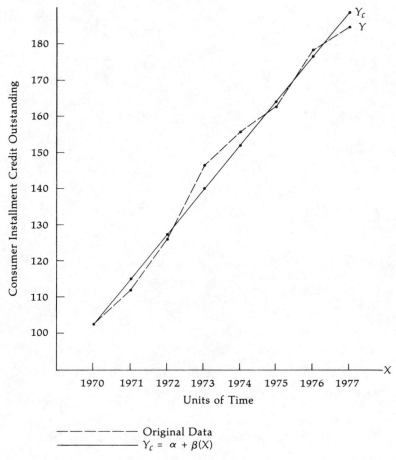

— — — — — Original Data
——————— $Y_c = \alpha + \beta(X)$

giving

$$4088.0 = 28\alpha + 98\beta$$
$$4606.5 = 28\alpha + 140\beta$$

To obtain the value for β, subtract the second equation from the first by changing the signs and adding:

$$
\begin{array}{rl}
4088.0 = & 28\alpha + 98\beta \\
-4606.5 = & -28\alpha - 140\beta \quad \leftarrow \text{(Change signs and add)} \\
\hline
-518.5 = & - 42\beta
\end{array}
$$

Therefore

$$\beta = \frac{-518.5}{-42} = 12.35 \text{ (rounded)}$$

Table 8-2   Calculation of Parameters for Arithmetic Straight Line Trend

1 Period	2[a] Y	3 X	4 (2 × 3)[a] XY	5 (3 × 3) X²
1970	101.9	0	0	0
1971	111.2	1	111.2	1
1972	126.8	2	253.6	4
1973	146.4	3	439.2	9
1974	155.4	4	621.6	16
1975	162.2	5	811.0	25
1976	178.8	6	1072.8	36
1977	185.3	7	1297.1	49
	$\Sigma Y = 1168.0$ $\bar{Y} = 146$	$\Sigma X = 28$	$\Sigma XY = 4606.5$	$\Sigma X^2 = 140$

[a] In billions of dollars.

Now substituting $\beta = 12.35$ in first normal equation:

$$1168 = 8\alpha + 28\ (12.35)$$
$$1168 = 8\alpha + 345.80$$
$$1168 - 345.80 = 8\alpha$$
$$822.20 = 8\alpha$$
$$102.78 = \alpha \text{ (rounded)}$$

Equation 8-1 for the Arithmetic Straight Line Trend now becomes

$$Y_c = 102.81 + 12.35(X).$$

It is calculated for the eight years of our sample in Table 8-3.

Where β is a positive figure, the data exhibit a rising secular trend; if

Table 8-3   Arithmetic Straight Line Trend

1 Period	2 Y[a]	3 $Y_c = 102.81 + 12.35(X)$
1970	101.9	$102.78 = 102.78 + 12.35(0)$
1971	111.2	$115.13 = 102.78 + 12.35(1)$
1972	126.8	$127.48 = 102.78 + 12.35(2)$
1973	146.4	$139.83 = 102.78 + 12.35(3)$
1974	155.4	$152.18 = 102.78 + 12.35(4)$
1975	162.2	$164.53 = 102.78 + 12.35(5)$
1976	178.8	$176.88 = 102.78 + 12.35(6)$
1977	185.3	$189.23 = 102.78 + 12.35(7)$

[a] In billions of dollars.

β were negative, the secular trend would be downward. Should the manager desire to project consumer credit for 1978, he need only add one time unit to the equation:

$$Y_c = 102.78 + 12.35(8)$$
$$= \$201.58 \text{ billion (1978 Consumer Credit Estimate).}$$

Figure 8-1 plots the original data and the Arithmetic Straight Line Trend.

Second-Degree Polynomial

This method describes a nonlinear secular trend, one that is concave or convex to the point of origin, that is, a curve with one change of direction. In form, a second degree curve is

$$Y_c = \alpha + \beta_1(X) + \beta_2(X^2) \tag{8-3}$$

The actual behavior of the trend depends upon whether the β_2 term is positive or negative. The values of the parameters—α, β_1, and β_2—are secured by solution of the following normal equations:

$$\Sigma Y = N\alpha + \beta_1\Sigma X + \beta_2\Sigma X^2$$
$$\Sigma XY = \alpha\Sigma X + \beta_1\Sigma X^2 + \beta_2\Sigma X^3 \tag{8-4}$$
$$\Sigma X^2Y = \alpha\Sigma X^2 + \beta_1\Sigma X^3 + \beta_2\Sigma X^4$$

For sake of illustration, let us apply this type of trend to the hypothetical data of Table 8-4, and note the difference in fit from that displayed in Figure 8-1.

Equation (8-4) now becomes

$$324.4 = 18\alpha + 153\beta_1 + 1{,}785\beta_2$$
$$2{,}958.4 = 153\alpha + 1{,}785\beta_1 + 23{,}409\beta_2$$
$$35{,}194.2 = 1{,}785\alpha + 23{,}409\beta_1 + 327{,}469\beta_2$$

Dealing with the first two equations above and eliminating the α term by multiplying the first equation by 8.5 we have

$$
\begin{array}{llll}
2{,}758.2 = 153\alpha + 1{,}300.5\beta_1 + 15{,}172.5\beta_2 & \text{(To subtract,} \\
2{,}958.4 = 153\alpha + 1{,}785\beta_1 + 23{,}409\beta_2 & \leftarrow \text{change signs} \\
\hline
-200.2 = - \phantom{1{,}30}484.5\beta_1 - \phantom{15{,}1}8{,}236.5\beta_2 & \text{and add)}
\end{array}
$$

Dealing with the second two equations above and eliminating the α term by multiplying the first equation by 11.666,

$$
\begin{array}{llll}
34{,}529.1 = 1{,}785\alpha + 20{,}823\beta_1 + 273{,}089\beta_2 & \text{(To subtract,} \\
35{,}194.2 = 1{,}785\alpha + 23{,}409\beta_1 + 327{,}469\beta_2 & \leftarrow \text{change signs} \\
\hline
-665.1 = \phantom{1{,}785\alpha} - \phantom{20{,}8}2{,}586\beta_1 - 54{,}380\beta_2 & \text{and add)}
\end{array}
$$

Table 8-4   Calculations for Nonlinear Second-Degree Trend[a]

Period	Y	X	XY	X^2	X^3	X^4	X^2Y
1960	12.4	0	0	0	0	0	0
1961	14.5	1	14.5	1	1	1	14.5
1962	13.2	2	26.4	4	8	16	52.8
1963	16.4	3	49.2	9	27	81	146.7
1964	17.3	4	69.2	16	64	256	276.8
1965	16.8	5	84.0	25	125	625	420.0
1966	16.6	6	99.6	36	216	1,296	597.6
1967	18.0	7	126.0	49	343	2,401	882.0
1968	21.4	8	171.2	64	512	4,096	1,369.6
1969	20.6	9	185.4	81	729	6,561	1,668.6
1970	18.4	10	184.0	100	1,000	10,000	1,840.0
1971	19.2	11	211.2	121	1,331	14,641	2,323.2
1972	20.0	12	240.0	144	1,728	20,736	2,880.0
1973	19.6	13	254.8	169	2,197	28,561	3,312.4
1974	19.0	14	266.0	196	2,744	38,416	3,724.0
1975	19.9	15	298.5	225	3,375	50,625	4,477.5
1976	20.3	16	324.8	256	4,096	65,536	5,196.8
1977	20.8	17	353.6	289	4,913	83,521	6,011.2
	324.4	153	2,958.4	1,785	23,409	327,469	35,193.7

$\Sigma Y = 324.4$ $\Sigma X^2 = 1,785$ $\Sigma X^2Y = 35,193.7$

$\Sigma X = 153$ $\Sigma X^3 = 23,409$

$\Sigma XY = 2,958.4$ $\Sigma X^4 = 327,469$

All Figures Rounded

[a] *Source:* hypothetical data.

Then eliminate the β_1 term by multiplying through by 5.33:

$$- \ 200.2 = - \ \ \ \ 484.5\beta_1 - \ \ 8,236.5\beta_2 \leftarrow \text{(Multiply this}$$
$$- \ 665.1 = - \ 2,586\beta_1 \ - 54,380\beta_2 \ \ \ \ \ \ \text{equation by 5.33)}$$

and

$$-1,067.1 = - \ 2,586\beta_1 \ - 43,898\beta_2 \ \ \ \ \text{(To subtract, change}$$
$$+ \ \ \ 665.1 = + \ 2,586\beta_1 \ + 54,380\beta_2 \leftarrow \text{signs and add)}$$
$$- \ \ \ 402 \ = \ \ \ \ \ \ \ \ \ \ \ \ \ + 10,482\beta_2$$
$$-0.038 \ \ = \beta_2$$

Substituting β_2 in the equation:

$$-200.2 = -484.5\beta_1 - 8,236.5(-0.038)$$
$$-200.2 = - \ 484.5\beta_1 + 313$$
$$-200.2 - 313 = - \ 484.5\beta_1$$
$$-513.2 \ \ \ \ \ \ \ \ = - \ 484.5\beta_1$$
$$1.06 \ \ \ \ \ \ \ \ \ = \beta_1$$

Substituting for β_1 and β_2 in the original equation, we obtain

$$324.4 = 18\alpha + 153(1.06) + 1,785(-0.038)$$
$$324.4 = 18\alpha + 162.2 - 67.8$$
$$324.4 - 162.2 + 67.8 = 18\alpha$$
$$230 = 18\alpha$$
$$12.78 = \alpha$$

Reverting to the original least squares equation in (8-3), we obtain

$$Y_c = 12.78 + 1.06(X) - 0.038(X^2)$$

The values of Y_c for our sample are given in Table 8-5.

A projection of the hypothetical data for 1978 becomes

$$19.54 = 12.78 + 1.06(18) - 0.038(324)$$

Figure 8-2 depicts the second-degree polynomial with the β_2 term a negative value. Observe that the curve is concave to the X axis and increases each time by decreasing amounts in the early periods. However, the second degree polynomial will decrease by increasing amounts after it reaches a peak value. If the β_2 term is a positive value, it would be increasing by increasing amounts and be convex to the ori-

Table 8-5   Nonlinear Secular Trend Second-Degree Polynomial[a]

1 Period	2[b] Y	3[b] $Y_c = 12.78 + 1.06(X) - 0.038(X^2)$
1960	12.4	$12.78 = 12.78 + 1.06(0) - 0.038(0)$
1961	14.5	$13.80 = 12.78 + 1.06(1) - 0.038(1)$
1962	13.2	$14.75 = 12.78 + 1.06(2) - 0.038(4)$
1963	16.4	$15.62 = 12.78 + 1.06(3) - 0.038(9)$
1964	17.3	$16.41 = 12.78 + 1.06(4) - 0.038(16)$
1965	16.8	$17.13 = 12.78 + 1.06(5) - 0.038(25)$
1966	16.6	$17.77 = 12.78 + 1.06(6) - 0.038(36)$
1967	18.0	$18.34 = 12.78 + 1.06(7) - 0.038(49)$
1968	21.4	$18.83 = 12.78 + 1.06(8) - 0.038(64)$
1969	20.6	$19.24 = 12.78 + 1.06(9) - 0.038(81)$
1970	18.4	$19.58 = 12.78 + 1.06(10) - 0.038(100)$
1971	19.2	$19.84 = 12.78 + 1.06(11) - 0.038(121)$
1972	20.0	$20.03 = 12.78 + 1.06(12) - 0.038(144)$
1973	19.6	$20.14 = 12.78 + 1.06(13) - 0.038(169)$
1974	19.0	$20.17 = 12.78 + 1.06(14) - 0.038(196)$
1975	19.9	$20.13 = 12.78 + 1.06(15) - 0.038(225)$
1976	20.3	$20.01 = 12.78 + 1.06(16) - 0.038(256)$
1977	20.8	$19.82 = 12.78 + 1.06(17) - 0.038(289)$

[a] *Source:* hypothetical data.
[b] Billions of dollars.

Figure 8-2   Nonlinear Secular Trend, Second-Degree Polynomial

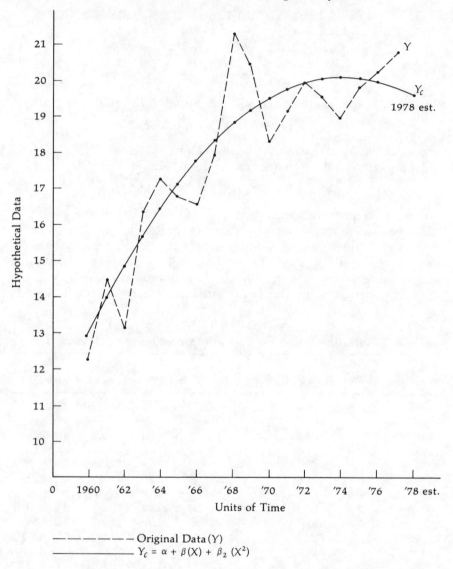

—————— Original Data (Y)
——————— $Y_c = \alpha + \beta(X) + \beta_2 (X^2)$

gin. Also, parabolic curves can be declining in the early stages when β_1 is negative and β_2 positive, and then reverse direction.

It is possible to construct third-degree polynomials $[Y_c = \alpha + \beta_1(X) + \beta_2(X^2) + \beta_3(X^3)]$ that would describe curves with two changes of direction. However, for polynomials of higher degree, the curves tend to follow the data too closely and become less descriptive of any trend that may be underlying the data.

Table 8-6   Conversion of Original Data to Logarithms

Year	Consumer Installment Credit[a] (Y)	log Value (Y)[b]
1970	101.9	2.0081742
1971	111.2	2.0461048
1972	126.8	2.1031193
1973	146.4	2.1655411
1974	155.4	2.1914510
1975	162.2	2.2100508
1976	178.8	2.2523675
1977	185.3	2.2678754

[a] In billions of dollars.
[b] Taken from the table of logarithm values.

Geometric Straight Line Trend

The original data may be increasing at a *constant rate* rather than by constant absolute amounts. The curve is described using logarithms:

$$\log Y_c = \log \alpha + \log \beta_1(X) \tag{8-5}$$

This is, of course, equation (1), with the original data converted into log values. The normal equations to solve for α and β are in like fashion converted to log values (see Table 8-6):

$$\Sigma \log Y = N \log \alpha + \log \beta \Sigma X$$
$$\Sigma X \log Y = \log \alpha \Sigma X + \log \beta \Sigma X^2 \tag{8-6}$$

After conversion the parameters α and β are obtained in the same manner as Table 8-2 (see Table 8-7).

Table 8-7   Calculation of Parameters for Geometric Straight Line Trend[a]

1 Year	2 Y	3 X	4 (2 × 3) XY	5 (3 × 3) X^2
1970	2.0081742	0	0	0
1971	2.0461048	1	2.0461048	1
1972	2.1031193	2	4.2062386	4
1973	2.1655411	3	6.4966233	9
1974	2.1914510	4	8.7655804	16
1975	2.2100508	5	11.0502520	25
1976	2.2523675	6	13.5141205	36
1977	2.2678754	7	15.8751270	49
	$\Sigma \log Y = 17.2446841$	$\Sigma X = 28$	$\Sigma X \log Y = 61.9540466$	$\Sigma X^2 = 140$

[a] *Source:* hypothetical data.

Table 8-8   Log Values of Secular Trend (Y_c)

1 Period	2 Log Values = log α + log $\beta(X)$
1970	2.0224473 = 2.0224473 + 0.0380394(0)
1971	2.0604867 = 2.0224473 + 0.0380394(1)
1972	2.0985261 = 2.0224473 + 0.0380394(2)
1973	2.1365655 = 2.0224473 + 0.0380394(3)
1974	2.1746049 = 2.0224473 + 0.0380394(4)
1975	2.2126443 = 2.0224473 + 0.0380394(5)
1976	2.2506837 = 2.0224473 + 0.0380394(6)
1977	2.2887231 = 2.0224473 + 0.0380394(7)

Using the data from Table 8-7, equation 8-6 becomes

$$17.244684 = 8\alpha + 28\beta$$
$$61.954046 = 28\alpha + 140\beta$$

Equation 8-6 is solved in the manner described on pages 150–152.
β equals 0.0380394 and α equals 2.0224473.
Filling in the α and β values in equation (8-5):

$$\log Y_c = 2.0224473 + 0.0380394(X) \qquad (8\text{-}7)$$

This expression will give the log values of consumer installment credit
as projected by the regression equation. However, the projected values
must then be reconverted back to natural numbers in order to secure the
secular trend running through the data. This is done using a table of
logarithms (Tables 8-8 and 8-9).

Figure 8-3 plots the Geometric Straight Line Trend. Since the curve
increases (or decreases) at a constant rate, it follows that it increases (or
decreases) by larger (or smaller) absolute amounts. Thus it will not plot

Table 8-9   Conversion of Log Values to Natural Numbers

1 Period	2 log Y_c	3[a] Y_c	4[a] Y
1970	2.0224473	105.3	101.9
1971	2.0604867	115.1	111.2
1972	2.0985261	125.5	126.8
1973	2.1365655	136.0	146.4
1974	2.1746049	149.5	155.4
1975	2.2126443	163.2	162.2
1976	2.2506837	178.1	178.8
1977	2.2887231	194.4	185.3

[a] Figures in columns 3 and 4 in billions of dollars.

Figure 8-3   Geometric Straight Line Trend

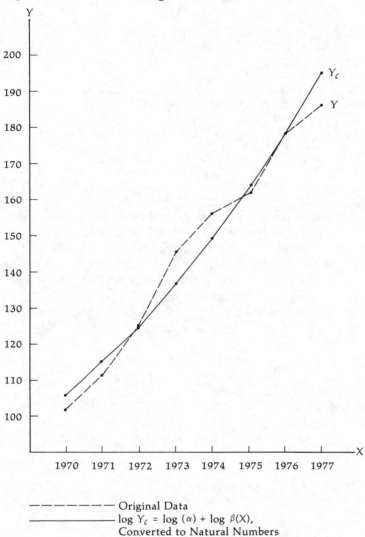

--------- Original Data
——————— log Y_c = log (α) + log β(X),
Converted to Natural Numbers

as a straight line except on semilog paper. The particular trend calculation which gives the best fit for the data under consideration depends
upon $\Sigma(Y - Y_c)^2$. The curve which yields the lowest sum of the residuals is the preferred choice.

On the other hand, the rate of growth implicit in the geometric trend
is often of interest to management. It is derived from the following
equation:

$$\log(1 + R) = \log \beta \qquad (8\text{-}8)$$

where R is the rate of growth per year. In the illustration, therefore,

$$\log(1 + R) = 0.0380394$$
$$1 + R = \text{antilog } 0.0380394$$
$$R = 1.091539\text{-}1$$
$$R = 0.09$$

Hence, we would estimate the rate of growth in Consumer Installment Credit as about 9% annually (rounded).

REMOVING THE TREND

In the management of long-term assets (capital budgeting) and in strategic planning, knowledge of underlying trends constitutes information of the highest order. For shorter-term decisions and working capital management, management's decisions can be greatly assisted by knowledge of how the business cycle and irregular influences affect the firm's sales. The problem, accordingly, becomes one of removing the trend from the original data. Recall the opening comments to this chapter that each time series (Y) comprises four elements: trend, seasonal, cyclical, and irregular movements. In the case of Consumer Installment Credit, the example employed annual data so that seasonal variations (intra-year movements in the data) can be ignored. This left the time series: $Y = T + C + I$. The influence of the trend can be removed by division:

$$\frac{T + C + I}{T}$$

leaving the cyclical and irregular influences. Table 8-10 uses the Arithmetic Straight Line Trend to illustrate the removal of the trend by division.

Table 8-10 Removal of Trend by Division[a]

1 Period	2 Y	3[a] Y_c	4 (2 ÷ 3) Actual Value as Percent of Trend
1970	101.9	102.78	0.99
1971	111.2	115.13	0.96
1972	126.8	127.48	0.99
1973	146.4	139.83	1.05
1974	155.4	152.18	1.02
1975	162.2	164.53	0.99
1976	178.8	176.88	1.01
1977	185.3	189.23	0.98

[a] Figures in columns 2 and 3 in billions of dollars.

Figure 8-4   Removal of Secular Trend by Division

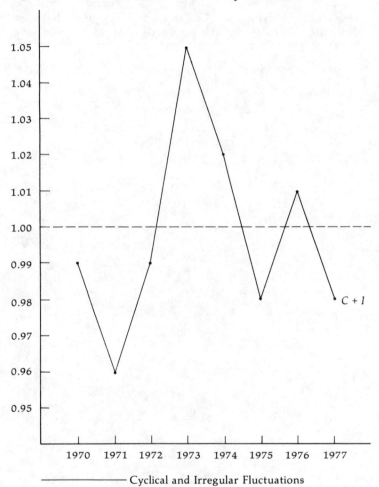

———————— Cyclical and Irregular Fluctuations

Figure 8-4 plots the cyclical and irregular fluctuations. Values below 1.00 indicate that consumer installment credit is below the average for the period covered. Similarly, values above 1.00 indicate the variable is performing at above average levels.

Several methods exist to remove the cyclical influence. However, since cyclical waves vary in duration and amplitude, the isolation of C from I rarely aids in the analysis of the movements in a given time series. Therefore, the components C and I are often reported in their combined form, as illustrated in Figure 8-4 and Table 8-10.

Table 8-11 Specific Seasonal Relatives[a]

1 Month	2 Demand Deposits	3 12-Month Moving Total	4 24-Month Centered Moving Total	5 (4 ÷ 24) Centered Moving Average	6 (2 ÷ 5) Specific Seasonal Relative
1976—Jan.	2.1				
Feb.	1.9				
Mar.	2.7				
Apr.	3.2				
May	3.2				
Jun.	3.0				
		29.9			
Jul.	2.5	+	59.1	2.46	1.02
		29.2			
Aug.	2.6		58.0	2.42	1.07
		28.8			
Sept.	2.6		57.3	2.39	1.09
		28.5			
Oct.	2.5		56.4	2.35	1.06
		27.9			
Nov.	1.9		55.1	2.30	0.83
		27.2			
Dec.	1.7		54.2	2.26	0.75
		27.0			
1977—Jan.	1.4		54.4	2.27	0.62
		27.4			
Feb.	1.5		54.8	2.28	0.66
		27.4			
Mar.	2.4		54.9	2.29	1.05
		27.5			
Apr.	2.6		55.4	2.31	1.11
		27.9			
May	2.5		56.5	2.35	1.06
		28.6			
Jun.	2.8		58.0	2.42	1.16
		29.4			
Jul.	2.9		59.7	2.49	1.16
		30.3			
Aug.	2.6		61.2	2.55	1.02
		30.9			
Sept.	2.7		62.8	2.62	1.03
		31.9			
Oct.	2.9		65.3	2.72	1.07
		33.4			
Nov.	2.6		68.4	2.85	0.91
		35.0			
Dec.	2.5		71.1	2.96	0.84
		36.1			

Table 8-11 (*Continued*)

1 Month	2 Demand Deposits	3 12-Month Moving Total	4 24-Month Centered Moving Total	5 (4 ÷ 24) Centered Moving Average	6 (2 ÷ 5) Specific Seasonal Relative
1978—Jan.	2.3		73.1	3.04	0.76
		37.0			
Feb.	2.1		74.6	3.11	0.68
		37.6			
Mar.	3.4		76.2	3.18	1.07
		38.6			
Apr.	4.1		78.7	3.28	1.25
		40.1			
May	4.1		81.8	3.41	1.20
		41.7			
Jun.	3.9		84.5	3.52	1.11
		42.8			
Jul.	3.9		86.6	3.61	1.08
		43.8			
Aug.	4.1		89.1	3.71	1.11
		45.3			
Sept.	3.5		91.4	3.81	0.92
		46.1			
Oct.	3.6		92.9	3.87	0.93
		46.8			
Nov.	3.5		94.5	3.94	0.89
		47.7			
Dec.	3.1		96.0	4.00	0.78
		48.3			
1979—Jan.	3.0		97.3	4.05	0.74
		49.0			
Feb.	3.1		99.0	4.13	0.75
		50.0			
Mar.	4.1		100.7	4.20	0.98
		50.7			
Apr.	4.2		101.5	4.23	0.98
		50.8			
May	4.6		102.6	4.28	1.07
		51.3			
Jun.	4.5		103.2	4.30	1.05
		51.9			
Jul.	4.2				
Aug.	4.6				
Sept.	4.6				
Oct.	4.1				
Nov.	4.4				
Dec.	3.1				

[a] *Source:* hypothetical data; data in columns 2–4 in millions of dollars.

163

SEASONAL VARIATIONS

Acquaintance with trend and cyclical movements, obviously helpful to the manager in short- and long-term planning, are not sufficient for the day-to-day operation of the firm. Here operational decisions (weekly or monthly or quarterly) come to the fore: the management of sales, accounts receivable, inventories, production schedules, and liquidity (cash and marketable securities) management. These cover the general problem of working capital. A firm must engage in long-term planning to survive, but the most common cause of business failure is traceable to inadequate working capital. Essential to working capital management are estimates of monthly variations in business activity, that is, seasonal movements.

Seasonal fluctuations result from climatic changes, institutional practices (such as income tax collection dates), or inherited customs and habits. Directly and indirectly they affect nearly all economic activity as fluctuations that occur within a year but that repeat themselves from year to year. For purposes of management, the objective is to separate seasonal variations from trend and cyclic influences and to measure their magnitude for planning purposes. For example, your bank must know the *normal monthly* (and weekly) inflow and outflow of deposits for each branch so that it can manage its reserve position and investment outlays. One of the better methods of identifying seasonal fluctuations is the ratio to moving average technique.

Ratio to Moving Average

The ratio to moving average is applied by means of the following steps:

1. Run a twelve-month moving total through the original monthly data in the manner of column 3 of Table 8-11.
2. Convert the twelve-month moving total to a twenty-four-month moving total as per column 4.
3. Divide the resulting twenty-four-month moving total by 24 (column 5).
4. Obtain the specific seasonal relative by dividing the original data in column 2 by the centered moving average in column 5.
5. The seasonal index may then be computed by either of two methods:
   A. Median average: Set up the specific seasonal relatives for each month as illustrated in Table 8-12; obtain the median average of specific seasonal relatives for each month and add the twelve monthly relatives; divide the resulting total into 1200 and multiply each median average by the ratio of

Table 8-12 Specific Seasonal Relatives Median and Arithmetic Mean

Specific Seasonal Relatives

	Jan.	Feb.	Mar.	Apr.	May	June	July	Aug.	Sept.	Oct.	Nov.	Dec.	Totals
1976							1.02	1.07	1.09	1.06	0.83	0.75	
1977	0.62	0.66	1.05	1.11	1.06	1.16	1.16	1.02	1.03	1.07	0.91	0.84	
1978	0.76	0.68	1.07	1.25	1.20	1.11	1.08	1.11	0.92	0.93	0.89	0.78	
1979	0.74	0.75	0.98	0.98	1.07	1.05							
(1) Median[a] average	74	68	105	111	107	111	108	107	103	106	89	75	1,164
(2) Adjusted seasonal index	76.22	70.04	108.15	114.33	110.21	114.33	111.24	110.21	106.09	109.18	91.67	77.25	1,200
(3) Average of specific seasonals	70.67	69.67	103.33	111.33	111.0	110.67	108.67	106.67	101.33	102.00	87.67	79.0	1,162.01
(4) Adjusted seasonal index	72.97	71.94	106.70	114.93	114.62	114.28	112.21	110.15	104.63	105.33	90.53	81.58	1,200

(1) Multiply median average by 1.031 (= 1,200/1,164) to generate adjusted seasonal index.
(2) Allow for minor difference in total of adjusted seasonal index due to rounding.
(3) Multiply average of specific seasonals by 1.0326 (= 1,200/1,162.01) to generate adjusted seasonal index.
(4) Allow for minor difference in total of adjusted seasonal index due to rounding.

[a] Median average for each month is obtained by dropping the highest and lowest averages for those years.

Table 8-13 Deseasonalized Bank Deposits[a]

1 1979	2 Actual Bank Deposits	3 Seasonal Relative[b]	4 (2 × 3) Deseasonalized Bank Deposits
Jan.	3.0	0.7622	2.29
Feb.	3.1	0.7004	2.17
Mar.	4.1	1.0815	4.43
Apr.	4.2	1.1433	4.80
May	4.6	1.1021	5.07
June	4.5	1.1433	5.14
July	4.2	1.1124	4.67
Aug.	4.6	1.1021	5.07
Sept.	4.6	1.0609	4.88
Oct.	4.1	1.0918	4.48
Nov.	4.4	0.9167	4.03
Dec.	3.1	0.7725	2.39

[a] Data in columns 2 and 4 in millions of dollars.
[b] Median average used (adjusted seasonal index).

the total median averages. This gives the seasonal index based upon median averages.

  B. Arithmetic mean: Repeat the process of 5A except that the monthly specific seasonal relative will be based upon the arithmetic mean (rather than the median) of the monthly specific seasonal averages. All computations are illustrated in Table 8-12.
6. Finally, deseasonalize the original data by multiplying figures on bank deposits by the seasonal relative. See Table 8-13.

Deseasonalizing data not only provides the manager with the trend and cyclical movements passing through the data (which may now be analyzed by the methods discussed earlier in the chapter) but further alerts him to variations in sales, accounts receivables, cash balances, and so on—or, in the instance of banking, with changes in his deposits—that accrue from seasonal patterns of customer behavior. The reader will also note that the averaging involved in the ratio-to-moving average technique tends to dampen irregular influences.

SUMMARY

The illustrating problems in this and other chapters have been worked out in detail to assist the reader's understanding of the assumptions and supporting theory behind a given statistical technique. Actually, all these techniques exist as "canned" computer programs that produce solutions in a few minutes. Some may also be solved quickly by a good-quality hand calculator. In either case, the manager must be in a position to interpret and question the validity of the results. Apropos of time series analysis he will wish to pose some basic questions:

1. How is the original data changing? At a constant absolute amount? At a constant rate? In some nonlinear fashion?
2. Is the business problem up for resolution a short term (one or two years) or a long term (five or more years) decision?
3. If long term, which method is used to measure the trend and does it best describe the original data?
4. If the business cycle weighs heavily on the decision, how has it been isolated from the other influences present in a time series?
5. If the decision turns on monthly (or quarterly) fluctuations in business activity, which method was employed to measure and remove seasonal fluctuations?
6. What is the source of the original data? Frequently, in a business situation, the desired data are not available and surrogate data must be obtained. This adds an element of uncertainty to the decision since the surrogate data are unlikely to match completely the requirements of the situation.
7. Is the base year and the time frame covered by the analysis appropriate to the decision requirements? Depending on the base year and time frame of the investigation, the results can show a rising or declining trend.

chapter 9

Associations and Correlations

A technique frequently used to assist management decisions is association and correlation analysis. Your market research department may use it to make the sales forecasts that serve as a basis for the preparation of operating budgets; manufacturing may utilize correlation in production control; and variations of the method are found in accounts receivable management, establishing credit terms, cash flow projections for capital budgeting, and so forth.

On a wider social plain, correlation analysis (or the use thereof) has influenced your life style in myriad ways: decisions to smoke or not to smoke, to diet or not to diet, to exercise or not—all of these generating prescriptions for a longer life span or at least one that seems longer. A forecast by the Nome Econometric Institute that next year's GNP will rise 3 percent just makes your day. A knowledge of the basics of correlation analysis, its limitations, and interpretation is a capability worth acquiring.

TERMINOLOGY OF CORRELATION

As the word implies, *correlation* concerns the "co-relation," or association, between a dependent (or explained) variable and one or more independent (explanatory) variables such that if we know (or can forecast) the value of the independent variable(s) we can estimate the value of the dependent variable.

Business usage tends to stress the importance of association rather than attempting to explain why knowing A enables us to predict the value of B. For example, in your firm you may observe that sales vary directly with discretionary customer income without completely delineating the reasons for this market phenomenon. It is sufficient that with an estimate of the change in discretionary consumer income you can forecast to some degree of accuracy the change in company sales. Other forms of research seek the causes underlying the association in order to uncover the presence of new explanatory variables and/or to avoid *nonsense correlations*. As an illustration of the latter, you might calculate a good correlation between the size of the prison population and the number of Ph.Ds in the population. You would not conclude, however, that the Ph.D. population is the cause of overcrowding in the local prison. Rather, they are more likely both functions of the growth in the total population as well as other socioeconomic factors. *Always watch for other variable(s) that may be jointly influencing the values of the independent variables in the analysis.* Statistical formulae are not unlike computers: garbage in, garbage out.

Statisticians classify correlation analysis into several subtopics:

1. *Simple correlation:* The association between one dependent and one independent variable.
2. *Multiple correlation:* The relationship between one dependent and two or more independent variables.
3. *Partial correlation:* The relationship between one of the variables in a multiple correlation and the dependent variables is examined.
4. *Linear correlation:* A straight line best describes the relationship between the variables; that is, if the data for each variable(s) were plotted on graph paper, the points would approximate a straight line.
5. *Nonlinear correlation:* The relationship between the variables best approximates a line with one or two changes of direction. For example, the line may slope upward, reach an apogee, and then level off.
6. *Positive correlation:* The value of the dependent and independent variables tend to move together over time. The relationship, however, may be coincident in time or one variable may lead or lag the movement of the other. For example, sales in the capital goods industries often lead changes in Gross National Product, turning down before a dip in the GNP and rising before GNP picks up—still a positive correlation exists between the two series.
7. *Negative correlation:* The dependent and independent variable(s) move in opposite directions; once again the correlation may depend on a lead or lag factor. For example, in the present recession (1979–?), high-technology stocks resisted the ambivalent behavior of the securities market.

These classes actually exist in combination. A simple correlation may be positive or negative, linear or nonlinear. The same is true of multiple correlations.

SIMPLE LINEAR CORRELATION

The previous chapter on time series developed a regression equation $[Y_c = \alpha + \beta(X)]$ in which the independent variable X represented units of time. In correlation analysis the same regression equation applies except that X now connotes some value other than units of time. Also the solution for α and β employs the familiar normal equations:

$$\Sigma Y = N\alpha + \beta\Sigma X$$
$$\Sigma XY = \alpha\Sigma X + \beta\Sigma X^2$$

(9-1)

where: Σ = signifies summation

N = the number of paired items entering the computation

α = the value of the regression line at its point of origin

β = the slope of the regression line or the typical change in the dependent variable that accompanies a unit change in the independent variable

X = actual value of the independent variable

Y = actual value of the dependent variable

Y_c = calculated value of Y based upon the regression equation

Hence, the regression line depicts an *average relationship between a dependent and independent variable based upon historical data.* This is a most important point in interpreting the results of correlation analysis.

By way of illustration, let us examine the data on sales and discretionary consumer income given in Table 9-1.

The firm wishes to use the data in forecasting. Assuming a linear relationship, a series of operations are performed (Table 9-2).

Substituting the data from Table 9-2 into equation 9-1 we obtain

$$608.8 = \quad 9\alpha + \quad 2,010\beta$$
$$136,699 = 2,010\alpha + 450,300\beta$$

Table 9-1   Basic Data Simple Linear Correlation[a,b]

Period	Company Sales	Discretionary Consumer Income
1970	50.2	200
1971	62.8	215
1972	76.4	220
1973	63.8	210
1974	67.1	230
1975	72.9	235
1976	66.8	225
1977	77.7	240
1978	71.1	235

[a] *Source:* hypothetical data.

[b] All figures in millions of dollars.

**Table 9-2 Data for Normal Equations Simple
Linear Correlation**[a,b]

1 Period	2 Sales (Y)	3 Discretionary Consumer Income (X)	4 (2 × 3) XY	5 (3 × 3) X^2
1970	50.2	200	10,040	40,000
1971	62.8	215	13,502	46,225
1972	76.4	220	16,808	48,400
1973	63.8	210	13,398	44,100
1974	67.1	230	15,433	52,900
1975	72.9	235	17,132	55,225
1976	66.8	225	15,030	50,625
1977	77.7	240	18,648	57,600
1978	71.1	235	16,708	55,225
	$\Sigma Y = 608.8$	$\Sigma X = 2,010$	$\Sigma XY = 136,699$	$\Sigma X^2 = 450,300$
	$\bar{Y} = 67.64$	$\bar{X} = 223.33$		

[a] *Source:* hypothetical data.
[b] All figures in millions of dollars.

The values of α and β are secured in the manner described on pages 150–152; β equals 0.523 and α equals -49.15.

We now have the values of α and β that can be used by the firm in the original regression equation to forecast 1979 sales. Let us assume the Department of Commerce or some private sector economic research firm or consultant estimates 1979 discretionary consumer income in the firm's marketing area at $260 million. Reverting to the regression equation:

$$Y_c = \alpha + \beta(X)$$
$$= -49.15 + 0.523(260)$$
$$= -49.15 + 136$$
$$= \$86.8$$

Based upon the historical relationship between company sales and discretionary consumer income, the firm would project 1979 sales at $86.8 million. Actually, in a realistic forecast situation, the analysis would have utilized quarterly or monthly data. It would also be necessary to update the values of α and β periodically, perhaps by adding the most recent year and dropping the earliest year.

All the same, the astute manager will surely raise the question, *How good a predictor is this simple linear equation for my company's sales?* After all, a forecasting technique may work for one company but not for another.

Testing the Quality of the Simple Linear Correlation

The objective is accomplished simply by putting the regression equation to work; that is, inputting the known values of the independent variable for the years 1970–1978, calculating the projected values of the dependent variable (Y_c), and then comparing the projected values (Y_c) with the actual values (Y) and noting the deviations (see Table 9-3). The Mean Absolute Deviation (MAD) would lead us to expect that the forecasted sales of $86.8 million will vary in either direction (plus/minus) by $3.32 million if the pattern of the past holds true for the future period. Whether a $3.32 million tolerance in the forecast is acceptable depends upon the firm's break-even point and the impact on the bottom line. If the company requires a more precise forecast other independent variables should be employed, or an alternative forecasting technique should be used.

The calculation of the variation between actual and projected sales in our illustration opens the door to more sophisticated measures of correlation quality. Three kinds of variation are discussed below.

Total Variation

This is the sum of the squared deviations of the Y values (actual values of the dependent variable) from the mean of $\bar{Y}$ or $\Sigma (Y - \bar{Y})^2$. Using the mean of $\bar{Y} = \$67.64$ from Table 9-2 we construct Table 9-4.

Table 9-3 Deviation of Projected and Actual Sales Simple Linear Correlation[a,b]

1 Period	2 Company Sales (Y)	3 Projected Sales (Y_c)	4 (2 − 3) ($Y - Y_c$)	5 (4 × 4) ($Y - Y_c$)²
1970	50.2	55.45 = −49.15 + 0.523(200)	− 5.25	27.56
1971	62.8	63.30 = −49.15 + 0.523(215)	− 0.50	0.25
1972	76.4	65.91 = −49.15 + 0.523(220)	+10.49	110.04
1973	63.8	60.68 = −49.15 + 0.523(210)	+ 3.12	9.73
1974	67.1	71.14 = −49.15 + 0.523(230)	− 4.04	16.32
1975	72.9	73.76 = −49.15 + 0.523(235)	− 0.86	0.74
1976	66.8	68.53 = −49.15 + 0.523(225)	− 1.73	2.99
1977	77.7	76.37 = −49.15 + 0.523(240)	+ 1.33	1.77
1978	71.1	73.76 = −49.15 + 0.523(235)	− 2.66	7.08

Mean Absolute Deviation, ignoring signs, $\dfrac{\Sigma(Y - Y_c)}{N} = \dfrac{29.9}{9} = 3.32$

Unexplained Variation $= \Sigma(Y - Y_c)^2 = \overline{176.48}$

[a] *Source:* hypothetical data.
[b] All figures in millions of dollars.

Table 9-4   Total Variation Simple Linear Correlation^{a,b}

1 Period	2 Y	3 $\bar{Y}$	4 (2 − 3) $(Y - \bar{Y})$	5 (4 × 4) $(Y - \bar{Y})^2$
1970	50.2	67.64	−17.44	304.15
1971	62.8	67.64	− 4.84	23.43
1972	76.4	67.64	+ 8.76	76.74
1973	63.8	67.64	− 3.84	14.74
1974	67.1	67.64	− 0.54	0.29
1975	72.9	67.64	+ 5.26	27.67
1976	66.8	67.64	− 0.84	0.71
1977	77.7	67.64	+10.06	101.20
1978	71.1	67.64	+ 3.46	11.97
			Total variation = $\Sigma(Y - \bar{Y})^2$ =	560.90

^{a} *Source:* hypothetical data.
^{b} All figures in millions of dollars.

Explained Variation

This represents that portion of the total variation that is accounted for by the behavior of the independent variable (X). It is the sum of the squared deviations of the Y_c values [the projected sales using the regression equation, $Y_c = \alpha + \beta(X)$] from the mean of $\bar{Y}$. Using these Y_c values we obtain an explained variation $[\Sigma(Y_c - \bar{Y})^2]$ of $383.02 million.

Unexplained Variation

The residual variation is unexplained in that it mirrors the effects of market forces over and above those explained by the fluctuations of the independent variable (X). Hence, to calculate the unexplained variation take the deviations between the actual sales (Y) and the forecasted sales (Y_c), square the deviations and summate. In short, the unexplained residual is $\Sigma(Y - Y_c)^2$. As previously calculated (Table 9-3) the result is $176.48 million.

Note that the algebraic sum of the deviations, $\Sigma(Y - Y_c)$, will always equal zero; that is, the regression line will always be a perfect fit (see Figure 9-1) even though the forecast error may be large. Also note that the total variation will always equal the sum of the explained and unexplained variations. In our case, therefore, $560.90 \approx 383.02 + 176.48$ millions of dollars, the difference due to rounding.

The calculation of the total, explained, and unexplained variations allows more precise measurement of the quality of the regression equation $[(Y_c = \alpha + \beta(X)]$ as a forecasting device of company sales. Several measures can be applied, and these are discussed in the following sections.

Figure 9-1 Simple Linear Correlation: Algebraic Sum of Deviations Using Values Given in Table 9-3

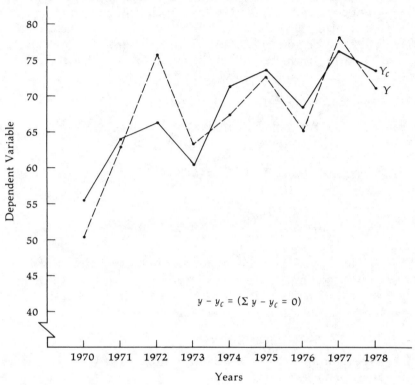

Coefficient of Correlation

The coefficient of correlation (R) is a relative measure of the relationship between two variables, that is, the degree of association between the dependent and independent variables:

$$R = \sqrt{\frac{\text{Explained Variation}}{\text{Total Variation}}}$$

$$= \sqrt{\frac{\Sigma(Y_c - \bar{Y})^2}{\Sigma(Y - \bar{Y})^2}} \qquad (9\text{-}2)$$

$$= \sqrt{\frac{383.02}{560.90}}$$

$$= 0.826$$

Interpretation of R depends upon the size of sample (the number of pairs, N). For our small sample ($N = 9$) we would have to go further before attempting a definitive assessment. In any event, for economic data a coefficient of correlation better than 0.75 is generally considered desirable. At this point, therefore, we would not be unimpressed with the association of company sales and discretionary consumer income.

The coefficient of correlation can vary from $+1$ for perfect positive correlation to -1 for perfect negative correlation. If $R = 0$, no correlation exists and the Y_c values will equal the mean of $\bar{Y}$. For the perfect case ($+1$ or -1), the explained variation equals the total variation.

Coefficient of Determination

Symbolized by R^2, the coefficient of determination is the simple ratio of the explained variation to the total variation. Thus,

$$R^2 = \frac{\text{Explained Variation}}{\text{Total Variation}}$$

$$= \frac{383.02}{560.90} \tag{9-3}$$

$$= 0.683$$

R^2 states that 68% of the total variation of the dependent variable is explained by discretionary consumer income or, in theoretical terms, the independent variable. R^2 is a more stringent test of association. Yet the manager may still question the significance of these tests.

F Test for Significance of the Regression Line

The F test uses variances as opposed to variations. The variance is simply the square of our old friend, the standard deviation, from Chapter 2.

$$F = \frac{\Sigma(Y_c - \bar{Y})^2/(K - 1)}{\Sigma(Y - Y_c)^2/(N - K)} \tag{9-4}$$

where K is the number of variables (two in simple correlation). Then,

$$F = \frac{383.02/(2 - 1)}{176.45/(9 - 2)}$$

$$= \frac{383.02/1}{176.48/7}$$

$$= \frac{383.02}{25.21}$$

$$= 15.19$$

The value of F must be compared with the appropriate statistic table (for the F distribution) to determine whether the regression line is significant at the 95% level; that is, whether there exists a 95% probability that the regression line yields a value greater than 0. As a general rule, however, when the number of observations (N) lies in the range of 6 to 10 (in our case, 9), the value of F must be greater than 6 for the regression line to be significant at the 95% level. The regression line, $Y_c = \alpha + \beta(X)$, therefore, satisfies the rule and the user could affirm with confidence that the slope of the regression line is greater than 0. His confidence would stand only a 5% chance of being misplaced.

Standard Error of the Slope

Is the regression line coefficient β significantly different from 0 or did it just occur by chance? Is the true value of β really different from 0? Or, if we suppose that the true value of β is 0, what is the likelihood that we would have obtained our specific value of β or a larger value? The measure needed to determine whether the true value of β is greater than 0 and the significance of the regression coefficient is the standard error of the coefficient—sometimes termed the standard error of the slope (S_β).

$$
\begin{aligned}
S_\beta &= \frac{\sqrt{\Sigma(Y - Y_c)^2/N - K}}{\sqrt{\Sigma(X - \bar{X})^2}} \\
&= \frac{\sqrt{176.48/(9 - 2)}}{\sqrt{1400.01}} \\
&= 0.134
\end{aligned}
\tag{9-5}
$$

where $\Sigma(X - \bar{X})^2$ is the sum of the squared deviation of the X values (independent variable) around the mean of $\bar{X}$.

With the value of one standard error for the regression coefficient β set at 0.134, the number of standard errors of β from 0 equals β/S_β, or $0.52/0.134 = 3.88$.

Interpretation depends upon the t distribution (Table 5-15). Generally, where there are at least five pairs, the computed regression coefficient β should be three or more standard errors (S_β) from 0 to be considered significant at the 95% level. For 15 pairs the t value should be at least 2. Thus we have evidence that our regression coefficient is significantly different from 0, that is, the actual value of β is almost certain to be greater than 0.

Confidence Interval of the Regression Coefficient

A further test of significance relates to the confidence interval for the regression coefficient. A 95% confidence interval gives a range within which the manager is 95% certain it contains the true value of β. If the value of β is 0.52, what is the range around this value (0.52) wherein the manager can be 95% certain of finding the true value of β? At the

95% level, the true value of the regression coefficient (β') approximates

$$\beta' = \beta \pm 1.96(S_\beta)$$
$$= 0.52 \pm 1.96(0.134) \qquad (9\text{-}6)$$
$$= 0.52 \pm 0.263$$

The true value of β', therefore, falls somewhere in the range 0.268 to 0.783. If the manager desired a range in which he could place 99% confidence, the multiplier would be 2.58, but the wider range entails loss of precision in the estimate.

Finally, how much confidence can the manager place in a specific forecast from the regression equation, $Y_c = -48.5 + 0.523(X)$?

Confidence Interval of a Specific Forecast

The standard error of the forecast (S_F) is

$$
\begin{aligned}
S_F &= \sqrt{\left[\frac{\Sigma(Y - Y_c)^2}{N - 2}\right]\left[1 + \frac{1}{N} + \frac{(X_F - \bar{X})^2}{\Sigma(X - X)^2}\right]} \\
&= \sqrt{\left[\frac{176.48}{9 - 2}\right]\left[1 + \frac{1}{9} + \frac{(260 - 223.3)^2}{1400.01}\right]} \\
&= \sqrt{\left[\frac{176.48}{9 - 2}\right]\left[1 + \frac{1}{9} + \frac{1344.89}{1400.01}\right]} \qquad (9\text{-}7) \\
&= \sqrt{[25.21][1 + 0.111 + 0.961]} \\
&= 5.02\sqrt{[2.073]} \\
&= 5.02(1.44) \\
&= 7.23
\end{aligned}
$$

where X_F is the forecast of the independent variable. Using equation (1) and with a discretionary income (X) of \$260, we have $Y_c = \$86.8$. Then the 95% confidence interval for our forecast of \$86.8 million in company sales will be \$86.8 $\pm$ 1.96(7.23). Hence, the manager can be 95% certain that the actual sales will be between \$72.63 and \$100.97 million.

In concluding the discussion of simple correlation analysis the reader should not overlook the key importance of the number of pairs (N). For the purpose of illustrating the calculations, the preceding discussion limited the number of observations to nine pairs. A sample of 30 pairs would have improved our confidence in the calculations and 100 even more so. As sample size increases, the range of the confidence interval becomes smaller. Any time the manager can obtain additional data points to compute the regression line, he should not overlook the opportunity to do so. However, confidence in the regression equation can also be improved by the addition of another independent variable. Note too the regression line may be a perfect fit ($R = +1$ or -1) and yet the regression equation might fail the test of significance.

MULTIPLE LINEAR REGRESSION

Multiple regression treats the relationship between one dependent and two or more independent variables as expressed by

$$Y_c = \alpha + \beta_1 X_1 + \beta_2 X_2 \qquad (9\text{-}8)$$

where: α = value of the regression line at its point of origin

β_1 = the typical change in the dependent variable that accompanies a unit change in the first independent variable (X_1)

β_2 = the typical change in the dependent variable that accompanies a unit change in the second independent variable (X_2)

As in the simple linear correlation the problem is to determine the value of α, β_1, and β_2 under the same assumption that a straight line best describes the relationship among the data. For this purpose, we use the not unfamiliar normal equations, drawing once again upon historical data:

$$\left.\begin{array}{l} \Sigma Y = N\alpha + \beta_1 \Sigma X_1 + \beta_2 \Sigma X_2 \\ \Sigma X_1 Y = \alpha \Sigma X_1 + \beta_1 \Sigma X_1^2 + \beta_2 \Sigma X_1 X_2 \\ \Sigma X_2 Y = \alpha \Sigma X_2 + \beta_1 \Sigma X_1 X_2 + \beta_2 \Sigma X_2^2 \end{array}\right\} \qquad (9\text{-}9)$$

Assume the firm adds housing starts to the data in the proceeding illustration, displayed in Table 9-5.

Substituting the data from Table 9-5 into equation) (9-9), we obtain

$$608.8 = 9\alpha + 2010\beta_1 + 16.4\beta_2$$
$$136{,}699 = 2010\alpha + 450{,}300\beta_1 + 3714\beta_2$$
$$1{,}146.8 = 16.4\alpha + 3714\beta_1 + 32.84\beta_2$$

The normal equations for multiple correlation are solved by the same process of successive reduction in the number of terms to the point where one of the parameters—α, β_1, or β_2—is solved; the remaining parameters are then obtained by working back by substitution. Obviously the number of calculations increase with the number of independent variables involved. A pocket calculator can reduce the tedium but the most expeditious alternative is a computer. Canned programs exist to handle the full range of regression analyses. For equation (9-9), using the data from Table 9-5, our computer gives us the following:

$$\alpha = 13.07$$
$$\beta_1 = 0.164$$
$$\beta_2 = 9.8$$

Substituting these into equation (9-8),

$$Y_c = 13.07 + 0.164(X_1) + 9.8(X_2)$$

Table 9-5 Basic Data: Multiple Linear Correlation[a]

1 Year	2 Sales[b] (Y)	3 Discretionary Consumer Income[b] (X_1)	4 Housing Starts[c] (X_2)	5 (2 × 3) X_1Y	6 (3 × 3) X_1^2	7 (3 × 4) X_1X_2	8 (2 × 4) X_2Y	9 (4 × 4) X_2^2
1970	50.2	200	1.0	10,040	40,000	200	50.2	1.00
1971	62.8	215	1.5	13,502	46,225	323	94.2	2.25
1972	76.4	220	2.5	16,808	48,400	550	191.0	6.25
1973	63.8	210	1.1	13,398	44,100	231	70.2	1.21
1974	67.1	230	1.7	15,433	52,900	391	114.1	2.89
1975	72.9	235	2.2	17,132	55,225	517	160.4	4.84
1976	66.8	225	1.6	15,030	50,625	360	106.9	2.56
1977	77.7	240	2.8	18,648	57,600	672	217.6	7.84
1978	71.1	235	2.0	16,708	55,225	470	142.2	4.00
	$\Sigma Y = 608.8$	$\Sigma X_1 = 2010$	$\Sigma X_2 = 16.4$	$\Sigma X_1Y = 136,699$	$\Sigma X_1^2 = 450,300$	$\Sigma X_1X_2 = 3714$	$\Sigma X_2Y = 1146.8$	$\Sigma X_2^2 = 32.84$
	$\bar{Y} = 67.64$	$\bar{X}_1 = 223.3$	$\bar{X}_2 = 1.82$					

[a] *Source:* hypothetical data.
[b] In millions of dollars.
[c] In millions of units.

180

As with the simple linear correlation, the manager must again raise the question: How good is the forecast? What is the typical error likely to accompany the forecast? Fortunately the tests for the quality of a multiple regression are mostly similar to those used in simple correlation.

Testing the Quality of Multiple Correlation

As with simple correlation, before we can evaluate the data it must be further processed (see Table 9-6).

Total Variation

Since the data are identical to that of Table 9-4, Y and $\bar{Y}$ are unchanged, the total deviation, $\Sigma(Y - \bar{Y})^2$, has the same value of 560.90 as in the simple linear correlation.

Explained Variation

$[\Sigma(Y_c - \bar{Y})^2]$, computed as before, is 486.05.

Unexplained Variation

$\Sigma(Y - Y_c)^2$, taken from Table 9-6, is 74.85. (See also Figure 9-2.)
   Thus, as before the total variation equals the explained plus the unexplained: $560.90 = 486.05 + 74.85$ (all data in millions of dollars).

Table 9-6   Deviation of Projected and Actual Sales
Multiple Linear Correlation[a,b]

1 Period	2 Company Sales (Y)	3 Projected Sales (Y_c)	4 (2 − 3) ($Y - Y_c$)	5 ($Y - Y_c$)²
1970	50.2	55.7 = 13.07 + 0.164(200) + 9.8(1)	−5.5	30.25
1971	62.8	63.0 = 13.07 + 0.164(215) + 9.8(1.5)	−0.2	.04
1972	76.4	73.6 = 13.07 + 0.164(220) + 9.8(2.5)	+2.8	7.84
1973	63.8	58.3 = 13.07 + 0.164(210) + 9.8(1.1)	+5.5	30.25
1974	67.1	67.4 = 13.07 + 0.164(230) + 9.8(1.7)	−0.3	.09
1975	72.9	73.2 = 13.07 + 0.164(235) + 9.8(2.2)	−0.3	.09
1976	66.8	65.6 = 13.07 + 0.164(225) + 9.8(1.6)	+1.2	1.44
1977	77.7	79.9 = 13.07 + 0.164(240) + 9.8(2.8)	−2.2	4.84
1978	71.1	71.2 = 13.07 + 0.164(235) + 9.8(2.0)	−0.1	.01

Mean Average Deviation, ignoring signs, $\Sigma \dfrac{(Y - Y_c)}{N} = \dfrac{18.1}{9} = 2.01$

Unexplained Variation $= \Sigma(Y - Y_c)^2 = \overline{74.85}$

[a] *Source:* hypothetical data.
[b] All figures in millions of dollars.

Figure 9-2 Multiple Linear Regression: Algebraic Sum of Deviations Using Data from Table 9-6

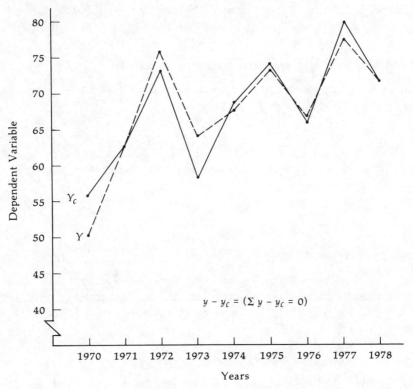

Coefficient of Correlation

$$R = \sqrt{\frac{\text{Explained Variation}}{\text{Total Variation}}}$$

$$= \sqrt{\frac{486.05}{560.90}} \tag{9-10}$$

$$= 0.93$$

Coefficient of Determination:

$$R^2 = \frac{\text{Explained Variation}}{\text{Total Variation}}$$

$$= \frac{486.05}{560.90} \tag{9-11}$$

$$= 0.86$$

F *Test for Significance of the Regression Line:*

$$F = \frac{\Sigma(Y_c - \bar{Y})^2/K - 1}{\Sigma(Y - Y_c)^2/N - K}$$

$$= \frac{486.05/3 - 1}{74.85/9 - 3}$$ (9-12)

$$= \frac{243.03}{12.48}$$

$$= 19.47$$

As in the case of the linear equation, where the sample size is six or more items, the F statistic should exceed a value of six to be significant. With the F statistic at 19.47, the manager has 95% assurance that the multiple regression equation exceeds zero.

Simple Correlation Matrix

In multiple correlation, the researcher can compute the individual coefficient of correlation for each of the pairs of variables and arrange the coefficients in a *correlation matrix*. In our forecasting case, a correlation coefficient could be computed for sales and discretionary consumer income, sales and housing starts, and discretionary consumer income and housing starts (see Table 9-7).

The data necessary to these calculations were obtained from Table 9-5 and the manner of calculation has been illustrated. The matrix tells the manager how the different variables are correlated and provides a basis for further tests of significance.

The correlation matrix, moreover, highlights the potential existence of a common computational problem in the use of business or economic data, that is, multicollinearity. This develops when two or more of the independent variables are highly correlated. Observe the correlation between housing starts and discretionary consumer income. Multicollinearity may result in overstatement of the coefficient of determination while at the same time the tests for significance of the individual regression coefficients may be very small, indicating these coefficients could as well be 0. In short, the objective in multiple correlation is to select

Table 9-7   Coefficient of Correlation Matrix—Three Variables

	Sales	Discretionary Consumer Income	Housing Starts
Sales	1.000	0.82	0.89
Discretionary Consumer Income	0.82	1.000	0.81
Housing Starts	0.89	0.81	1.000

independent variables that are highly correlated with the dependent variable but not with each other.

Standard Error of the Slope

Adjusting equation (9-5) for multiple regression, the standard error of the slope (S_β) becomes

$$S_\beta = \frac{\sqrt{\Sigma(Y - Y_c)^2/N - K}}{\sqrt{\Sigma(X - \bar{X})^2}} \tag{9-13}$$

Then, for the first independent variable, discretionary consumer income:

$$S_{\beta 1} = \frac{\sqrt{74.85/9 - 3}}{\sqrt{1400.01}}$$

$$= \frac{3.53}{37.42}$$

$$= 0.094$$

and for the second independent variable, housing starts:

$$S_{\beta 2} = \frac{\sqrt{74.85/9 - 3}}{\sqrt{2.96}}$$

$$= \frac{3.53}{1.72}$$

$$= 2.05$$

Observe that the denominator changes for each independent variable (X_1 and X_2) due to the difference in the sums of the squared deviations.

Similar again to the simple linear correlation, if we suppose that the true value of β is 0, what is the likelihood that we would have obtained our specific value of β or a larger value? Having calculated the value of one standard error of β, the expression β/S_β indicates the number of standard errors the calculated value β is from 0. Thus, for the first independent variable, discretionary consumer income, $0.164/0.094 = 1.74$; that is, the value of the regression coefficient, β_1, is less than two standard errors from 0. For the second independent variable, $9.8/2.05 = 4.78$, that is, the value of the regression coefficient, β_2, is almost 5 standard errors from 0.

Following the rule previously established that where there are at least five pairs, computed regression coefficient, β, should be three or more standard errors from 0 to be considered significant at the 95% level, we may assert that β_2 is significant and that the coefficient, β_1, could be 0. The value of β_1 could have occurred by chance. Therefore, the first explanatory variable (X_1) should not be included in the analysis since its slope may not be different from zero. The second explanatory variable (X_2) should be included since its slope is different from zero.

The value of alpha can be subjected to the same type of probing. Could alpha's value be the result of chance? The standard error of the intercept (S_α) equals:

$$S_\alpha = \frac{\sqrt{\Sigma(Y - Y_c)^2/(N - K)}}{\sqrt{1/N}}$$

$$= \frac{\sqrt{74.85/(9 - 3)}}{\sqrt{1/9}} \qquad (9\text{-}14)$$

$$= \frac{3.53}{0.33}$$

$$= 10.70$$

Applying the same procedure to α, $13.07/10.70 = 1.22$—the intercept is less than two standard errors from 0.

Accordingly, the value of alpha might also be the consequence of chance. The low values in the tests of significance in the individual regression coefficients could well be the result of the marked degree of multicollinerity between the two independent variables, discretionary consumer income and housing starts.

Confidence Interval of the Regression Coefficients

In equation (9-6), we denoted a range of values, that would have an approximate 95% confidence level of containing the true value of the coefficient (β), that is,

$$\beta' = \beta \pm 1.96(S_\beta) \qquad (9\text{-}15)$$

For discretionary consumer income,

$$\beta' = 0.164 \pm 1.96(0.094)$$
$$= 0.164 \pm 0.184$$

For housing starts,

$$\beta' = 9.8 \pm 1.96(2.05)$$
$$= 9.8 \pm 4.02$$

Confidence Interval of a Specific Forecast

Multiple regression necessitates some modification in determining the standard error of the forecast. Equation (9-7) is thus revised as follows:

$$S_F = \sqrt{\left[\frac{(\Sigma Y - Y_c)^2}{N - K}\right]\left[\left(1 + \frac{1}{N}\right) + \frac{(X_F - \bar{X}_1)^2}{\Sigma(X_1 - \bar{X}_1)^2} + \frac{(X_F - \bar{X}_2)^2}{\Sigma(X_2 - \bar{X}_2)^2}\right]}$$

$$= \sqrt{\left[\frac{74.85}{9 - 3}\right]\left[\left(1 + \frac{1}{9}\right) + \frac{(260 - 223.3)^2}{1400.01} + \frac{(3 - 1.82)^2}{2.96}\right]} \qquad (9\text{-}16)$$

$$= 3.53\sqrt{1.111 + 0.962 + 0.470}$$

$$= 3.53(1.595)$$

$$= 5.629$$

If $X_1 = 260$ and $X_2 = 3$, the regression equation would project next period sales at \$85.11 million. However, rather than a single discrete value, management planning would be facilitated by a range within which the actual sales are apt to fall. After all, the one certainty about a forecast is that it will in some degree miss the mark. The standard error of the forecast (S_F) serves this function. At a 95% level of certainty, actual sales (Y') should lie within \$85.11 $\pm$ 5.63, or a range of \$79.48 to \$90.74. Obviously, this datum is now a valuable input to working capital management (liquidity, inventory, and receivables), arranging short-term financing, production planning, and assessing the impact of different levels of sales on the bottom line.

Assumptions of Multiple Regression Analysis

When using quantitative methods as a basis for business decision making, the manager must be alert to the assumptions underlying a particular statistical technique. These should conform to the reality of the business environment. If they do not, the quantitative results may appear superficially acceptable but totally worthless, with possible dire effects on short- or long-term planning. A quantitative technique can become a trap if the decision maker does not keep the underlying assumptions in the forefront.

Multiple regression analysis rests upon four assumptions:

1. As in simple correlation, the methodology assumes a linear relationship between the dependent variable (Y) and each of the independent variables $(X_1, X_2,$ and so forth). It is possible, however, to transform some nonlinear relationships into a linear relationship but the method lies beyond the scope of the present discussion.

2. The second assumption is constant variance of errors, $(Y - Y_c)^2/N$, as the independent variable(s), X, increases. If the variance remains the same over the range of observations, the assumption is met (Figure 9-3A). By contrast, if the residuals, $Y - Y_c$, manifest a definite pattern in magnitude or in sign (plus or minus), the assumption is violated (Figures 9-3B,C).

3. The residuals are independent of one another; each residual is independent of the one before and after it. If, on the other hand, the residuals cluster in plus and minus groups and form a wavelike pattern, the data are not likely to fit the assumption. When the independence assumption is violated, a serial correlation or autocorrelation exists among successive residual values as the independent variable increases (See Figure 9-3C). The cause may lie in the omission of an important independent variable or the use of an incorrect regression form. The pres-

Figure 9-3 Constant Variance Assumption

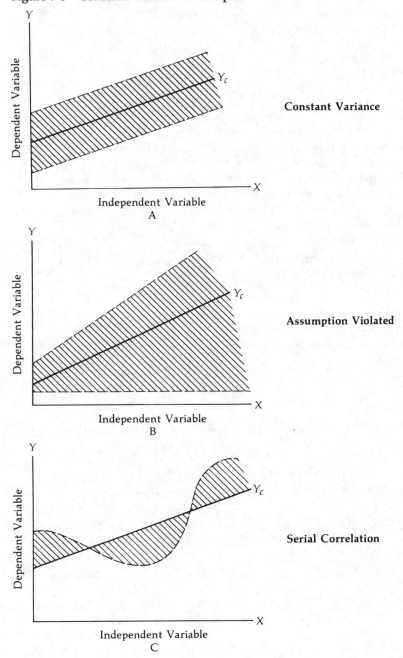

Constant Variance

Assumption Violated

Serial Correlation

ence of autocorrelation will generate incorrect variances, vitiate tests of significance, and lead to an incorrect estimate of the coefficient of determination (R^2).

4. The residuals are normally distributed. The assumption is generally met with a sample size of 30 or more. If the assumption is not met, the tests of significance and the confidence intervals developed from them will not apply.

Looking back over our forecasting case—a deliberately flawed illustration in terms of data selection but correct in terms of the technical working of the regression line—we can see immediately for both the simple and multiple regression the need for a larger sample. In the multiple correlation the correlation matrix gave evidence of a strong multicollinearity, and the residuals of the multiple correlation failed the test of normal distribution. Graphing the original variables will generally indicate the presence or lack of a linear relationship only in the case of a simple regression. However, graphing the regression line and the residuals is a quick screening test on the extent to which the other assumptions are met in multiple regression.

ADVANTAGES OF CORRELATION ANALYSIS

Regression analysis demands greater effort than the evaluation techniques of Chapter 8. Nonetheless, it offers the prospect of greater rewards.

1. Correlation analysis allows for quantitative evaluation of market forces and company marketing actions and permits inclusion of company marketing plans (advertising expenditures, promotion strategies, new products), brand preferences, exports, and industry economics as predictors of sales levels.
2. If turning points in the explanatory variables can be foreseen, then turning points in company sales can be predicted.
3. Regression analysis will lead to more accurate forecasting, provided that independent variables can be projected with reasonable accuracy while minimizing multicollinearity and avoiding autocorrelation.
4. It may be the only feasible technique for new products or for long-term forecasts.
5. It is subject to cumulative improvement and refinement with time and experience.
6. It allows for the isolation and analysis of errors.

DISADVANTAGES OF CORRELATION ANALYSIS

1. More in-depth knowledge of market forces is required for correlation analysis than for extrapolation techniques, such as time series projections.
2. It is more costly in computation time, extent of data required, and competence of personnel.
3. It may not be possible to forecast dependent variables with the accuracy required to improve on extrapolation techniques.
4. Historical data may not be available on many important variables.
5. Coefficients are still based upon historical relationships and may not quickly respond to new influences entering the market. It is essential to keep updating the model with new data and/or new independent variables and to recalculate the parameters—α, β_1, β_2, and so forth.
6. Correlation analysis is not easily understood by personnel unfamiliar with statistical techniques.

SUMMARY

Our summary will take the form of a series of questions that the manager might pose after receiving a report with conclusions inferred from a regression analysis:

1. Are there other variables influencing the values of the independent variable(s) or that could be added to improve the predictability of the regression equation?
2. What type of correlation is assumed? Linear or nonlinear? Simple or multiple regression?
3. Depending on the response to the second query, what assumptions are made and do they accord with the external environment?
4. How frequently are the parameters—α, β_1, β_2—updated?
5. Are changes in the historical relationship among the variables anticipated?
6. How much confidence can be placed in the estimates produced by the regression equation? What is the coefficient of correlation and the coefficient of determination? Are the regression equation and the coefficients significant? What is the probability that the latter are not significantly different from zero? What is standard error of the β values? What is the confidence in-

terval for each of the β values? How much confidence can be placed in a specific forecast? What is the standard error of the forecast?

7. Finally, when correlation analysis is used in forecasting, the manager should inquire as to possible feedback effects. A forecast is made before decisions on advertising expenditures, price adjustments, promotional campaigns, and the like. When these decisions are made, the forecast must be adjusted to reflect the impact of the new situation. If this modification is not made, the original forecast can become misleading when used as a basis for making other decisions. Moreover, the original forecast can no longer be used as a basis for evaluating the accuracy of the forecasting technique.

An understanding of correlation analysis is important not only for its immediate utility in quantifying business problems but it also provides the basis for more advanced techniques, such as the Box–Jenkins models and multivariate analysis. These latter, however, lie beyond the concerns of a primer in quantitative methods.

SECTION VI
Classifying Things

chapter 10

Discriminant Analysis

Linear discriminant analysis extends the subject matter of Chapter 9 on associations. Similar to the regression technique, Linear Discriminant Analysis (LDA) uses independent or explanatory variables to predict fluctuations in a dependent or explained variable. Unlike regression analysis, LDA does not attempt to forecast a future value of the dependent variable. Rather, it calculates discriminant functions to classify the dependent variable as belonging to separate categories or groups. Based upon the classification, management proceeds to render a judgment.

LDA is a powerful tool in situations where classification is prerequisite to decision making. These commonly include judging the credit worthiness of customers, predicting defaults and/or bankruptcies, selecting employees, assessing the success of business combinations, evaluating different forecasting techniques, and so on.

GENERAL DESCRIPTION

Applying LDA to credit management, for example, let us assume a firm wishes to establish some cutoff point to guide decisions on extending credit. The credit manager's experience dictates that a customer's past record of payment best indicates his future credit worthiness. Using this criterion, he classifies his customers into two groups: good and bad credit risks. The good risks are assigned a credit score (S) of 1 and the poor risks a credit score of 0.[1]

Each account is analyzed to identify key variables in establishing a

---

[1] LDA is used to illustrate the value of discriminant analysis in certain business situations. The manager with an interest in the subject matter should review other available techniques which may better conform to the circumstances of his problem.

credit rating. For example, one study specified nine independent variables (X) as most significant in credit scoring[2]:

X_1—percentage of suppliers reporting slow payments,
X_2—percentage of suppliers reporting COD terms,
X_3—percentage of suppliers reporting accounts in for collection,
X_4—percentage of suppliers reporting credit refused,
X_5—percentage of suppliers reporting selling account three years or more,
X_6—highest amount of credit granted,
X_7—past due amount owed supplier,
X_8—composite credit rating given by Dun & Bradstreet, and
X_9—appearance of physical premises.

Some or all of the identified characteristics become independent variables in the familiar multiple, linear regression equation:

$$S = \alpha + \beta_1 X_1 + \beta_2 X_2 + \beta_3 X_3 + \ldots + \beta_n X_n \qquad (10\text{-}1)$$

Associating the Ss on the Xs in the manner of the previous chapter yields the beta values (β). When a new customer applies for credit, the credit manager combines his X values with the related beta values as computed to determine the applicant's score. A previously fixed cut off score establishes which group the new customer belongs; that is, a good credit risk or a poor risk.

Illustration

Assume the credit manager selects independent variables X_1, X_2, and X_3 as the significant explanatory variables for his firm in granting credit. In Table 10-1, a sample of ten customers is chosen from the files and subdivided into two groups[3]:

Step 1—Determine the Values of α and β

We use the form of equation (10-1) for one dependent and three independent variables:

$$\begin{aligned}
\Sigma S &= N\alpha + \beta_1 \Sigma X_1 + \beta_2 X_2 + \beta_3 X_3 \\
\Sigma X_1 S &= \alpha \Sigma X_1 + \beta_1 \Sigma X_1^2 + \beta_2 \Sigma X_1 X_2 + \beta_3 \Sigma X_1 X_3 \\
\Sigma X_2 S &= \alpha \Sigma X_2 + \beta_1 \Sigma X_1 X_2 + \beta_2 \Sigma X_2^2 + \beta_3 \Sigma X_2 X_3 \\
\Sigma X_3 S &= \alpha \Sigma X_3 + \beta_1 \Sigma X_1 X_3 + \beta_2 \Sigma X_2 X_3 + \beta \Sigma X_3^2
\end{aligned} \qquad (10\text{-}2)$$

[2] David C. Ewert, "Trade Credit Management: Selection of Accounts Receivable Using a Statistical Model," Paper No. 236, March 1969, Purdue University: Institute for Research in Behavioral, Economic and Management Sciences.

[3] We limited the number of explanatory variables and the size of the sample to reduce the number of calculations. Actually, a larger number of variables and a larger sample would enhance the validity of the model. Since the calculations are likely to be performed by computer, the analyst should experiment to include all variables necessary to optimize results.

Table 10-1 Sample Illustration[a]

Customer	X_1	X_2	X_3	Credit Risk (S)
Estimation Sample				
A	0.10	0.50	0.01	S = 1
B	0.40	0.10	0.15	S = 0
C	0.15	0.60	0.05	S = 1
D	0.05	0.45	0.03	S = 1
E	0.35	0.15	0.10	S = 0
Control Sample				
F	0.15	0.45	0.03	S = 1
G	0.15	0.60	0.00	S = 1
H	0.10	0.53	0.01	S = 1
I	0.40	0.10	0.20	S = 0'
J	0.45	0.05	0.15	S = 0

[a] *Source:* hypothetical data.

Inserting the values from Table 10-2 into equation (10-2),

$$3 = 5\alpha + 1.05\beta_1 + 1.8\beta_2 + 0.34\beta_3$$
$$0.30 = 1.05\alpha + 0.3175\beta_1 + 0.2550\beta_2 + 0.1050\beta_3$$
$$1.55 = 1.8\alpha + 0.2550\beta_1 + 0.8450\beta_2 + 0.0785\beta_3 \qquad (10\text{-}3)$$
$$0.09 = 0.34\alpha + 0.1050\beta_1 + 0.0785\beta_2 + 0.0360\beta_3$$

The normal equations are solved with the procedures illustrated in Chapters 8 and 9. We do not repeat the process at this point but simply state the solution:

$$\alpha = 0.3326$$
$$\beta_1 = -1.327$$
$$\beta_2 = 1.245$$
$$\beta_3 = 1.438$$

Inserting these parameters in equation (10-1),

$$S = 0.3326 - 1.327X_1 + 1.245X_2 + 1.438X_3 \qquad (10\text{-}4)$$

Step 2—Determine the Credit Scores of the Estimation Group

We apply equation (10-4) to the estimation group comprising companies A through E; that is, we insert the X_1, X_2, and X_3 values for each company to determine the credit score. For example, for Company A

$$S = 0.3326 - 1.327(0.10) + 1.245(0.50) + 1.438(0.01)$$
$$= 0.3326 - 0.1327 + 0.6225 + 0.01438 \qquad (10\text{-}5)$$
$$= 0.837$$

Repeating the procedure for all members of the estimation group we construct Table 10-3.

Table 10-2 Calculation of Variables from Equation (10-2) for the Estimation Sample[a]

Company	S	X_1	X_2	X_3	X_1^2	X_2^2	X_3^2
A	1	0.10	0.50	0.01	0.0100	0.2500	0.0001
B	0	0.40	0.10	0.15	0.1600	0.0100	0.0225
C	1	0.15	0.60	0.05	0.0225	0.3600	0.0025
D	1	0.05	0.45	0.03	0.0025	0.2025	0.0009
E	0	0.35	0.15	0.10	0.1225	0.0225	0.0100
$\Sigma S = 3$		$\Sigma X_1 = 1.05$	$\Sigma X_2 = 1.80$	$\Sigma X_3 = 0.34$	$\Sigma X_1^2 = 0.3175$	$\Sigma X_2^2 = 0.8450$	$\Sigma X_3^2 = 0.0360$

X_1X_2	X_1X_3	X_2X_3	X_1S	X_2S	X_3S
0.0500	0.0010	0.0050	0.10	0.50	0.01
0.0400	0.0600	0.0150	0.00	0.00	0.00
0.0900	0.0075	0.0300	0.15	0.60	0.05
0.0225	0.0015	0.0135	0.05	0.45	0.03
0.0525	0.0350	0.0150	0.00	0.00	0.00
$\Sigma X_1X_2 = 0.2550$	$\Sigma X_1X_3 = 0.1050$	$\Sigma X_2X_3 = 0.0785$	$\Sigma X_1S = 0.30$	$\Sigma X_2S = 1.55$	$\Sigma X_3S = 0.09$

[a] Source: hypothetical data.

196

Table 10-3   Credit Scores: Estimation Group[a]

Company	Credit Score (Rounded)	Good/Bad Risk
A	0.837	1
B	0.142	0
C	0.952	1
D	0.870	1
E	0.199	0

[a] *Source:* hypothetical data.

The model as structured gives credit scores (S) between 0 and 1. The reader will observe, however, the same underlying assumption common to all associative analysis: the future will be much like the past. Given this assumption our simplified example distinguishes quite sharply between good and bad credit risks.

Step 3 —Determine the Credit Scores of Control Group

Applying equation (10-4) to the control group, companies F through J, we construct Table 10-4.

Again the model clearly distinguishes between good and bad risks.

Step 4 —Set Up Cumulative Probability Distribution of Scores for Estimation and Control Groups

We are now ready to construct a cumulative probability distribution (Table 10-5).

None of the good risks scored below .217 and none of the bad risks scored 0.737 or above. There is a zero probability of a good risk scoring 0.217 or below and a bad risk scoring 0.737 or better. Actually, as credit managers will attest, some good risks score below the dividing line between the categories and some bad risks score well. Our model would have manifested like characteristics with a larger sample. It is for management to determine the cutoff score dividing good and bad credit risks. Experience will naturally constitute an important judgmental

Table 10-4   Credit Scores: Control Group[a]

Company	Credit Score (Rounded)	Good/Bad Risk
F	0.737	1
G	0.881	1
H	0.874	1
I	0.217	0
J	0.013	0

[a] *Source:* hypothetical data.

Table 10-5 Cumulative Probability Distribution of Companies Receiving a Given Credit Score or Lower[a]

Credit Score	Good Risk (%)	Bad Risk (%)
0.013	0	10
0.142	0	20
0.199	0	30
0.217	0	40
0.737	50	0
0.837	60	0
0.870	70	0
0.874	80	0
0.881	90	0
0.952	100	0

[a] *Source:* hypothetical data.

factor. However, the pressure to expand sales may induce management to lower the cutoff score and accept the risk of an increase in late payments or defaults.

The Ewert study referred to above sampled 507 customers from the credit files of a manufacturer: 298 good risks and 209 bad risks. The cumulative probability distribution for this group is given in Table 10-6.

Mao offers an illustration of how Ewert's data may be employed by a credit manager. Suppose a credit manager knows that 90 percent of his customers are good risks (A_1) and 10 percent, poor risks (A_2). A credit applicant receives a score of 0.226. What is the probability the applicant will default? The probability that a good risk will score 0.226 or less is 0.02. Therefore, $A_1 = 0.90 \times 0.02 = 0.018$. The probability of a bad risk scoring .226 or less is 0.36. Hence, $A_2 = 0.36 \times 0.10 = 0.036$. Using the formula, $A_2/(A_1 + A_2)$, $0.036/(0.018 + 0.036) = 0.67$. The credit manager, if he accepted the account, runs a 67 percent chance of default.[4]

Step 5—Setting Up a Cutoff on Credit Risk

If the credit manager knows that a particular account runs a 67 percent probability of default, how does this information relate to other variables entering his decision?

Bear in mind the use of discriminant analysis does not eliminate the need for managerial judgment. Some credit managers follow the policy that accepting a bad credit risk is far more costly than rejecting a good customer. Other managers place a higher premium on the loss of a good customer and would consequently set a lower cutoff score so that more

[4] James C. T. Mao, *Corporate Financial Decisions*, Palo Alto, CA: Pavan Publishers, 1976, pp. 260–263.

Table 10-6   Cumulative Probability Distribution of Firms Receiving a Given Credit Score or Lower[a]

Credit Score	Good Risk (%)	Bad Risk (%)
0.208	0	35
0.226	2	36
0.298	5	49
0.356	6	58
0.543	16	76
0.577	17	82
0.596	20	85
0.699	34	97
0.763	49	99
0.898	75	100

[a] *Source:* Ewert, p. 17.

customers would be accepted. Since no model is perfect, the manager's philosophy and experience shapes in significant measure company policy.

On the other hand, "sharp pencil risk return analysis" also enters the decision. Suppose I_F designates the profit on a sale to customer F. Then,

$$I_F = S_F - CS_F - B_F \tag{10-6}$$

where: S_F = sales to customer F
   C = ratio of incremental costs to incremental sales
   B_F = bad-debt losses

B_F equals the sales to F with a probability of default (P_F) and zero loss with a probability of $1 - P_F$. This means that the expected value of B_F is equal to $P_F S_F$. Therefore, taking the expected value of both sides of equation (10-6),

$$E(I_F) = (1 - C)S_F - P_F S_F \tag{10-7}$$

Suppose a customer applies for credit of \$10,000 and has a credit score of 0.596 on Table 10-6. The company's experience indicates that 90 percent of the customers are good risks (A_1) and 10 percent default (A_2). The ratio of incremental costs to incremental sales is 30 percent. What is the expected profit on the sale?

The probability that a good risk (A_1) will score 0.596 or less is 0.20 (Table 10-6). Hence, $A_1 = 0.90 \times 0.20 = 0.18$. The probability that a poor risk will score 0.596 or less is 0.85; therefore, $A_2 = 0.85 \times 0.10 = 0.085$. The customer presents a default probability of $.085/(0.18 + 0.085)$, or 32 percent.

Completing equation (10-7),

$$E(I_F) = (1 - 0.30)\$10{,}000 - (0.32)(\$10{,}000)$$
$$= \$7{,}000 - \$3{,}200 \qquad (10\text{-}8)$$
$$= \$3{,}800$$

The larger the risk, the smaller the expected profit.

From this point, either of two decision rules could be instituted. If the firm wishes simply to maximize expected profit, it will accept all credit accounts that have a positive expected profit. Mao, however, recommends a modification of the traditional maximization rule in financial management. He suggests the firm accept all credit accounts with a positive expected profit subject to the constraint that total expected bad debts not exceed some specified percentage of total sales.[5]

A firm with a predominant number of small accounts, roughly the same size, may find it more expeditious to calculate the expected profit per dollar of sales. This necessitates modifying equation (10-7) as follows:

$$\frac{E(I_F)}{S_F} = 1 - C - P_F \qquad (10\text{-}9)$$

Using the same data,

$$\frac{E(I_F)}{\$10{,}000} = 1 - 0.30 - 0.32$$
$$\frac{\$3{,}800}{\$10{,}000} = 0.38 \qquad (10\text{-}10)$$

For customer F, the expected profit per dollar of sales is 38¢, or—as in equation (10-8)—$3,800 on an investment of $10,000.

Since the larger the risk the smaller the expected profit, the firm can rank credit customers by expected profit per dollar of sales and by risk. As expected profit decreases, the expected bad debt loss per dollar of sales increases. The manager may decide how far down the list to go by applying either of the two decision criteria mentioned above.

A firm with a few large customers has a quite different perspective. The major issue here does not concern the maximum bad debt level acceptable for all credit customers but rather the maximum possible loss on a given account and how that impacts on the firm's own financial survival. If a given loss could throw the firm into insolvency, it might choose to reject the application even given a very small probability of default. Expected profit and probability of default are all germane but the credit manager's judgment is the crucial factor in the situation.

[5] James C. T. Mao, *Corporate Financial Decisions*, Palo Alto, CA: Pavan Publishers, 1976, p. 265.

SUMMARY

We have used credit management to illustrate LDA in solving management problems. It takes little imagination to envision the potential of LDA in evaluating selection procedures for new employees, or in assessing the effectiveness of the firm's forecasting techniques, or in forecasting bankruptcies, and so on. One must only be able to define success and failure, assign to them a quantitative value, and identify the explanatory variables accounting for success and failure. However, since the topic emanates from the subject matter of correlation analysis, the manager can pose the same questions he would if confronted with the results of any correlation analysis:

1. Is the relationship between the variables linear or nonlinear? LDA need not suppose a linear relationship. A nonlinear relationship might result in a better classification.
2. Would the addition of other explanatory variables add to the accuracy of classification?
3. Are the parameters—α, β_1, β_2, . . ., β_n—periodically updated?
4. How much confidence can be placed in the credit scores yielded by the regression equation?
5. How is the system modified as between large and small accounts?
6. Is the system applied mechanistically or are the firm's salesman asked for inputs in marginal cases?
7. If the firm is introducing a new product, management may wish to lower cutoff scores to facilitate sales of the innovation.
8. Similarly, during a downturn in the business cycle, the firm may choose to loosen credit standards on marginal accounts rather than face the certain losses of idle plant and facilities.

By this time, the reader may assert that, by using explanatory variables to classify people, organizations, and techniques based upon historical experience, LDA really does predict the future. The response must be in the affirmative. Nowhere is this predictive function more palpable than in the use of financial ratios spanning a number of fiscal years to forecast the ultimate ability of a firm to pay its maturing debts or to collapse into bankruptcy. Moreover, when such a model is used by creditors and financial institutions in deciding to extend or withdraw credit, the prediction can become a self-fulfilling prophecy. The withdrawal of credit may in itself precipitate the bankruptcy.

SECTION VII
Another Approach

chapter 11

Nonparametric Statistics

The statistical methods employed in our previous chapters are termed parametric techniques. Parametric methods involve underlying assumptions about the population studied, usually that sample observations are drawn randomly from large populations and, therefore, the sampling distributions are normally shaped. Sample observations from such populations, accordingly, were tested against the values on Table 5-14 to identify the parameters or characteristics of the particular population in which the businessman evinced interest; for example, sales, variable costs, cash flows, and the like.

The assumption of "normalcy," the reader will agree, should not be applied universally to business and economic data. True, the beta advocates in portfolio management assert that changes in stock market prices occur randomly and are normally distributed. The sales of certain products and samplings of production runs for quality control may show a similar randomness. On the other hand, the bulk of business-oriented data are more likely to be shaped by seasonal, cyclical, and trend factors, management decisions, consumer attitudes, and so on. There are techniques in parametric statistics for addressing this problem but it remains as a troublesome factor in the utilization of statistical methods in business decision making.

Not so with nonparametric techniques. As the term implies, non-parametrics does not make restrictive assumptions concerning the sampling distribution. Normalcy is not presumed. Freed of this inhibiting condition, nonparametric methodologies relate to a wide range of business situations and are easier to understand and to apply. They involve *rank* and *order* rather than numerical values. Hence, they afford a handy tool where the manager has very little sample information on the population or when the information available to him classifies observations by description rather than quantitatively.

Since we are departing from the conventional use of numerical values, it is convenient to look at the different types of measurement scales.

TYPES OF MEASUREMENT SCALES

Categorical Scales

Such scales use numbers only to indicate to which class or category an observation belongs. For example, in Chapter 10, on Linear Discriminant Analysis, good risks were given an arbitrary value of 1 and bad risks, a value of 0.

Ordinal Scales

These rank observations according to their relative importance. Ordinal values tell us whether something is more than or less than without specifying by how much. Thus, a survey may ask participants to rank competing products as their first choice, second choice, and so on. Employees may be asked to rank certain aspects of their work environment by a preference order. Ordinal rankings reflect subjective reactions not susceptible to direct, quantitative measurement.

Interval Scales

Here, numbers gain added significance. Interval scales use numbers to show both order and difference between two or more series. A scale or series has a unique zero point and method of defining an interval of change. Differences between scale values can be expressed as multiples of one another.

The familiar scales for temperature are interval scales. Hence, 100°C is 100% warmer than 50°C; 75°F is 50% warmer than 50°F.

Ratio Scales

In order to establish the ratio of two measurements, the ratio scale requires the calculation of a natural zero point. We could not say, for example, that the difference between 50°C and 25°F represents a 2:1 ratio. The scales lack a common zero point. However, we observe that

$$°F = (9/5)°C + 32 \qquad (11\text{-}1)$$

It now becomes feasible to calculate ratios between the two series if we first convert 50°C to the Fahrenheit scale:

$$°F = (9/5)(50°) + 32° = 122° \qquad (11\text{-}2)$$

Then the ratio of 122°F (50°C) to 25°F is 4.88:1.

Nonparametric techniques are suitable for categorical and ordinal measurements. They can also be adapted to interval and ratio scale measurements where the distribution of the population is unknown or not specified for the analysis. However, when nonparametric methods are applied in situations where parametric techniques could be used, they suffer some disadvantages. The use of ordering or ranking as opposed to the actual numerical values of the observations results in the loss of a certain amount of information. For example in testing for significance at the 5 percent level, the probability of a Type II error would be greater for the nonparametric test than for the parametric test. On the other hand, the nonparametric tests may instill greater confidence because they are not dependent on restrictive assumptions that may be wholly unrealistic in the given situation. Nevertheless, if the assumptions of parametric statistics fit the characteristics of the population under study, the use of numerical values in the observations will yield superior results to those achieved by nonparametric techniques.

THE SIGN TEST

The sign test is an example of one nonparametric method. The test depends not on quantitative magnitudes but on the signs (positive or negative) of observed differences in ranking.

Suppose a panel of 100 automotive engineers is asked to evaluate two prototypes of new designs, A and B, that are to be marketed as passenger vehicles. Each engineer ranks the two prototypes on a scale of 1 (for best) to 5 (for worst). The engineers are to consider the appropriateness of the two designs for family use. Table 11-1 records their scores.

The immediate response suggests adoption of design B. But are the rank scores significantly different? Refer back to the discussion on the null hypothesis (Chapter 7). In this case, we can take the null hypothesis to mean that plus and minus signs are equally likely in the rankings so that the tabulation should produce an approximately equal distribution of signs. In short, with an equal number of plus and minus signs, the rankings are not significantly different. If a large number of one or the other sign comes up, the null hypothesis would be rejected.

If p is the assumed probability of obtaining a plus sign, then the null hypothesis is stated as:

$$H_0: p = 0.50 \text{ (Null Hypothesis)}$$
$$H_1: p \neq 0.50 \text{ (Alternative Hypothesis)} \tag{11-3}$$

Where p is the proportion of positive signs and q, the proportion of negative signs, the mean of the sampling distribution (μ_p) is expressed:

$$\mu_p = p = 0.50; \quad q = (1 - p) = (1 - 0.50) = 0.50$$

Table 11-1   Rank Scores Assigned to Two New Designs[a]

1 Engineering Panel	2 Design A Ranking	3 Design B Ranking	4 Sign of Difference (+ = B; − = A)
A	4	1	+
B	3	2	+
C	3	3	0 (tie score)
D	1	4	−
E	2	3	−
F	4	1	+
G	3	2	+
H	2	1	+
I	1	2	−
J	3	2	+

and so on, for 100 engineers

Summary of Results
for 100 Engineers

+ scores	60
− scores	30
ties	10
Total	100

[a] *Source:* hypothetical data.

and the standard deviation (excluding tie rankings):

$$\sigma_{\bar{p}} = \sqrt{\frac{pq}{N}} = \sqrt{\frac{(0.50)(0.50)}{90}} = 0.0527 \qquad (11\text{-}4)$$

The actual sample data from the engineers gives the proportion of plus signs ($\bar{p}$) as 60/90 = 0.667. Therefore,

$$Z = \frac{\bar{p} - p}{\sigma_{\bar{p}}} = \frac{0.667 - 0.50}{0.0527} = 3.169 \qquad (11\text{-}5)$$

Performing the test of significance at the 5 percent probability level, we would reject the null hypothesis when the Z value is less than -1.96 or more than $+1.96$. Since the actual value of Z equals $+3.169$, the null hypothesis is rejected. The conclusion that the engineers prefer design B stands.

Some observations on the Sign Test are appropriate:

1. Although the company obviously could have evaluated the two designs on the basis of engineering data, it solicited the subjective reactions of engineers to the designs as general passenger vehicles. It thereby substituted ordinal values for numerical values.

2. The parameters of the population were not available or specified prior to the sample. The test did not require the underlying population of pluses and minuses to be normally distributed.
3. The test is simple and direct.
4. The method is obviously germane to situations where management seeks employee reactions to new personnel programs, market research into customer opinions, and so on.

MATCHED PAIRS SIGNED TEST

The sign test recorded the differences between matched pairs of observations without attempting to quantify the disparities except by the designation of plus or minus. The matched pairs signed test, on the other hand, measures the magnitude of the differences between pairs of observations. The distinction is useful when the paired observations can be numerically measured and then ranked.

For example, assume that after introduction of a new automotive transmission, the number of warranty transmission claims in ten major cities changes as in Table 11-2.

The actual quantitative differences in transmission claims between the old and new products are given in column 4 of Table 11-2. These differences are first ranked without regard to sign in column 5 (with ties assigned a ranking halfway between the rank for which they are tied and the following rank). In column 6, the rankings are assigned plus or minus values, depending on the original difference. Finally, the ranks are summed for each plus–minus distribution.

Again, at first glance, the sample data would give credence to the assertion that the new transmission had succeeded in reducing warranty claims. Claims declined from 775 to 755. The statistician, on the other hand, will interpose the question of whether the differences in rankings are significant. The null hypothesis, in this instance, presumes the samples reflect identical population distributions: $H_0: \Sigma(+) = \Sigma(-)$. That is, the positive and negative differences are symmetrical about a mean of 0. The test statistic is the smaller of the two rank summations: $\Sigma(+) = 11.5$ from Table 11-2. With a small sample (excluding ties, $N - 1 = 10 - 1 = 9$), the critical values of T are given in Table 11-3.

Table 11-3 should be read as follows: for nine matched pairs, at the 5 percent significance level for a two tailed test, $T \leq 5$. These values, however, are maximum values for T. Up to the T value, the test statistic is significant and the null hypothesis is rejected. Above the T value, the null hypothesis is accepted. In the illustration the test statistic exceeds the T value, that is, $11.5 > 5$, and the null hypothesis is accepted. The introduction of the new transmission had no significant impact on warranty claims.

Table 11-2 Matched Pairs Signed Test: Warranty Transmission Claims[a]

1 Cities	2 Old Transmission	3 New Transmission	4 (3 − 2) Difference (d)	5 Rank[b]	6 Signed Rank Rank(+)	6 Signed Rank Rank(−)
A	80	77	−3	4.5		−4.5
B	92	70	−22	9		−9
C	90	110	+20	8	+8	
D	73	73	0	0	0	0
E	80	72	−8	7		−7
F	65	62	−3	4.5		−4.5
G	60	61	+1	1	+1	
H	62	64	+2	2.5	+2.5	
I	83	78	−5	6		−6
J	90	88	−2	2.5		−2.5
	Total 775	755			$\Sigma(+) = 11.5$	$\Sigma(-) = 33.5$

[a] *Source:* hypothetical data.
[b] In ascending order, based on size of difference (ignoring sign). Identical differences are both assigned rank halfway between that and following rank (that is, tie for second rank becomes 2.5).

Table 11-3   Critical Values[a] of T: Wilcoxon Matched-Pairs Signed-Ranks Test[b]

	Level of Significance for One-Tailed Test					Level of Significance for One-Tailed Test			
	0.05	0.025	0.01	0.005		0.05	0.025	0.01	0.005
	Level of Significance for Two-Tailed Test					Level of Significance for Two-Tailed Test			
N	0.10	0.05	0.02	0.01	N	0.10	0.05	0.02	0.01
5	0	—	—	—	28	130	116	101	91
6	2	0	—	—	29	140	126	110	100
7	3	2	0	—	30	151	137	120	109
8	5	3	1	0	31	163	147	130	118
9	8	5	3	1	32	175	159	140	128
10	10	8	5	3	33	187	170	151	138
11	13	10	7	5	34	200	182	162	148
12	17	13	9	7	35	213	195	173	159
13	21	17	12	9	36	227	208	185	171
14	25	21	15	12	37	241	221	198	182
15	30	25	19	15	38	256	235	211	194
16	35	29	23	19	39	271	249	224	207
17	41	34	27	23	40	286	264	238	220
18	47	40	32	27	41	302	279	252	233
19	53	46	37	32	42	319	294	266	247
20	60	52	43	37	43	336	310	281	261
21	67	58	49	42	44	353	327	296	276
22	75	65	55	48	45	371	343	312	291
23	83	73	62	54	46	389	361	328	307
24	91	81	69	61	47	407	378	345	322
25	100	89	76	68	48	426	396	362	339
26	110	98	84	75	49	446	415	379	355
27	119	107	92	83	50	466	434	397	373

[a] The T value denotes the smaller sum of the ranks for differences of the same sign. For any given number of ranked differences, the computed value of T is significant if it is equal to or less than the table value.

[b] Source: A. J. Hughes and E. E. Grawoig, Statistics: A Foundation for Analysis. Reading, MA: Addison-Wesley Publishing Co., 1971.

With respect to Table 11-3, recall that the parametric t test for paired observations assumed a normal distribution for the underlying population of differences. Table 11-3, listing the T values for paired observations by rank, makes no assumption concerning the shape of the underlying population. Likewise, whereas Chapter 9 described correlation analysis using parametric techniques, nonparametric techniques also permit the calculation of a correlation coefficient using the rankings of two variables in lieu of their actual values (see Table 11-4).

Table 11-4   Rank Correlation Coefficient[a]

1 Income Per Household (X)	2 Rank (X)	3 Number of Households Per 1000 Riding Public Transport (Y)	4 Rank (Y)	5 Difference in Ranks (d)	6 d²
$10,044	1	41.0	9	−8	64
$10,048	2	31.4	5	−3	9
$10,085	3	34.0	8	−5	25
$13,560	6	31.6	6	0	0
$13,470	5	29.5	4	1	1
$14,650	7	27.8	1	6	36
$16,330	9	29.1	3	6	36
$14,940	8	28.5	2	6	36
$12,380	4	33.0	7	−3	9
					$\Sigma d^2 = \overline{216}$

[a] *Source:* hypothetical data.

The coefficient of rank correlation is derived from

$$R = 1 - \frac{6\Sigma d^2}{N(N^2 - 1)} \tag{11-6}$$

where: R = the coefficient of rank correlation
d = difference in ranks $(X - Y)$
d^2 = square of rank differences
N = number of paired observations
N^2 = square of number of paired observations

Hence,

$$R = 1 - \frac{6(216)}{9(81 - 1)}$$

$$R = 1 - \frac{1296}{720} \tag{11-7}$$

$$= 1 - 1.80$$

$$= -0.80$$

The coefficient of rank correlation may vary from $+1$ to -1, the same range as the coefficient of correlation. A plus one indicates perfect direct correlation, the two variables being ranked exactly the same way and $d^2 = 0$. A minus one indicates a perfect inverse correlation, the two variables being ranked perfectly opposite. As a rule, a positive value in the rank correlation coefficient indicates more agreement in the rankings than disagreement. The closer the coefficient is to plus one or minus one the stronger the agreement; proximity to zero signifies weak agreement.

Actual numerical values may be ranked (the example in Table 11-4) or the rankings may reflect the opinions of individuals on two variables of interest to management. The rankings may be made from lowest to highest or highest to lowest. Either way will not change the coefficient of rank correlation.

The significance of the coefficient of rank correlation can be tested in the usual manner. Testing the results of Table 11-4, the null hypothesis would state that $R = 0$ and no correlation in the ranked data exists. The t statistic is used:

$$t = \frac{R}{\sqrt{(1 - R^2)/(N - 2)}}$$
$$= \frac{-0.80}{\sqrt{(1 - 0.64)/(9 - 2)}} \qquad (11\text{-}8)$$
$$= \frac{-0.80}{0.227}$$
$$= -3.524$$

Referring to the t distribution (Table 5-15) and testing significance at the 5 percent level, for 7 degrees of freedom ($N - 2 = 9 - 2$) the t value is 2.365. Note that the test statistic is the critical t less than 0 and the critical t greater than 0. If the calculated t falls between the critical t's—in this case, -2.365 to $+2.365$—H_0 is accepted. If the calculated t is less than the critical t left or more than the critical t right, H_0 is rejected. Since the calculated t statistic is less than the table value ($-3.524 < -2.365$), we reject the null hypothesis and conclude that the coefficient of rank correlation is significant—that a positive correlation exists between the two variables. At the 5 percent level, we have a 95 percent probability of being correct in this judgment, that is, that the coefficient of rank correlation is *significantly greater than zero*.

Another illustration will suffice to demonstrate the utility of rank correlation in a business setting. Suppose a firm wishes three supervisors to rank five employees in terms of initiative. The supervisors rankings are given in Table 11-5.

How might the firm determine the correlation between the ranks assigned by the supervisors? Correlations between the three possible pairings of supervisors are first obtained (Tables 11-6–11-8).

In summary, the supervisors' coefficients of rank correlation are:

Supervisor 1 and 2	$+0.875$
Supervisor 1 and 3	$+0.825$
Supervisor 2 and 3	$+0.900$

Table 11-5   Supervisors' Rankings of Employees' Initiative[a]

Employee	Supervisor's 1 Ranking	Supervisor's 2 Ranking	Supervisor's 3 Ranking
A	3.5	4	4
B	1	2	2
C	2	1	1
D	3.5	3	4
E	5	5	4

[a] *Source:* hypothetical data.

Are they significantly different from zero? Is the null hypothesis ($R = 0$) correct at the 5 percent level? Applying equation (11-8) successively, we have

$$t = \frac{0.875}{\sqrt{[1 - (0.875^2)]/(5 - 2)}} = 3.13$$

$$t = \frac{0.825}{\sqrt{[1 - (0.825^2)]/(5 - 2)}} = 2.528$$

$$t = \frac{0.90}{\sqrt{[1 - (0.90^2)]/(5 - 2)}} = 3.577$$

Table 11-6   Supervisor's 1 and 2 Rankings; Coefficient of Rank Correlation[a]

1 Employee	2 Supervisor 1	3 Supervisor 2	4 (2 − 3) d	5 d²
A	3.5	4	−0.5	0.25
B	1	2	−1.0	1.00
C	2	1	+1.0	1.00
D	3.5	3	+0.5	0.25
E	5	5	0.0	0.00
				$\Sigma d^2 = 2.50$

$$R = 1 - \frac{6\Sigma d^2}{N(N^2 - 1)}$$

$$= 1 - \frac{6(2.50)}{5(5^2 - 1)}$$

$$= 1 - \frac{15}{120}$$

$$= 1 - 0.125$$

$$= +0.875$$

[a] *Source:* hypothetical data.

Table 11-7 Supervisor's 1 and 3 Rankings; Coefficient of Rank Correlation[a]

1 Employee	2 Supervisor 1	3 Supervisor 3	4 (2 − 3) d	5 d^2
A	3.5	4	−0.5	0.25
B	1	2	−1.0	1.00
C	2	1	+1.0	1.00
D	3.5	4	−0.5	0.25
E	5	4	+1.0	1.00
				$\Sigma d^2 = \overline{3.50}$

$$R = 1 - \frac{6(3.50)}{5\,(5^2 - 1)}$$

$$= 1 - \frac{21}{120}$$

$$= 1 - 0.175$$

$$= +0.825$$

[a] *Source:* hypothetical data.

From the t distribution (Table 5-15) the t value corresponding to 3 degrees of freedom ($N - 2 = 5 - 2$) is 3.182. Thus only the coefficient of rank correlation for the rankings of supervisors 2 and 3 is significantly greater than zero. For the paired rankings of supervisor 1 with super-

Table 11-8 Supervisor's 2 and 3 Rankings; Coefficient of Rank Correlation[a]

1 Employee	2 Supervisor 2	3 Supervisor 3	4 (2 − 3) d	5 d^2
A	4	4	0	0
B	2	2	0	0
C	1	1	0	0
D	3	4	−1	1
E	5	4	+1	1
				$\Sigma d^2 = \overline{2}$

$$R = 1 - \frac{6(2)}{5\,(5^2 - 1)}$$

$$= 1 - \frac{12}{120}$$

$$= 1 - 0.10$$

$$= +0.90$$

[a] *Source:* hypothetical data.

visors 2 and 3, the null hypothesis is accepted. For these rankings, the null hypothesis states the coefficient of rank correlation is de facto zero, not significantly greater than zero. The apparent consensus of opinion is open to question. However, since supervisors 2 and 3 are in closest agreement, the firm might accept the majority rule as the basis for a decision. Both 2 and 3 agree that employee C displays the greatest initiative.

CHI-SQUARED TEST FOR INDEPENDENCE

In the chapter on probabilities much emphasis was placed on the distinction between independent and dependent variables. We had to classify variables as independent or dependent in order to calculate the individual or joint probabilities. In business forecasting, the researcher seeks explanatory relationships between dependent and independent variables. Market research is similarly interested in the issue of independence. The chi-squared distribution test for independence is tailored to determine whether two variables are related or whether they are independent. The variables can be measured using categorical scales, ordinal scales, interval scales, or ratio scales. Moreover, no assumption is made regarding the underlying population, whether it is normal or otherwise. This places the chi-square test in the purview of nonparametric statistics.

Chi-square utilizes the familiar contingency table. In Chapter 4, a contingency table was used to illustrate types of probabilities (reproduced here as Table 11-9).

The chi-squared test modifies the contingency table by calculating the expected frequency for each cell. The expected frequency for each cell is found by multiplying the relevant row total by the relevent column total and dividing that product by the sum total of all events. For example,

$$\frac{(55)\ (100)}{185} = 29.73$$

for the 15% yield cell. Table 11-10 is the modified contingency table.

Table 11-9 Contingency Table[a]

Boeing \ General Motors	Yields 15%	Yields 25%	Total Events
15%	30	70	100
25%	25	60	85
Total Events	55	130	185

[a] *Source:* hypothetical data.

Table 11-10   Chi-Square Contingency Table [a]

General Motors Boeing	Yields 15%	Yields 25%	Total Events
15%	30/29.73	70/70.27	100
25%	25/25.27	60/59.73	85
Total Events	55	130	185

[a] *Source:* hypothetical data.

If we determine the expected frequency for a given cell, the expected frequency for the remaining cell in the same row is the difference between the calculated expected frequency and the row total, that is, $55 - 29.73 = 25.27$. Generally, as the expected and observed frequencies gravitate closer, the independence of the variables is confirmed.

Thus, the computed value of chi-squared statistic is

$$\text{Chi-square} = \sum_{i=1}^{n} \frac{[F_i - E(F_i)]^2}{F_i} \tag{11-9}$$

where: F_i = the observed frequencies in a given cell (i)
$E(F_i)$ = the expected frequencies in a given cell (i)
N = number of cells in contingency table

Hence,

$$\text{Chi-Square} = \frac{(30 - 29.73)^2}{29.73} + \frac{(25 - 25.27)^2}{25.27}$$
$$+ \frac{(70 - 70.27)^2}{70.27} + \frac{(60 - 59.73)^2}{59.73} \tag{11-10}$$
$$= 0.00245 + 0.00288 + 0.00104 + 0.00122$$
$$= 0.0076$$

The computed value of Chi-Square must be compared against the Table of Chi-Square Values (Table 11-11) according to the degrees of freedom. The degree of freedom equals the number of rows in the contingency table minus one times the number of columns minus one. In the contingency table above, there are two columns and two rows. Therefore, the degree of freedom equals $(2 - 1) \times (2 - 1) = 1$. From Table 11-11, for one degree of freedom, the Chi-Square value is 3.841 at the 5 percent level of significance. If the computed Chi-Square statistic is less than the table value, the variables are independent. For our illustration, the two variables—the separate yields on General Motors and Boeing common stock—are patently independent.

Table 11-11   Chi-Square Distribution[a]
(Selected Numbers)

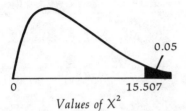

Values of X^2

Example In a chi-square distribution with $v = 8$ degrees of freedom, the area to the right of a chi-square value of 15.507 is 0.05.

Degrees of Freedom v	Area in Right Tail				
	0.20	0.10	0.05	0.02	0.01
1	1.642	2.706	3.841	5.412	6.635
2	3.219	4.605	5.991	7.824	9.210
3	4.642	6.251	7.815	9.837	11.345
4	5.989	7.779	9.488	11.668	13.277
5	7.289	9.236	11.070	13.388	15.086
6	8.558	10.645	12.592	15.033	16.812
7	9.803	12.017	14.067	16.622	18.475
8	11.030	13.362	15.507	18.168	20.090
9	12.242	14.684	16.919	19.679	21.666
10	13.442	15.987	18.307	21.161	23.209

[a] If the computed value of Chi-Square is less than the critical value in the table (the white area under the curve), then the two variables are independent. If the computed Chi-Square exceeds the critical value on the table (the shaded area under the curve), then a relationship exists between the variables.

Source: Fisher and Yates: *Statistical Tables for Biological, Agricultural and Medical Research,* published by Oliver and Boyd Ltd. Edinburgh, (selected numbers and illustration from Table IV).

SUMMARY

The field of nonparametrics has other similar techniques to offer; however, the basic concept does not change. Most are easier to use and understand than comparable parametric techniques. In addition, depending on the nature of the data analyzed, the advantages of nonparametrics can offset its disadvantages. What is lost in precision may be regained in added realism concerning the characteristics of the population studied.

Nonparametrics are especially useful in assessing attitudes of personnel and customers in situations where subjective reactions are important. Since the leadership role is an essential function of management, subjective reactions to company decisions may be more important than inputs on prices, cost, interest rates, and the like. How much of output per manhour depends on worker attitudes as opposed to capital investment per worker? Whatever, the manager should not fall into the trap of considering nonparametrically derived information as "soft data" and parametric analysis as hard data. On the other hand, if presented with nonparametric data, he should carefully explore the quality of the results:

1. Which nonparametric technique was used?
2. Which measuring scale was employed?
3. Were the results statistically significant? Was hypothesis testing applied before acceptance or rejection of sample values?

Recall that in our illustrations there appeared in two cases an apparent concensus in the rankings that did not stand up under testing. Generally, we are testing the assertion that no correlation exists in the rankings (null hypothesis) and any apparent correlation is not significantly greater than zero. Without testing in this manner, the manager may set policy using spurious information.

SECTION VIII

The Computer and Quantitative Analysis for Business Decisions

chapter 12

The Computer and Managerial Statistics

The statistical models discussed in the preceding chapters have been programmed for quick calculation by computer. In addition, the models frequently are combined with other formulations to facilitate decision making in complex situations. Referred to as "Software Packages," service firms market a wide variety of programs covering topics in the major functions of business—finance and accounting, production, marketing, and personnel management. Elsewhere in the chapter, we shall refer to some leading software suppliers and their programs which incorporate statistical models.

This chapter does not focus on the internal operations of digital computers or their recordkeeping capacities. We view the computer simply as a calculator that will accept a large number of instructions at one time. The set of instructions that constitutes a detailed description of the job to be performed is called a *program*. A program must be prepared in a form acceptable to the computer such as *punched cards, magnetic tape, console typewriter,* or *magnetic disk*. The value of the computer output depends upon the validity the statistical model put into the program format and the quality of the data base.

Computerization does not diminish management responsibility. Quite the opposite. It adds another dimension to management. Not every manager has formal training in accounting, for example, but it would be a rare manager who could not comprehend the financial statements of his firm. Similarly, although managers need not qualify as programmers or statisticians they should understand the process sufficiently to interpret the results and avoid pitfalls. Computers do not make decisions. Similar to the accounting system, the information revolution spawned by computers raises the level of debate and narrows the area of uncertainty. Yet decision making involves more than information—management's experience, judgment, and objectives are crucial.

TYPES OF PROGRAMS

Among the programs pertinent to business problems, not all enjoy equal acceptance. In some instances, the level of sophistication may inhibit across-the-board usage; other types of programs require further refinement; still others may be too costly for widespread implementation. Here, we shall concentrate only on those programs that have gained a respectable level of recognition within the business community.

Linear Programming (LP)

The LP model is the most widely known and used program in business. Roccaferrera offers two definitions of LP, one from the perspective of the economist and one from the mathematician:

> An economist may define linear programming as a method for allocating a group of limited resources in a manner which satisfies a certain group of competing demands under known and fixed limitations.
> A mathematician may be more technical in defining linear programming by saying that it is a process of solving specific problems in which an objective function must be maximized or minimized, considering a set of definitive restrictions and limited resources.[1]

Requirements of Linear Programming

Whatever definition you prefer, business applications of LP and its variations require the fulfillment of certain basic requirements:
An Objective Function. The LP solution seeks to *maximize* or *minimize* a defined variable. A number of examples illustrate the notion:

1. In capital budgeting, which combination of projects will *maximize* the net present value (NPV) of the investment or the rate of return on the investment?
2. In inventory management, what size inventory will *minimize* the carrying charges of inventory and concurrently service the needs of customers?
3. Where two or more product lines are manufactured, what is the product mix that will *optimize* profits?

[1] Giuseppe M. Ferrero di Roccaferrera, *Operation Research Models for Business and Industry*, Cincinnati: South-Western Publishing Co., 1964, p. 296.

4. In liquidity management, what is the optimum cash investment to *minimize* the loss of income from holding cash?
5. In managing long-term debt, what is the appropriate refunding
   sequence to *minimize* the cost of debt over some time frame.

Quantitative Measurement. The relationship among the elements in
the objective function must be described in quantitative terms: dollars,
units of output, weights, time, and so on.
Alternate Choice. It must be possible to choose among the elements of
the objective function in order to maximize or minimize the defined
variable.
Linear Relationships. The relationship between the elements of
the problem—within the objective function and accompanying
constraints—must be linear. See the discussion of simple linear correlation in Chapter 9. If all changes in one variable (X) result in changes in
another variable (Y) such that the Y values plot as a straight line, a
linear relationship exists between X and Y. The linear relationship requires no more than first-degree equations: $Y_c = \alpha + \beta(X)$.[2]

Assumptions of Linear Programming

The requirements of LP applications derive from the assumptions of
the methodology:

1. The objective function and constraints are expressed in linear
   equations.
2. The parameters of the problem in the objective function and
   constraints are specified and not subject to variation. The pris-
   tine LP model assumes certainty.
3. All decision variables must be stated in positive values. Non-
   negative values are ruled out.
4. A single objective function is maximized or minimized.
5. The LP model assumes continuous rather than discrete variables. The data are divisible into fractions and choice is not
   confined to units of zero or one.
6. Resources to be allocated are homogeneous or qualitatively
   equal. No qualitative differences exist between each hour of
   work or quantity of materials.
7. The linear assumption implies proportionality. For example,
   increasing (or decreasing) the number of direct labor hours ex-
   pended on a given product results in a stated proportionate increase (or decrease) in output.

[2] Giuseppe M. Ferrero di Roccaferrera, *Operation Research Models for Business
and Industry*, Cincinnati: South-Western Publishing Co., 1964, pp. 296–300.

8. Changes in production methods, economies of scale, and the like do not affect the parameters set forth in the model.
9. The system is additive: the total resources utilized equals the sum of the resources used by each activity.
10. LP elements are independent. Variables, resources, and operations do not interact with each other.[3]

Obviously, the realities of business activity do not always match the assumptions of the LP formulation. This does not rule out the usefulness of LP for the decision maker. The issue is one of degree. Judgment alone can assess whether departures from assumptions are so substantive as to make useless the employment of LP in particular business situations. Short of this borderline, LP can contribute approximate answers to complex problems and/or help focus on the preferred solution.

LP Formulation

Assume a firm produces AM and FM/AM radio sets. Each AM radio costs $0.50 in wages and $0.50 in materials and sells at $3 per set. Each AM/FM radio incurs $2.50 in wages and $1.50 in materials. These sell at $7. The contribution margin (excess of incremental revenues over incremental costs or the contribution to fixed costs and/or profit) for AM sets is $2 per unit and $3 per unit for AM/FM sets. The firm can sell all that it can produce at the market prices designated. The firm has $30 in working capital and 20 hours of machine time. Each AM radio requires 3 hours of machine time. Each AM/FM set requires 2 hours of machine time. *What combination of AM and AM/FM sets will maximize the contribution margin?*

Objective Function **(Z).** The element to be maximized (Z) is defined:

$$\text{Max } Z = C_1(X_1) + C_2(X_2) \tag{12-1}$$

where: C_1 = unit contribution margin on AM sets
X_1 = number of AM units
C_2 = unit contribution margin on AM/FM sets
X_2 = number of AM/FM sets

Therefore,

$$\text{Max } Z = \$2(X_1) + \$3(X_2)$$

Constraints or Restrictions. The contribution margin is to be maximized within the limitations set by working capital ($30) and available

[3] John J. Clark, Thomas J. Hindelang, and Robert E. Pritchard, *Capital Budgeting,* New York: American Institute of Certified Public Accountants, Inc., 1979, p. 220.

machine time (20 hours). The nonnegativity assumption imposes a further constraint. These constraints are expressed as follows:

$3(X_1) + 2(X_2) \leq 20$ (available machine time)
$\$1(X_1) + \$4(X_2) \leq \$30$ (available working capital compared to   (12-2)
    variable unit production costs of \$1 for
    AM sets and \$4 for AM/FM sets.)
$X_i \geq 0$, where $i = 1, 2$ (nonnegativity condition;
    X values must be positive numbers)

Observe the constraints take the form of inequalities (less than or equal to/more than or equal to). The maximum solution may not exceed the constraints or restrictions placed upon the objective function.

What the Computer Does

The simple problem in our illustration can be solved graphically or by use of a pocket calculator using the simplex method. However, the problem was solved in a few minutes using the Apple III computer and a program written in Basic Language. The Apple III is a micro, or firm-specific, computer for the resolution of particular management problems.

The inequalities of the constraints are converted into equalities by the introduction of slack variables (S). The new variable (S) is added (or subtracted) to each inequality to absorb the difference (positive or negative) between the left and right sides of the inequality and so convert it to an equality. Thus, slack variables may be plus or minus. Introducing the *slack variables* into the constraints, we have:

$$3(X_1) + 2(X_2) + S_1 = 20$$
$$\$1(X_1) + \$4(X_2) + S_2 = \$30$$
(12-3)

To solve for the values of X_1 and X_2 that will satisfy the objective function, the computer goes through a series of iterative procedures in the form of tableaus starting from the original matrix (Table 12-1).

Starting with the original matrix, the last column (termed, the *constant column*) shows the constraints on the objective function (the right-hand side of the inequalities 20 and \$30). In the last tableau (Iteration #2), the constant column contains the maximum value of Z and the values of X_1 and X_2. Hence, if the firm produces two AM units and seven AM/FM units, it will maximize the contribution margin at \$25.

$$\text{Max } Z = C_1(X_1) + C_2(X_2)$$
$$= \$2(2) + \$3(7)$$
$$= \$25 \text{ Maximum Contribution Margin}$$

Table 12-1   LP Problem One: Two Constraints

Max $Z = +2X_1 + 3X_2$
Subject to
$+3X_1 + 2X_2 \leq 20$
$+1X_1 + 4X_2 \leq 30$

$X_1 - X_2 \geq 0$

Original matrix

				Constant column	
− 2.000	− 3.000	+ 0.000	+ 0.000	+ 0.000	←—Index row
+ 3.000	+ 2.000	+ 1.000	+ 0.000	+20.000	
+ 1.000	+ 4.000	+ 0.000	+ 1.000	+30.000	

Constraint	Basic variable
1	3
2	4

Iteration #1

− 1.250	+ 0.000	+ 0.000	+ 0.750	+22.500
+ 2.500	+ 0.000	+ 1.000	− 0.500	+ 5.000
+ 0.250	+ 1.000	+ 0.000	+ 0.250	+ 7.500

Constraint	Basic variable
1	3
2	2

Iteration #2

				Constant column	
+ 0.000	+ 0.000	+ 0.500	+ 0.500	+25.000	←—Index row
+ 1.000	+ 0.000	+ 0.400	− 0.200	+ 2.000	
+ 0.000	+ 1.000	− 0.100	+ 0.300	+ 7.000	

Constraint	Basic variable
1	1
2	2

Optimal solution

The optimal value of Z is $Z^* = 25$
The *basic variables* are
Basic var, $X_1^* = 2$
Basic var, $X_2^* = 7$

All other variables = 0

The second and third rows of columns 1 and 2 contain the parameters of the constraint equations (3,2 and 1,4) in the original matrix. In the last tableau (Iteration #2), these values are replaced by $+1$, 0 and 0, $+1$ respectively. The shift is significant. The presence of $+1$ and 0 indicates that X_1 and X_2 are *basic variables*. A basic variable has a value of $+1$ in one of the rows and zeros elsewhere in the column for that variable. Plus one means the basic variable takes on the value in the same row of the last column (constant column): $X_1 = 2$ and $X_2 = 7$. The remaining variables, which do not have the $+1/0$ sequence, are nonbasic and have a zero value in the solution.

The second and third rows of column 3 and 4 are reserved for the slack variables (S_1 and S_2). In the original matrix, these are $+1$ and 0 for S_1 in the first constraint equation and 0 and $+1$ for S_2 in the second constraint. In the last iteration, the $+1/0$ sequence is replaced by other values signifying these are nonbasic variables. The constant column contains the computed values of each iteration.

The presence of negative values in the first two columns of the index row indicates the need for further iteration to achieve the objective function goal. The presence of zero values in the index row means the objective of the program has been achieved. Positive values show how much the contribution margin might decrease if one more unit of X_1 or X_2 were produced.

Negative numbers in columns 3 and 4 of the index row signify that while the objective function has been maximized *under the existing constraints* a change in the latter could improve the contribution margin. The situation encourages experimentation using *shadow prices* to assess the effects of changing the constraints. Shadow prices measure the amount by which the value of the objective function would increase if the constraints were lifted by one unit. For example, if the available machine time were increased by 1 hour, this would increase Z by $0.50; if available working capital were increased by $1, Z would also increase by $0.50. To put the matter another way, shadow prices show the maximum amount management would be willing to pay to acquire one additional unit of a resource or have a constraint relaxed by one additional unit. At some point, relaxation of constraints will cease to have an incremental effect on Z. At this point, the index row will read zero in all columns except the last column. This represents the *optimal solution*. No further improvement in the contribution margin is possible given the parameters in the objective function ($2 and $3) and the constraint inequalities (3 and 2; $1 and $4).

However, the decision maker can further probe the situation by sensitivity analysis. One approach asks the question how much can the original values (20 and $30) in the last columns change without changing the variables in the solution (2 and 7). Or in relation to the objec-

Table 12-2   LP Problem Two: Three Constraints

Max $Z = +2X_1 + 3X_2$
Subject to
$+1X_1 + 2X_2 \leq 6$
$+3X_1 + 2X_2 \leq 20$
$+1X_1 + 4X_2 \leq 30$

$X_1 - X_2 \geq 0$

Original matrix

					Constant column	
− 2.000	− 3.000	+ 0.000	+ 0.000	+ 0.000	+ 0.000 ←	Index
+ 1.000	+ 2.000	+ 1.000	+ 0.000	+ 0.000	+ 6.000	row
+ 3.000	+ 2.000	+ 0.000	+ 1.000	+ 0.000	+20.000	
+ 1.000	+ 4.000	+ 0.000	+ 0.000	+ 1.000	+30.000	

Constraint	Basic variable
1	3
2	4
3	5

Iteration #1

− 0.500	+ 0.000	+ 1.500	+ 0.000	+ 0.000	+ 9.000
+ 0.500	+ 1.000	+ 0.500	+ 0.000	+ 0.000	+ 3.000
+ 2.000	+ 0.000	− 1.000	+ 1.000	+ 0.000	+14.000
− 1.000	+ 0.000	− 2.000	+ 0.000	+ 1.000	+18.000

Constraint	Basic variable
1	2
2	4
3	5

Iteration #2

					Constant column	
+ 0.000	+ 1.000	+ 2.000	+ 0.000	+ 0.000	+12.000 ←	Index
+ 1.000	+ 2.000	+ 1.000	+ 0.000	+ 0.000	+ 6.000	row
+ 0.000	− 4.000	− 3.000	+ 1.000	+ 0.000	+ 2.000	
+ 0.000	+ 2.000	− 1.000	+ 0.000	+ 1.000	+24.000	

Constraint	Basic variable
1	1
2	4
3	5

230

Table 12-2 (*Continued*)

Optimal solution

The optimal value of Z is $Z^* = 12$
The *basic variables* are
Basic var, $X_1^* = 6$
Basic var, $S_2^* = 2$
Basic var, $S_3^* = 24$

All other variables $= 0$

---

tive function, how much might the coefficients ($2 and $3) increase or decrease without affecting the solution ($25).

LP Formulation: Three-Constraint Problems

Let us add another constraint to the problem above. Each AM radio costs $0.50 in wages and $0.50 in materials and sells at $3 per set. Each AM/FM radio incurs $2.50 in wages and $1.50 in materials. These sell at $7. The contribution margin for AM sets is $2 per unit and $3 for AM/FM sets. The firm can sell all that it can produce at the market prices designated. The firm has $30 in working capital, 20 hours of machine time, and 6 hours of assembly time. Each AM radio requires 3 hours of machine time and 1 hour of assembly time. Each AM/FM set requires 2 hours of machine time and 2 hours of assembly time. *What combination of AM/FM sets will maximize the contribution margin?*

Objective Function (Z). From Expression (12-1),

$$\text{Max } Z = \$2(X_1) + \$3(X_2)$$

Constraints

$$1(X_1) + 2(X_2) \leq 6 \text{ (Available assembly time)}$$
$$3(X_1) + 2(X_2) \leq 20 \text{ (Available machine time)}$$
$$\$1(X_1) + \$4(X_2) \leq \$30 \text{ (Available working capital)} \quad (12\text{-}4)$$
$$X_i \geq 0, \quad \text{where } i = 1, 2, \ldots \text{ (Nonnegativity assumption)}$$

Slack Variables

$$1(X_1) + 2(X_2) + S_1 = 6$$
$$3(X_1) + 2(X_2) + S_2 = 20 \quad (12\text{-}5)$$
$$\$1(X_1) + \$4(X_2) + S_3 = \$30$$

Computer Solution. Table 12-2 reproduces the iterations leading to the maximum value of Z (the contribution margin) given the imposed constraints. Substituting into equation (12-1),

$$\text{Max } Z = C_1(X_1) + C_2(X_2)$$
$$\$12 = \$2(6) + \$3(0) \tag{12-6}$$

The best the firm might do, given the constraints, is to produce six AM units and no AM/FM sets. This can be established by taking the *basic variables* in the computer printout ($X_1 = 6$, $S_2 = 2$, and $S_3 = 24$) and substituting them into equation (12-5):

$$1(6) + 2(0) + 0 = 6$$
$$3(6) + 2(0) + 2 = 20 \tag{12-7}$$
$$\$1(6) + \$4(0) + 24 = \$30$$

The solution, while best for the circumstances, appears hardly satisfactory. The presence of a positive value in column 2 of the index row tells us that manufacturing one unit of X_2 violates a constraint and/or reduces the contribution margin. Assembly time is obviously the bottleneck. Production of one unit of X_2 would cause assembly time consumed to exceed the 6 hour constraint. To stay within the assembly time constraint and produce one unit of X_2 would require the sacrifice of two units of X_1. In terms of the contribution margin, two units of X_1 equals one unit of X_2. But the trade-off would leave unused machine time of 6 hours. Moreover, the maximum solution also leaves management with $24 of excess working capital. Whatever the technical problem the solution raises questions about the efficient use of resources.

Three Variables and Four Constraints

Assume the following balance sheet for Titanic Manufacturing, Inc.:

Assets		Liabilities and Equity	
Cash	$300	Notes Payable:	
Accounts receivables	$100	Bank A	$120
Plant and equipment	$400	Bank B	$ 80
		Bonds payable	$500
		Net worth	$100
	$800		$800

Titanic produces three products:

	Machine Time	Assembly Time
Sonar set (X_1)	5 hours	8 hours
Loran set (X_2)	4 hours	2 hours
VHF radios (X_3)	6 hours	4 hours

Titanic has 200 hours of machine time available and 120 hours of assembly time. The contribution margin by product line is

	X_1 Sonar Set	X_2 Loran Set	X_3 VHF Radio
Selling price	$22	$6	$10
Variable manufacturing cost	$20	$2	$ 4
Contribution margin	$ 2	$4	$ 6

The company also pays out $40 in overhead charges. The loan at Bank B must be paid immediately but the loan at Bank A can be renewed. A licensing agreement prohibits the production of more than 10 units of X_2 and/or X_3. What combination of outputs will maximize the contribution margin?

Objective Function

$$\text{Max } Z = \$2(X_1) + \$4(X_2) + \$6(X_3) \qquad (12\text{-}8)$$

Constraints

$$
\begin{aligned}
5(X_1) + 4(X_2) + 6(X_3) &\leq 200 \text{ (Capacity constraint)} \\
8(X_1) + 2(X_2) + 4(X_3) &\leq 120 \text{ (Capacity constraint)} \\
(X_2) + (X_3) &\leq 10 \text{ (Legal constraint)} \qquad (12\text{-}9) \\
20(X_1) + 2(X_2) + 4(X_3) &\leq 160 \text{ (Financial constraint)} \\
X_i &\leq 0, \quad \text{where } i = 1, 2, \ldots \text{ (Nonnegativity constraint)}
\end{aligned}
$$

The financial constraint is calculated:

Gross working capital	$400
Less	
Payment of Bank B loan	80
Total	$320
Less	
Payment of overhead expense	40
Total	$280
Less	
Bank A liability	120
Net working capital	$160

Table 12-3 presents the LP solution. The firm will maximize its contribution margin by producing six units of X_1 (sonars) and ten units of X_3 (VHF sets):

$$
\begin{aligned}
\text{Max } Z &= \$2(X_1) + \$4(X_2) + \$6(X_3) \\
&= 2(6) + 4(0) + 6(10) \qquad (12\text{-}10) \\
&= \$72 \text{ (Maximum Contribution Margin).}
\end{aligned}
$$

Table 12-3 LP Problem Three: Four Constraints

Max $Z = +2X_1 + 4X_2 + 6X_3$
Subject to
$+5X_1 + 4X_2 + 6X_3 \le 200$
$+8X_1 + 2X_2 + 4X_3 \le 120$
$+0X_1 + 1X_2 + 1X_3 \le 10$
$+20X_1 + 2X_2 + 4X_3 \le 160$

$X_1 - X_3 \ge 0$

Original matrix

							Constant column
− 2.00	− 4.00	− 6.00	+ 0.00	+ 0.00	+ 0.00	+ 0.00	+ 0.00 ← Index row
+ 5.00	+ 4.00	+ 6.00	+ 1.00	+ 0.00	+ 0.00	+ 0.00	+200.00
+ 8.00	+ 2.00	+ 4.00	+ 0.00	+ 1.00	+ 0.00	+ 0.00	+120.00
+ 0.00	+ 1.00	+ 1.00	+ 0.00	+ 0.00	+ 1.00	+ 0.00	+ 10.00
+ 20.00	+ 2.00	+ 4.00	+ 0.00	+ 0.00	+ 0.00	+ 1.00	+160.00

Constraint	Basic variable
1	4
2	5
3	6
4	7

Iteration #1

							Constant column
− 2.00	+ 2.00	+ 0.00	+ 0.00	+ 0.00	+ 6.00	+ 0.00	+ 60.00
+ 5.00	− 2.00	+ 0.00	+ 1.00	+ 0.00	− 6.00	+ 0.00	+140.00
+ 8.00	− 2.00	+ 0.00	+ 0.00	+ 1.00	− 4.00	+ 0.00	+ 80.00
+ 0.00	+ 1.00	+ 1.00	+ 0.00	+ 0.00	+ 1.00	+ 0.00	+ 10.00
+ 20.00	− 2.00	+ 0.00	+ 0.00	+ 0.00	− 4.00	+ 1.00	+120.00

Constraint	Basic variable
1	4
2	5
3	3
4	7

Iteration #2

							Constant column
+ 0.00	+ 1.80	+ 0.00	+ 0.00	+ 0.00	+ 5.60	+ 0.10	+ 72.00
+ 0.00	− 1.50	+ 1.00	+ 0.00	− 5.00	− 0.25		+110.00
+ 0.00	− 1.20	+ 0.00	+ 1.00	+ 0.00	− 2.40	− 0.40	+ 32.00
+ 0.00	+ 1.00	+ 0.00	+ 0.00	+ 1.00	+ 0.00		+ 10.00
+ 1.00	− 0.10	+ 0.00	+ 0.00	− 0.20	+ 0.05		+ 6.00

← Index row

Constraint	Basic variable
1	4
2	5
3	3
4	1

Optimal solution

The optimal value of Z is $Z^* = 72$
The basic variables are

Basic var, $S_1^* = 110$
Basic var, $S_2^* = 32$
Basic var, $X_3^* = 10$
Basic var, $X_1^* = 6$

All other variables = 0

235

Looking at the constraints,

$$
\begin{aligned}
5(X_1) + 4(X_2) + 6(X_3) &\leq 200 \ \text{(Capacity} \\
5(6) \ + 4(0) \ + 6(10) &= \ \ 90 \ \text{constraint)}
\end{aligned}\Bigg\}
$$

$$
\begin{aligned}
8(X_1) + 2(X_2) + 4(X_3) &\leq 120 \ \text{(Capacity} \\
8(6) \ + 2(0) \ + 4(10) &= \ \ 88 \ \text{constraint)}
\end{aligned}\Bigg\}
$$

$$
\begin{aligned}
(X_2) + \ \ (X_3) &\leq \ \ 10 \ \text{(Legal con-} \\
(0) \ + \ \ (10) &= \ \ 10 \ \text{straint)}
\end{aligned}\Bigg\}
$$

$$
\begin{aligned}
\$20(X_1) + \$2(X_2) + \$4(X_3) &\leq \ \ 160 \ \text{(Financial} \\
\$20(6) \ + \$2(0) \ + \$4(10) &= \$160 \ \text{constraint)}
\end{aligned}\Bigg\}
$$

(12-11)

Titanic obviously suffers from excess capacity. Increased output would improve the profit picture. While the licensing agreement limits the production of Loran and/or VHF sets, since no Loran sets are to be produced, the presence of excess capacity would suggest the financial constraint is the actual restriction on profitability. Each dollar increase in the financial constraint would increase profits by $0.10.

Titanic should conduct a sensitivity analysis by gradually raising the financial constraint and determining the increment in the contribution margin. At the point where the increment in the contribution margin equals the incremental cost of new financing, the optimal output combination is reached.

Integer Programming (IP)

The LP cases discussed assume the decision variable is continuous. For capital budgeting problems, however, the continuity assumption complicates the solution. Capital projects, with few exceptions, are indivisible; that is, we must take all of the project or reject it. We cannot accept slices of a capital project as we would purchase shares of stock. IP, on the other hand, imposes a 0–1 choice as a constraint on the selection of projects, $X_i = 0$ or 1 $(i = 1, 2, \ldots)$. Subject to this 0–1 constraint along with such other constraints that might be imposed, the objective function in IP asks the following questions: What is the combination of capital projects that will maximize NPV or the rate of return on investment? Which projects should be accepted and which rejected?

However, discarding the continuity assumption of the LP model places certain limitations on integer programming. IP does not provide a useful set of shadow prices or marginal values since the marginality concept loses meaning in face of discontinuous decision variables. Small increments to the available budgetary amounts have no effect on the optimum portfolio combination until another preferred set of integer values becomes feasible.

Suppose a firm has the following capital projects under consideration:

Project	NPV	Investment	Accounting Rate of Return
1	$ 17	$ 100	0.10
2	$ 20	$ 200	0.20
3	$ 4	$ 50	0.40
4	$138	$1,000	0.35
5	$120	$ 900	0.45
6	$ 27	$ 400	0.30
7	$150	$1,100	0.43
		$3,750	

Management, however, has a limit on the funds available for investment of $2,500 and requires a minimum accounting rate of return of 30 percent. What is the best combination of projects to maximize NPV subject to the imposed restrictions?

Using integer programming, the objective function is

$$\text{Max } Z = 17(X_1) + 20(X_2) + 4(X_3) + 138(X_4)$$
$$+ 120(X_5) + 27(X_6) + 150(X_7) \tag{12-12}$$

and the constraints are

$$100(X_1) + 200(X_2) + 50(X_3) + 1000(X_4) + 900(X_5) + 400(X_6)$$
$$+ 1,100(X_7) \leq \$2,500 \text{ (Capital constraint)}$$
$$0.10(X_1) + 0.20(X_2) + 0.40(X_3) + 0.35(X_4) + 0.45(X_5) \tag{12-13}$$
$$+ 0.30(X_6) + 0.43(X_7) \geq 0.30 \text{ (Rate of return constraint)}$$
$$X_i = [0, 1] \text{ (0 or 1 requirement)}$$

The optimal solution subject to the imposed restrictions under 0–1 integer programming is

Project	NPV	Investment	Accounting Rate of Return
4	$138	$1,000	0.35
6	$ 27	$ 400	0.30
7	$150	$1,100	0.43
	$315	$2,500	0.36

Accepting projects 4, 6, and 7 will maximize NPV and exceed the minimum accounting rate of return.

Goal Programming (GP)

Where a large number of elements enter into a decision or a large number of capital projects are up for selection, LP and IP allow simultaneous consideration of many variables. However, they are limited by their unidimensional objective function that maximizes or minimizes a single criterion as NPV, profit, cost, and so forth. Business decisions do not usually depend on a single criterion. Market and financial managers may have aims other than the maximization of NPV; under certain conditions in the capital markets, a maximized NPV may not improve shareholder wealth. Other conflicting objectives in the short run could include acceptance of losses to penetrate new markets, need to maintain target growth rates, stability of accounting earnings, and desire to reduce the payback period of a capital budget.

The attraction of GP is its ability to evaluate simultaneously a hierarchy of objectives and determine the penalties or gains of achieving one objective at the cost of deviating from other goals. A hierarchy of multiple objectives is incorporated in the program and the objective function strives to minimize the deviations from the several goals sought according to a priority ranking scheme. In effect, GP takes the constraints of the LP model and elevates them to the rank of objectives or goals varying in degree of importance.

Management specifies the hierarchy of goals and assigns weights according to the importance of each goal. The goals may involve conflicting objectives, with under- or overachievement of a goal being penalized, so that the decision maker seeks to come as close as possible to a desired target(s). Thus, some slack variables in GP represent deviations from the stated goals and determine the value of the objective function according to the priority structure established.

By way of comparison, between LP and GP, assume a company has two divisible projects, X and Y, under consideration. Fifteen manhours are available to manage the projects; each unit of X absorbs 3 manhours and each unit of Y, 1 manhour. Management stipulates a minimum accounting profit of $16 or better; each unit of X will yield a $10 accounting profit; each unit of Y, $6. Management has $300 available for investment; each unit of X will absorb $50 and Y, $100. Subject to these constraints, the firm wishes to maximize NPV: each unit of X has an NPV of $10 and Y, $8. However, a minimum NPV of $75 is desired.

LP Formulation

Objective Function

$$\text{Max NPV} = \$10X + \$8Y \tag{12-14}$$

Constraints

$$3X + 1Y \le 15 \text{ (manhours)}$$
$$\$50X + \$100Y \le \$300 \text{ (capital constraint)} \tag{12-15}$$
$$\$10X + \$6Y \ge \$16 \text{ (accounting profit)}$$

GP Formulation

The following goals are immediately distinguishable:

to *minimize* the manhour requirements within the limit of 15;
to *maximize* the accounting profit with a minimum requirement of
$16;
to *minimize* capital investment with a limit set at $300; and
to *maximize* NPV with a minimum requirement of $75.

Objective Function

$$\text{Min } P_1 d_1^+ + P_2 d_2^- + P_3 d_3^+ + P_4 d_4^- \tag{12-16}$$

Constraints

$$
\begin{aligned}
3X + 1Y + d_1^+ &= 15 \text{ (manhours)} \\
10X + 6Y + d_2^- &= 16 \text{ (accounting profit)} \\
50X + 100Y + d_3^+ &= 300 \text{ (capital constraint)} \\
10X + 8Y + d_4^- &= 75 \text{ (NPV)} \\
X, Y, d_1^+, d_2^-, d_3^+, d_4^- &\geq 0
\end{aligned}
\tag{12-17}
$$

where: d_1^+ and d_3^+ = upside deviations from goals 1 and 3
d_2^- and d_4^- = downside deviations from goals 2 and 4
P_1, P_2, P_3, and P_4 = priority coefficients in the function (values assigned by management)
all d values are non-negative numbers

The GP objective function provides a solution that will minimize the deviations among the multiple goals. In this respect, the program can be run with different sets of priorities (P_is) to spotlight the trade-offs among goals. *After the insertion of the priority values, the formulation can be run as a typical LP program.* Let us assume that management assigns the following values to priority coefficients in the objective function: $P_4 = 4$, $P_3 = 3$; $P_2 = 1$, and $P_1 = 2$.

Table 12-4 presents the standard LP solution[1] to the problem:

$$
\begin{aligned}
\text{Max NPV} &= 10X_1 + 8Y \\
&= 10(4.8) + 8(0.6) \\
&= 52.8
\end{aligned}
\tag{12-18}
$$

and for the constraint:

$$
\left.
\begin{aligned}
3X + 1Y &\leq 15 \text{ (manhours constraints)} \\
3(4.8) + 1(0.6) &= 15
\end{aligned}
\right\}
$$

$$
\left.
\begin{aligned}
\$50X + \$100Y &\leq \$300 \text{ (capital constraint)} \\
\$50(4.8) + \$100(0.6) &= \$300 \\
\$10X + \$6Y &\geq \$16 \text{ (accounting profit)} \\
\$10(4.8) + 6(0.6) &= \$51.6
\end{aligned}
\right\}
\tag{12-19}
$$

All constraints are satisfied.

[1] Project Y in Table 12-4 is designated X_2.

Table 12-4 LP Formulation Preliminary to Goal Programming

Max $Z = +10X_1 + 8X_2$
Subject to
$+3X_1 + 1X_2 \leq 15$
$+50X_1 + 100X_2 \leq 300$
$+10X_1 + 6X_2 \geq 16$

$X_1 - X_2 \geq 0$

Original matrix

− 10.00	− 8.00	+ 0.00	+ 0.00	+ 0.00	+ 1.00	+ 0.00
+ 3.00	+ 1.00	+ 1.00	+ 0.00	+ 0.00	+ 0.00	+ 15.00
+ 50.00	+100.00	+ 0.00	+ 1.00	+ 0.00	+ 0.00	+300.00
+ 10.00	+ 6.00	+ 0.00	+ 0.00	− 1.00	+ 1.00	+ 16.00
+ 0.00	+ 0.00	+ 0.00	+ 0.00	+ 0.00	+ 1.00	+ 0.00

Constraint	Basic variable
1	3
2	4
3	6

Modified original matrix

− 10.00	− 8.00	+ 0.00	+ 0.00	+ 0.00	+ 1.00	+ 0.00
+ 3.00	+ 1.00	+ 1.00	+ 0.00	+ 0.00	+ 0.00	+ 15.00
+ 50.00	+100.00	+ 0.00	+ 1.00	+ 0.00	+ 0.00	+300.00
+ 10.00	+ 6.00	+ 0.00	+ 0.00	− 1.00	+ 1.00	+ 16.00
− 10.00	− 6.00	+ 0.00	+ 0.00	+ 1.00	+ 0.00	− 16.00

Constraint	Basic variable
1	3
2	4
3	6

Iteration #1

+ 0.00	− 2.00	+ 0.00	+ 0.00	− 1.00	+ 2.00	+ 16.00
+ 0.00	− 0.80	+ 1.00	+ 0.00	+ 0.30	− 0.30	+ 10.20
+ 0.00	+ 70.00	+ 0.00	+ 1.00	+ 5.00	− 5.00	+220.00
+ 1.00	+ 0.60	+ 0.00	+ 0.00	− 0.10	+ 0.10	+ 1.60
+ 0.00	+ 0.00	+ 0.00	+ 0.00	− 0.00	+ 1.00	+ 0.00

Constraint	Basic variable
1	3
2	4
3	1

Table 12-4 (*Continued*)

Iteration #2

+ 3.33	+ 0.00	+ 0.00	+ 0.00	− 1.33	+ 2.33	+ 21.33
+ 1.33	+ 0.00	+ 1.00	+ 0.00	+ 0.17	− 0.17	+ 12.33
−116.67	+ 0.00	+ 0.00	+ 1.00	+ 16.67	− 16.67	+ 33.33
+ 1.67	+ 1.00	+ 0.00	+ 0.00	− 0.17	+ 0.17	+ 2.67

Constraint	Basic variable
1	3
2	4
3	2

Iteration #3

− 6.000	+ 0.000	+ 0.000	+ 0.080	+ 0.000	+ 1.000	+24.000
+ 2.500	+ 0.000	+ 1.000	− 0.010	+ 0.000	+ 0.000	+12.000
− 7.000	+ 0.000	+ 0.000	+ 0.060	+ 1.000	− 1.000	+ 2.000
+ 0.500	+ 1.000	+ 0.000	+ 0.010	+ 0.000	+ 0.000	+ 3.000

Constraint	Basic variable
1	3
2	5
3	2

Iteration #4

+ 0.000	+ 0.000	+ 2.400	+ 0.056	+ 0.000	+ 1.000	+52.800
+ 1.000	+ 0.000	+ 0.400	− 0.004	+ 0.000	+ 0.000	+ 4.800
+ 0.000	+ 0.000	+ 2.800	+ 0.032	+ 1.000	− 1.000	+35.600
+ 0.000	+ 1.000	− 0.200	+ 0.012	+ 0.000	+ 0.000	+ 0.600

Constraint	Basic variable
1	1
2	5
3	2

Optimal solution

The optimal value of Z is $Z^* = 52.8$
The basic variables are
Basic var, $X_1^* = 4.8$
Basic var, $S_3^* = 35.6$
Basic var, $X_2^* = 0.6$

All other variables = 0

Given the priorities assigned to the goals, the solution, which would minimize the deviations from the goals, suggested that if the amount available for investment *were increased by* $170, 4.0665 units of X and 2.667 units of Y should be accepted. This would raise the accounting profit to $56.67 and NPV to $62. The manpower constraint approximates the budgeting allocation of 15. In short, the GP format presented to management an optimal set of trade-offs among the stated goals and priorities.

The reader will observe the initial presentation took the form of an LP program. After conversion to GP format, we had modified the objective function from "Max NPV" to "Min $P_1 d_1^+$," and so on, but still subject to constraints. Thus the computer ran the problem as an LP program. This

Table 12-5   Arithmetic Mean and Related Measures

```
WAIT..
READY
TAPE

READY
900 DATA 184.90,197.65,205.47,209.05,212.44,212.95,214.13,
901 DATA 215.50,188.13,199.35,206.49,209.55,211.75,213.16,
902 DATA 214.50,216.20,190.34,201.05,206.83,210.07,2122←.27,
903 DATA 213.63,214.83,216.35,192.04,202.53,208.00,210.25,
904 DATA 212.44,213.63,214.83,216.40,194.42,204.11,209.04,
905 DATA 210.74,212.44,213.99,215.34,216.86
KEY

READY
RUN

STAT01      18:18      CEIR

NUMBER      SUM          SUM-OF-SQUARES      MEAN        VARIANCE
   40       8323.65           1.73488E  6    208.091     71.7182

STD. DEV.    STD. ERROR OF THE MEAN      COEFF. OF VARIATION
 8.46866           1.33901                        4.06969E-2

OUT OF DATA LINE #294

RUNNING TIME: 00.8 SECS

READY
BYE
OFF AT 18:19
```

is because both IP and GP are variations of the basic LP approach, obtained in each case by relaxing one of the LP assumptions. Other more sophisticated programs have been similarly formulated by relaxing a particular assumption underlying LP. These lie beyond the scope of our introductory efforts.

Finally, for the record, it took 97 seconds to run the first LP formulation and the GP revision.

COMING FULL CYCLE

We began the discussion of managerial statistics with the topic of averages. Along the way such concepts as the mean, the standard deviation, variance, standard error of the mean, and coefficient of variation were introduced. Even using a pocket calculator to calculate these measures would cut into your work day. Now let us assume the following data and a few seconds to spare:

Data Table

184.90	206.49	212.27	214.83
197.65	209.55	213.63	216.40
205.47	211.75	214.83	194.42
209.05	213.16	216.35	204.11
212.44	214.50	192.04	209.04
212.95	216.20	202.53	210.74
214.13	190.34	208.00	212.44
215.50	201.05	210.25	213.99
188.13	206.83	212.44	215.34
199.35	210.07	213.63	216.86

Table 12-5 represents the computer printout of the statistical measures noted in the preceding paragraph. Note the running time.

Table 12-6   Frequency Distribution[a]

Class Interval (Five Units)	Frequency (F)	Class Midpoint
180–184.99	1	182.49
185–189.99	1	187.49
190–194.99	3	192.49
195–199.99	2	197.49
200–204.99	3	202.49
205–209.99	7	207.49
210–214.99	17	212.49
215–219.99	6	217.49
	40	

[a] *Source:* hypothetical data.

Table 12-6 places the same data in the frequency distribution format.

Suppose the data in Table 12-6 were fed to the computer with a request for the arithmetic mean, median, geometric mean, harmonic mean, and sundry measures of absolute and relative dispersion. Table 12-7 represents the printout.

Table 12-7   Measures of Central Tendency and Dispersion

```
PROBLEM NAME: STATFR***
WAIT..
READY
900 DATA 8,5,0
901 DATA 1,1,4,2,2,7,17,6
902 DATA 182.49,187.49,192.49,197.49,202.49,207.49,212.49,217.49
RUN


STATFR      18:35     CEIR


SUM OF FREQUENCIES=                                        40
MEASURES OF CENTRAL TENDENCY
          ARITHMETIC MEAN=                                207.74
          MEDIAN=                                         210.872
          GEOMETRIC MEAN=                                 207.541
          HARMONIC MEAN=                                  207.334


MEASURES OF ABSOLUTE VARIATION, SKEWNESS, AND KURTOSIS
          STANDARD DEVIATION=                             8.94078
          VARIANCE=                                       79.9375
          SKEWNESS=                                       −841.219
          KURTOSIS=                                       21936.2


MEASURES OF RELATIVE VARIATION, SKEWNESS, AND KURTOSIS
          COEFFICIENT OF VARIATION                        4.30383
          BETA 1=                                         1.38537
          ALPHA 3=                                        1.17702
          BETA 2 OR ALPHA 4=                              4.29448E-2


TEST OF SIG. DIFF. BETW. S-MEAN AND POP. MEAN
          STANDARD ERROR OR MEAN=                         1.43167

RUNNING TIME: 01.8 SECS

READY
BYE
OFF AT 18:37
```

SUMMARY

The various formulations in mathematical programming obviously constitute a powerful tool in decision making for the manager with a basic understanding of the concepts involved. The manager who can interpret the computer printout and who knows the capabilities of the type of program involved not only has a recommended solution before him but also the opportunity to test in what ways that solution could be improved upon.

The manager need not be a programmer any more than he need be a statistician. But he should be able to work knowledgeably with both by defining his objective(s) and the restrictions in the way of achieving that objective(s). When he receives the printout, he can then pose fundamental questions regarding the solution:

1. What type of program was employed? A linear or nonlinear program? A Zero–One Integer Program? A Goal Program?
2. What are the elements making up the objective function? Does the relationship among these elements satisfy the assumptions of the program employed?
3. Is the objective specified a maximization or minimization function?
4. Have all the constraints on the objective function been identified and accurately defined?
5. Can the identified solution be improved by lifting one or more of the constraints? If so, will the cost of lifting a constraint be overbalanced by improvement in the objective function solution?
6. What are the constraints that constitute bottlenecks to the improvement in the solution?
7. Can the program be transformed from a single objective function to one allowing for the influence of other goals? If goal programming is feasible, what additional objectives enter the picture and what trade-offs among the goals can be made to serve the wider interests of the firm?

This chapter has provided a brief introduction to various programming models to alert managers of the potentials in mathematical programming for decision making. No longer are these tools the exclusive province of large corporations with the resources to support extensive computer installations. The advent of minicomputers and timesharing offers comparable techniques to medium and small business. It is hoped that the reader will build upon this overview by pursuing the selected references in the bibliography and by exploring the innovations in hardware and software coming on to the market. Apropos of the latter, Commodore Business Machines has published a *Commodore Software Encyclopedia*, "listing most of the software offerings known to Commodore as of this printing" (1981). Another valuable source of information on hardware and software is *Infosystems*, published monthly by Hitchcock Publishing Company. Datapro publishes extensive directories on software, updated monthly, which provide "uniformly written software product profiles" to assist the user in selecting the most effective software applications pertinent to the firm's needs. Sentry Database Publishing, publishers of *Software News*, conducts an information service to bring "together buyers and sellers of computer software." Many of these organizations maintain a consulting service to handle specific business problems.

bibliography

General Statistics and Managerial Statistics

The following readings represent a stepped up discussion of the topics included in our introductory volume.

Brabb, E. F., and Livingston, E. J., A Decision Analysis Approach to Business Statistics, *Decision Sciences*, Vol. 7, No. 3, July 1976, pp. 538–546.

Bradley, J. V., *Distribution-Free Statistical Tests*, Englewood Cliffs, NJ: Prentice-Hall, Inc., 1968.

Campbell, Stephen K., *Flaws and Fallacies in Statistical Thinking*, Englewood Cliffs, NJ: Prentice-Hall, Inc., 1974.

Chatterjee, Sambit, and Price, Bertram, *Regression Analysis by Example*, New York: John Wiley and Sons, 1977.

Chou, Ya-Lun, *Statistical Analysis with Business and Economic Applications*, New York: Holt, Rinehart and Winston, Inc., 1975.

Cochran, William G., *Sampling Techniques*, 3rd ed., New York: John Wiley and Sons, Inc., 1977.

Crask, M. R., and Perreault, W. D., Jr., Validation of Discriminant Analysis in Marketing Research, *Journal of Marketing Research*, Vol. 14, No. 1, Feb. 1977, pp. 60–68.

Ekeblad, Frederick A., *The Statistical Method, Applications of Probability and Inference to Business and Other Problems*, New York: John Wiley and Sons, Inc., 1962.

Gibbons, J. D., *Nonparametric Statistical Inference*, New York: McGraw-Hill Book Co., 1971.

Hamburg, Morris, *Statistical Analysis for Decision Making*, 2nd ed., New York: Harcourt Brace Jovanovich, Inc., 1977.

Heinze, David, *Fundamentals of Managerial Statistics*, Cincinnati: South-Western Publishing Co., 1980.

Kraft, C. H., and van Eeden, C., *A Nonparametric Introduction to Statistics*, New York: Macmillan Publishing Co., 1968.

Mansfield, Edwin, *Managerial Economics and Operations Research,* New York: W. W. Norton & Co., 1980.

Mason, Robert D., *Statistical Techniques in Business and Economics,* 3rd ed., Homewood, IL: Richard D. Irwin, Inc., 1982.

Mills, Frederick C., *Statistical Methods,* New York: Holt, Rinehart and Winston, 1955.

Moroney, M. G., *Facts from Figures,* Baltimore, MD: Penguin Books, Inc., 1951.

Newton, Byron, *Statistics for Business,* Chicago, IL: Science Research Associates, Inc., 1963.

Noether, G. E., *Elements of Nonparametric Statistics,* New York: John Wiley & Sons, Inc., 1967.

Pfaffenberger, Roger C., and Patterson, James H., *Statistical Methods for Business and Economics,* Homewood, Il: Richard D. Irwin, Inc., 1981.

Savage, Leonard J., *The Foundation of Statistics,* New York: John Wiley and Sons, Inc., 1954.

Schlaifer, Robert, *Probability and Statistics for Business Decisions,* NY: McGraw-Hill Book Co., Inc., 1959.

Schutte, Jerald G., *Everything You Always Wanted to Know About Statistics but Were Afraid to Ask,* Englewood Cliffs, NJ: Prentice-Hall, Inc., 1977.

Spurr, William A., and Bonini, Charles P., *Statistical Analysis for Business Decisions,* Homewood IL: Richard D. Irwin, 1973.

Stockton, John R., and Clark, Charles T., *Introduction to Business and Economic Statistics,* Cincinnati: South-Western Publishing Co., 1980.

Tanur, Judith M., *Statistics: A Guide to the Unknown,* San Francisco: Holden-Day, Inc., 1976.

Weaver, Warren, *Lady Luck, the Theory of Probability,* New York: Doubleday & Co., Inc., 1963.

Some Special Applications of Managerial Statistics

The readings below deal with particular business operations employing statistical techniques. The list is only illustrative, not definitive.

Altman, Edward I., Financial Ratios, Discriminant Analysis and the Prediction of Corporate Bankruptcy, *Journal of Finance,* Vol. 23, Sept. 1968, pp. 589–609.

Arens, Alvin A., and Loebbecke, James K., *Applications of Statistical Sampling to Auditing,* Englewood Cliffs, NJ: Prentice-Hall, 1981.

Beaver, William H., Market Prices, Financial Ratios, and the Prediction of Failure, *Journal of Accounting Research,* Vol. 6, Autumn 1968, pp. 179–192.

Butler, William F., and Kavesh, Robert A., *How Business Economists Forecast,* 3rd ed., Englewood Cliffs, NJ: Prentice-Hall, Inc., 1966.

Clark, John J., Clark, Margaret T., and Elgers, Pieter T., *Financial Management: A Capital Market Approach*, Boston: Holbrook Press, Inc., 1976.

Clark, John J., Elgers, Pieter, and Hindelang, Thomas, *Statistics for Accountants*, New York, American Institute of Certified Public Accountants, Inc., 1979.

Clark, John J., Hindelang, Thomas J., and Pritchard, Robert E., *Capital Budgeting*, Englewood Cliffs, NJ: Prentice-Hall, Inc., 1979.

Clark, John J., and Speagle, Richard E., *Publishing Financial Forecasts: Benefits, Alternatives, Risks*, Philadelphia: Laventhol and Horwath, 1974.

Deakin, Edward B., A Discriminant Analysis of Predictions of Business Failure, *Journal of Accounting Research*, Vol. 10, Spring 1972, pp. 167–179.

Dun & Bradstreet, Inc., *Ten Keys to Basic Credits and Collections*, New York: 1973.

Eisenbeis, Robert A., Pitfalls in the Application of Discriminant Analysis in Business Finance and Economics, *Journal of Finance*, Vol. 32, June, 1977, pp. 875–900.

Ernst and Whinney, *Audit Sampling*, New York: 1980.

Grant, Eugene L., *Statistical Quality Control*, 4th ed., New York: McGraw-Hill Book Co., Inc., 1972.

Hassan, Nabil, Marquette, R. Penny, and McKeon, Joseph M., Jr., Sensitivity Analysis: An Accounting Tool for Decision-Making, *Management Accounting*, Vol. 59, No. 10, April 1978, pp. 43–50.

Lewellen, Wilbur G., and Edmister, Robert O., A General Model for Accounts Receivable Analysis and Control, *Journal of Financial and Quantitative Analysis*, Vol. 8, March 1973, pp. 195–206.

Liddell, R. S., The Computer in Practice, *Accountancy % London*, Vol. 86, No. 980, April 1975, p. 60.

Mao, James C. T., *Corporate Financial Decisions*, Palo Alto, CA: Pavan Publishers, 1976.

Mehta, Dileep R., *Working Capital Management*, Englewood Cliffs, NJ: Prentice-Hall, Inc., 1974, Chaps. 1–3.

Monroe, Kent B., and Della-Bitta, Albert J., Models for Pricing Decisions, *Journal of Marketing Research*, Vol. 12, No. 3, Aug. 1978, pp. 413–428.

Monroe, Kent B., and Della-Bitta, Albert J., *Reviewing Financial Forecasts*, New York: American Institute of Certified Public Accountants, 1980.

United States Department of Commerce, *Statistical Abstract of the United States* (Annually).

Wheelwright, Steven C., and Spyros, Makridakis, *Forecasting Methods for Management*, 3rd ed., New York: John Wiley and Sons, 1980.

Computers and Managerial Statistics

Listed below are some software bureaus and articles and/or books that address the particular significance of computers in the work of managerial statistics.

Broaddus, Alfred, Linear Programming: A New Approach to Bank Portfolio Management, *Monthly Review*, Federal Reserve Bank of Richmond, November, 1972.
Buckley, William M., Adapting to Computer Age Sends Executives to School, *The Wall Street Journal*, February 23, 1981.

Case, Howard, Managing the Data Center, *Data Management*, Vol. 13, No. 10, Oct. 1974, pp. 21–25.
Clark, John J., Elgers, Pieter, and Hindelang, Thomas, *Programming for Accountants*, New York: American Institute of Certified Public Accountants, 1979.
Commodore Software Encyclopedia, Commodore Business Machines, Inc., 681 Moore Rd. King of Prussia, PA 19406.

Datapro, Datapro Research Corp., 1805 Underwood Blvd., Delran, NJ 08075.
Davis, Gordon B., *An Introduction to Electronic Computers*, New York: McGraw-Hill Book Co., 1965.
Di Roccaferrara, Giuseppe M. Ferrero, *Operations Research Models for Business and Industry*, Cincinnati: South-Western Publishing Co., 1964.

Infosystems, Hitchcock Publishing Co., Hitchcock Bldg., Wheaton, IL 80187.

Jacobs, Sanford L., Experts Say Computerization Raises Risk of Embezzlement, *The Wall Street Journal*, February 23, 1981.

Moskowitz, Howard R., Computer Modeling Can Help Develop New Consumer Products Faster, Cheaper, *Marketing News*, Vol. 14, No. 12, Dec. 12, 1980, p. 8.

Schleef, Harold J., Using Linear Programming for Planning Life Insurance Purchases, *Decision Sciences*, (July 1980) pp. 522–534.
Seamans, Lyman H., Jr., "Increasing Productivity with Computers," *The Personnel Administrator*, Vol. 20, No. 3, May, 1975, pp. 44–46.
Software News, Sentry Database Publishing, 5 Kane Industrial Dr., Hudson, MA 01749.

Taylor, Bernard W. III, and Anderson, Paul F., Goal Programming Approach to Marketing/Production Planning, *Industrial Marketing Management*, Vol. 8, No. 2, April 1979, pp. 136–144.

glossary

arithmetic average, or mean the sum of all the values in a series divided by the total number of values.

averages measures of central tendency where values cluster to typify the series.

coefficient of correlation (R) a relative measure of the relationship between two variables, showing the degree of association between the dependent and independent variables expressed as a percentage.

coefficient of determination (R)^2 the percentage of the total variation in the dependent which is explained by the independent variable.

coefficient of variation a relative measure of dispersion that shows for absolute values, the standard deviation as a percent of the arithmetic mean.

computer program a set of instructions detailing the job to be performed, and prepared in a form acceptable to the computer. There are different types of programs, such as linear, goal, and integer programming.

conditional probability the probability of one event occurring, given that another related event has occurred.

continuous variable a variable that can assume an infinite number of values.

correlation concerns the strength of the association between a dependent (or explained variable) and one or more independent (explanatory variables).

cyclical fluctuations in time series, a wavelike fluctuation about the trend which may vary in length and amplitude from one cycle to another.

discrete variable a variable that can assume only a specified finite number of values.

expected value the weighted arithmetic mean of a random variable; in a probability distribution the weights are the respective probabilities of the values that the individual variables can assume.

frequency distribution or table division of the population into classes, recording the number of cases or frequencies that fall in each class of data.

geometric mean the Nth root of the product of all values in a series; alternately, the antilog of the arithmetic average of the logarithms of the values in the series.

harmonic mean the reciprocal of the average of the reciprocals of the individual values in a series (that is, each value divided into 1).

interval estimate the probability of a population parameter falling within a particular range of values.

irregular fluctuation in a time series, a completely unsystematic fluctuation, not part of the trend, cyclical, or seasonal components of the series.

joint probability the probability of events occurring simultaneously.

linear correlation the relationship between the dependent and indepen-

251

dent variables is described by a straight line or constant association.

linear programming a technique that seeks to maximize or minimize a defined variable, within certain specified constraints, where the relationship of the variables in the problem is linear.

linear regression a technique that shows to what extent the value of dependent variable is expected to change with a change of one unit in the inependent variable, shown by the slope of the straight line.

mean absolute deviation the average or typical deviation of all observations from the mean value, without considering plus or minus signs in deviations.

median the "centralmost," or middle, value in a series of data arrayed from the lowest to highest values.

mode the most probable value in a series, as it occurs or is repeated most frequently in a set of observations.

multicollinearity a situation existing when two or more independent variables are highly correlated.

multiple correlation deals with the relationship between one dependent and two or more independent variables.

negative correlation the dependent and independent variables move in opposite directions at the same rate or in a lead-lag relationship.

nonlinear correlation the relationship between variables is described by a line with one or two changes of direction, which may slope upward, reach a peak and slope downward.

null hypothesis (H_0) in statistical testing, the null hypothesis or statement assumes there is "no significant difference" between the value of population parameter being tested and the value of the statistic computed from the sample drawn from the population. When the null hypothesis is rejected, the alternate hypothesis is accepted.

partial correlation deals with the relationship between one of the indepen-

dent variables in multiple correlation and the dependent variable.

point estimate designates a single value to identify a population parameter.

population or universe represents the totality of data collected on a problem, which falls within the framework of the problem under study, from which sample information is drawn.

positive correlation the values of the dependent and independent variables tend to move together over time, either stepwise or with a lead-lag relationship.

probability distribution deals with all possible values of a random variable and their probability of occurrence. The various types of probability distributions are binomial, Poisson, hypergeometric, t or Student distribution, chi-square, and F distribution.

random variable a variable that takes on different numerical values due to chance or randomly.

sample a selected portion drawn from an entire population or universe from which inferences are made about that population.

seasonal variation in a time series a regular recurring pattern of fluctuations occurring for periods of less than one year.

second-degree polynomial a nonlinear secular trend (a curve) with one change of direction, either concave or convex to the origin.

secular trend in a time series, a long-term sweep of data, either growth or decline.

simple correlation concerns the association between one dependent and one independent variable.

simple random sample a sample drawn from a population where every item in the population has the same chance of being selected in the sample.

skewness tendency of a distribution to be nonsymmetrical. Skewness can be positive or negative where the averages are influenced to the right or left side of the distribution.

standard deviation gives the measure of dispersion of data from their mean in units of original data and is calculated as the square root of the variance.

time series consists of observations of a quantitative variable recorded over successive increments of time.

Type I error is rejection of the null hypothesis when it is correct.

Type II error accepting a false null hypothesis.

variance a measure of dispersion, calculated as the arithmetic mean of the squared deviation of the individual values about their mean.

Index

Addition rule, 62
Alternative hypothesis, 130, 207
Antilog, 17; *see also* Logarithms
Arithmetic average (mean), 11–13, 38, 251
  grouped data, 38
  ungrouped data, 9–11
    limitations, 11
    uses, 11
    weighted, 12, 38
Arithmetic straight line trend, 151–153
Associations, 169–190; *see also* Correlation
Autocorrelation, 186–187
Averages, 9–25, 251
  grouped data, 35–42
    computational, 38–40
    positional, 40–42
  ungrouped data, 9–25
    computational, 9–21
    positional, 21–25
Averaging time rates: *see* Harmonic mean

Bayesian Theory, 76–77
  posterior (revised) probabilities, 77
  prior probabilities, 77
Binomial distribution, 81–89
  assumptions, 81
  binomial coefficient, 82–83
  cumulative binomial distribution, 88
  mean, 89
  standard deviation, 89
  table of binomial probabilities, 85–87

Categorical scales, 206
Central Limit Theorem, 113, 124
Chi-square distribution (χ^2), 106–108, 216–218
  confidence interval for population variance, 106

Chi-square distribution (χ^2) (*cont.*)
  table of values, 107, 218
  test for independence, 216–217
Clark, John J., 226n
Cluster sampling, 115–116
Coefficient of
  correlation (R), 175, 182, 251
  determination (R^2), 176, 182–183, 251
  rank correlation, 212–214
  skewness, 50
  variation (V), 32, 251; *see also* Relative dispersion
Commodore Business Machines, 246
Commodore Software Encyclopedia, 246
Computers, 223–246
  programs, 223–243
    defined, 223
    goal programming, 237–243
    integer programming, 236–237
    linear programming, 224–236
  software, 223, 246
Computational averages, 38–40
  arithmetic mean, 10, 38
  geometric mean, 13, 39
  harmonic mean, 20, 39–40
Conditional probability, 60, 251
Conditional probability rule, 64
Confidence intervals (levels) for
  chi-square distribution, 106–108
  normal distribution, 99–104
  t distribution (Student's), 104–106
Continuous random variable, 104, 251
Correlation, 169–190
  advantages, 188
  disadvantages, 189
  linear correlation analysis, 171–178
  multiple correlation analysis, 178–188
  types, 170
Covariance, 66–68

Credit analysis, 193–200
Critical ratio, 135–143
Cumulative frequency distribution, 42
Cyclical fluctuations, 194, 251; *see also*
    Time series

Deciles: *see* Quartile deviation
Decision tree, 72–74
Degrees of freedom, 105, 143, 218
Dependent variable, 169, 171
Di Roccaferrera, Guiseppe M. Ferrero,
    225*n*
Discrete probability distributions, 81–99
    binomial, 81–89
    hypergeometric, 89–94
    Poisson, 94–99
Discrete variable, 251
Discriminant analysis, 193–201
Dispersion: *see* Variability

Ewert, David, 194*n*, 198
Expected value, 61, 251

Factorials, 95
Frequency distribution (table), 243, 251
    characteristics of, 47–52
    construction of, 35–38
    cumulative, 42–43
    relative, 42–43
F test for significance, 176–183

Geometric mean, 13–20, 39
    grouped data, 39
    ungrouped data, 13–20
Geometric straight line trend, 157–160
Goal programming, 237–243

Harmonic mean, 20–21, 39, 251
Hindelang, Thomas, 226*n*
Hitchcock Publishing Co., 246
Hypergeometric distribution, 89–94
Hypothesis testing, 129–145

Infosystems, 246
Integer programming, 236–237
Interquartile range, 27
Interval estimate, 251; *see also* Confidence
    interval
Interval scales, 206
Inventory management, 69–72
Irregular fluctuations, 251; *see also* Time
    series

Law of large numbers, 114
Level of significance, 131–132
Linear correlation, 171–178, 251
Linear discriminant analysis (LDA), 193–
    201
Linear programming, 224–236
    assumptions, 225
    format, 224
    formulation, 226
Logarithms, 15–18

Managerial statistics, 4
Mao, James C. T., 198*n*, 199*n*, 200
Matched pairs signed test, 209–211
Mean absolute deviation (MAD), 28–29,
    47
Median, 21, 40–41, 252
    grouped data, 40–41
    ungrouped data, 21–23
    limitations, 24
    uses, 24
Mode, 23–25, 41–42, 252
    grouped data, 41–42
    ungrouped data, 23–25
    limitations, 24
    uses, 24
Multicollinearity, 183, 185, 252
Multiple correlation, 178–188, 252
Multiple linear regression, 179, 186, 194–
    195
Multiplication rule, 64

Negative correlation, 170, 252
Nonlinear correlation, 170, 252
Nonparametric statistics, 205–219
Normal curve, 47; *see also* Frequency dis-
    tribution
Normal distribution, 99–104
    areas under, 100
    assumptions of, 103
    table of areas, 102
Null hypothesis, 129–130, 207, 209, 252

Objective function, 224
Ordinal scales, 206

Parametric techniques, defined, 205
Partial correlation, 252
Percentiles: *see* Quartile deviation
Point estimate, 120, 252
Poisson distribution, 94–99
Poisson probability table, 98

Population, 4, 252
  parameters, 119–120, 121, 123, 127
  standard deviation, 107
Portfolio management, 66–69, 205
Positive correlation, 170, 252
Positional averages, 21–25, 40–42
  median, 21–23, 40–41
  mode, 23–25, 41–42
Pritchard, R., 226n
Probability, 57–78
  classical, 58
  concepts of, 57–58
  conditional, 60
  cumulative, 73
  events, 59–60
  joint, 60
  marginal, 60
  objective, 75
  posterior, 76–79
  prior, 76
  rules, 61–66
  subjective, 59, 75–77
Probability distribution(s), 79–109, 252
  binomial, 81–89
  chi-square, 106–108
  continuous, 80, 99–108
  discrete, 80, 99
  hypergeometric, 89–94
  multivariate, 80
  normal, 99–104
  Poisson, 94–99
  t distribution, 104–106
  univariate, 80

Quality control, 72
Quartile deviation, 26

Random variables, 4, 79, 99, 100, 252
Range, 25, 44
Rates of change: *see* Geometric mean
Ratio scales, 206
Ratio to moving average, 164–166
Regression analysis, 150–160, 171–172, 179–182
  arithmetic straight line trend, 150–153
  geometric straight line trend, 157–160
Relative changes: *see* Geometric mean
Relative dispersion, 30
Relative frequency distribution, 43

Sample, 113, 252
  and population, 113

Sample size, 120–125
Sample variance, 106, 107
Sampling, 113–128, 252
  error, 115
  cluster, 115–116
  convenience, 177
  judgment, 117
  nonrandom, 117
  random, 114–117
  stratified, 115
  systematic, 116–117
Seasonal variation(s), 149, 164, 252; *see also* Time series
  deseasonalized data, 165–166
Second-degree polynomial, 153–157, 252
Secular trend, 149–161; *see also* Time series
Semi-interquartile range: *see* Quartile deviation
Sentry Database Publishing, 246
Serial correlation, 186
Shadow prices, 229
Sigma, 30
Sign test, 207–209
Simple correlation, 171–178, 252
Skewness, 49–52, 252
Slack variable, 227
Software News, 246
Standard deviation, 30, 31, 47
Standard error, 132–135, 177–185
  of forecast, 178, 185
  of intercept, 185
  of mean, 132–135
  of slope, 177–178
Statistical inference: *see* Hypothesis testing
Student's: *see* t Distribution
Sum of probabilities rule, 61

Table of random numbers, 117–118
Tchebycheff's Theorem, 114, 121, 124
T critical values, 211, 213–215
t Distribution, 104–106
Test of significance, 208
Testing statistic, 135–143
Time series, 149–167, 253
Two-tailed test, 135, 140–141
Type I error, 130, 253
Type II error, 130–131, 207, 253

Universe: *see* Population

Variability, 25–47
  average deviation methods, 28–30, 46–47
  distance measures, 25–28, 44–45
Variance, 30, 106, 253
Variation, 173–174, 181
  explained, 174, 181

Variation (*cont.*)
  unexplained, 173, 181

Wilcoxon matched pairs test, 211

Z value, 101–103, 124–125

274547

519.5 Clark, John J.

A statistics primer
for managers

DATE			

19.95